The Community Engagement Professional in Higher Education

The subject of this book, the research project on the community engagement professional, was done under the auspices of Campus Compact and through the diligent work of the Scholar-in-Residence and Research Follows.

Scholar-in-Residence

Lina D. Dostilio, University of Pittsburgh

Research Fellows

Lane Perry, Western Carolina University
Ashley Farmer-Hanson, Buena Vista University
Kira Pasquesi, University of Iowa
Kortney Hernandez, Loyola Marymount University
Sean Crossland, Salt Lake Community College
Tait Kellogg, Tulane University
Laura Martin, University of Mississippi
Shannon Chamberlin, University of Arkansas, Little Rock
Johanna Phelps-Hillen, University of South Florida
Melissa Quan, Fairfield University
Romy Hübler, University of Maryland, Baltimore County
Laura Weaver, Indiana Campus Compact
Jodi Benenson, University of Nebraska Omaha
Kevin Hemer, Iowa State University
Kara Trebil, University of Denver

The Community Engagement Professional in Higher Education

A Competency Model for an Emerging Field

Edited by
LINA D. DOSTILIO

BOSTON, MASSACHUSETTS
Distributed by Stylus Publishing, LLC

COPYRIGHT © 2017 BY CAMPUS COMPACT

Published by Campus Compact
45 Temple Place
Boston, MA 02111

All rights reserved. No part of this book may be reprinted or reproduced in any form or by any electronic, mechanical, or other means, now known or hereafter invented, including photocopying, recording, and information storage and retrieval, without permission in writing from the publisher.

Library of Congress Cataloging-in-Publication Data
Names: Dostilio, Lina D., editor.
Title: The community engagement professional in higher education: a competency model for an emerging field / edited by Lina D. Dostilio. Description: Boston, MA : Campus Compact, 2017. | Includes bibliographical references and index.
Identifiers: LCCN 2016038863 (print) |
LCCN 2016059182 (ebook) |
 ISBN 9781945459023 (cloth : alk. paper) |
 ISBN 9781945459030 (pbk. : alk. paper) |
 ISBN 9781945459047 (library networkable e-edition) |
 ISBN 9781945459054 (consumer e-edition)
Subjects: LCSH: Community and college--United States. | Universities and colleges--United States--Public services. | Universities and colleges--Public relations--United States. | Service learning--United States.
Classification: LCC LC238 .C665 2017 (print) |
LCC LC238 (ebook) | DDC 378.1/03--dc23
LC record available at https://lccn.loc.gov/2016038863

13-digit ISBN: 978-1-945459-02-3 (cloth)
13-digit ISBN: 978-1-945459-03-0 (paperback)
13-digit ISBN: 978-1-945459-04-7 (library networkable e-edition)
13-digit ISBN: 978-1-945459-05-4 (consumer e-edition)

Printed in the United States of America

All first editions printed on acid-free paper
that meets the American National Standards Institute
Z39-48 Standard.

> Bulk Purchases
>
> Quantity discounts are available for use in workshops and for staff development.
> Call 1-800-232-0223

First Edition, 2017

This book is dedicated to the community-oriented faculty, student leaders, and staff who early on eked out spaces for community engagement within postsecondary education, and to the community-based stakeholders who urged and mentored campuses to open themselves up to wider public concerns. By many accounts, their efforts were radical and they were often marginalized. Through shared work, they built community with each other. Through their collegiality, shared commitment to social justice, frank critique, and commiseration, they wove together a set of understandings of how colleges and universities could practically engage their civic purposes. They passed on their experiences, the scars and the joys, to those of us who came later into formal roles to support this work. It is only because of their grassroots, visionary efforts that we have actual jobs dedicated to supporting community engagement in postsecondary education, not to mention a proliferation of centers, senior administrative positions, scholarly literature, grant programs, and national dialogues. We dedicate this emerging work to the people who have shaped us and our craft: our mentors, teachers, and friends. We hope we do you and the work justice.

CONTENTS

1. AN EXPLANATION OF COMMUNITY ENGAGEMENT
   PROFESSIONALS AS PROFESSIONALS AND LEADERS   1
   Lina D. Dostilio and Lane G. Perry

2. PLANNING A PATH FORWARD   27
   Identifying the Knowledge, Skills, and Dispositions of Second-Generation
   Community Engagement Professionals
   Lina D. Dostilio

3. CRITICAL PERSPECTIVES AND COMMITMENTS
   DESERVING ATTENTION FROM COMMUNITY
   ENGAGEMENT PROFESSIONALS   56
   Kortney Hernandez and Kira Pasquesi

4. PROGRAM ADMINISTRATION AND EVALUATION   79
   Ashley J. Farmer-Hanson

5. ENVISIONING, LEADING, AND ENACTING
   INSTITUTIONAL CHANGE FOR THE PUBLIC GOOD   98
   The Role of Community Engagement Professionals
   Romy Hübler and Melissa Quan

6. ATTRIBUTES OF COMMUNITY ENGAGEMENT
   PROFESSIONALS SEEKING TO INSTITUTIONALIZE
   COMMUNITY-CAMPUS ENGAGEMENT   118
   Laura Weaver and B. Tait Kellogg

7. SUPPORTING STUDENT CIVIC LEARNING AND
   DEVELOPMENT   139
   Jodi Benenson, Kevin M. Hemer, and Kara Trebil

8. HIGH-QUALITY COMMUNITY-CAMPUS PARTNERSHIPS 161
   Approaches and Competencies
   Laura Martin and Sean Crossland

9. COMPETENCIES COMMUNITY ENGAGEMENT
   PROFESSIONALS NEED FOR FACULTY DEVELOPMENT 179
   J. Shannon Chamberlin and Johanna Phelps-Hillen

   EDITOR AND CONTRIBUTORS 201

   INDEX 207

Chapter One

AN EXPLANATION OF COMMUNITY ENGAGEMENT PROFESSIONALS AS PROFESSIONALS AND LEADERS

Lina D. Dostilio and Lane G. Perry

Community engagement professionals (CEPs) (Dostilio, 2016; Dostilio & McReynolds, 2015; Jacoby & Mutascio, 2010; McReynolds & Shields, 2015) are professional staff whose primary job is to support and administer community-campus engagement. There is very little empirical literature about CEPs, yet there is abundant literature on the practices of community-university engagement. Little is written on the professionalization or shared dispositions and competencies of CEPs (Dostilio, 2016). Some resources have been instrumental in helping CEPs grow professionally, such as Jacoby and Mutascio's (2010) reflective guide for community service-learning professionals and Campus Compact's professional development institutes titled *Diving In: Institute for New Community-Service Learning Professionals* and *Diving Deep: Institute*

for Experienced Civic and Community Engagement Practitioners. More recently, Bartha, Carney, Gale, Goodhue, and Howard (2014) curated a collection of pieces on intermediary administrative engagement work stemming from a series of workshops and roundtable conversations at the 2012 and 2013 Imagining America conferences. The collection included a manifesto and series of myths, manifestations, and stories that outline the underappreciated and undercharacterized role of staff committed to higher education's public engagement. McReynolds and Shields (2015) edited a volume written by participants in one of the *Diving Deep* institutes, which synthesized their experiences as a model for professional development. Keith (2015) explored the concept of democratic civic professionals in her work on *social partnerships*, though the term and accompanying consideration of the profession were framed broadly to include anyone within postsecondary education whose work engaged the public. Despite these foundational guides and programs, there has been little empirical and systematically constructed understanding of CEPs within the community-campus literature.

This book presents a review of community-campus engagement practice literature, from which we endeavored to infer competencies and attributes that may be shared among CEPs at a general level and by focus—such as those CEPs who specialize in building community-campus partnerships; those who specialize in faculty development; or those who have multiple responsibilities, such as facilitating partnerships *and* faculty development. This review, an attempt to systematically uncover the knowledge, skills, and dispositions that the literature suggests are necessary to promote the practices of community-campus engagement, is the first step in a multiphase inquiry. Our hope is that the findings here and of future phases of the project will open up myriad researchable questions about CEPs that can be undertaken to build a knowledge base about this group of stakeholders so key to community-campus engagement.

We write this as a group of practitioners, perhaps better described as practitioner-scholars, who are interested in better understanding and improving the practice of CEPs as a step in the ultimate goal of involving higher education in the work of a more peaceful, just, and sustainable world. Within this chapter, we lay out the nature of community engagement staff as those who span a continuum of technical service staff to change agents, the latter being considered CEPs. We then offer reflections on the role of CEPs as change-oriented leaders, using their positions within the middle spaces of their organizations to catalyze change and greater realization of postsecondary education's civic purpose.

The first generation of community engagement staff were often viewed as those who performed tasks limited to instrumental functions, such as coordinating logistic support. Those kinds of staff positions continue today, even in light of a shift to a second generation of community engagement practice (Welch & Saltmarsh, 2013). It could be perceived that there is little need to reflect critically on the civic purposes of their daily work or to seek professional development that prepares them to be scholarly practitioners. These staff may exist for a variety of reasons. Perhaps the role was conceived by institutional leaders who are unfamiliar with civically oriented forms of community engagement. Perhaps this is one staff position within a larger engagement unit whose scope of work is very narrow, such as a transportation coordinator (though we argue that there would be room to involve that coordinator in dialogue about the profession and about his or her deepening identity as a CEP). Perhaps it is a newly graduated student who has seemingly fallen into engagement work, by virtue of his or her desire to work with college students. In each instance, the need for this project becomes evident. We may well have staff whose roles are limited to instrumental functions—indeed, instrumental support is necessary for community-campus engagement—but it is a piece within the larger mosaic of change-oriented civic work. Staff whose energy, professional identity, and growth trajectory bring them to change-oriented and civically oriented community engagement are considered community engagement *professionals* as explained in this chapter. Our hope is that for those staff whose roles have been constructed in ways that limit their participation in the civic enterprise this project and others (Bartha et al., 2014; McReynolds & Shields, 2015) might expose individuals and institutions to a more nuanced understanding of what such staff positions might grow into and be given some indication of how to cultivate and support that growth.

Community Engagement Practitioners as Professionals

This chapter is focused on professional or administrative staff whose primary responsibility is to support community engagement initiatives within American higher education. We propose that a naming shift from *practitioner* to *professional* more accurately describes our current and evolving experiences of this work, although this is not yet the preferred nomenclature within professional engagement associations. In the early days of the International Association for Research on Service-Learning & Community Engagement (IARSLCE), members were often classified as researchers, graduate students, or practitioners (though more recently there is less rigid categorization). Engagement staff and faculty who did not produce research were considered practitioners. In the past, Campus Compact referred to engagement staff as *service-learning directors* or *community service directors* (SLDs/CSDs), although this categorization is also changing to acknowledge the number of staff who either (a) do not carry the title of director or (b) have portfolios of community engagement work broader than service-learning or community service activities. The Engagement Scholarship Consortium (previously the National Outreach Scholarship Conference) has the Outreach and Engagement Practitioners Network. Despite a history of referring to these positions as *practitioners* or *staff*, the practice field and those in it may be better served by moving toward using the word *professional* when describing our work.

While there is no absolute consensus on the definition of a *professional* (Scanlon, 2011), there is some agreement about professionals having a specialized body of knowledge and practice methods distinct from others (Bowman, West, Berman, & Van Wart, 2004; Eraut, 1994; Evetts, 2006). Profession is a historical concept (see Dingwall, 2008, for a comprehensive history and evolution of professions), at one point denoting a very narrow framing of highly specialized knowledge and professional preparation typical of doctors, lawyers, and clergy. In a postmodern and socially interconnected society, defining a profession by the degree of exclusivity of its knowledge base is no longer possible (Scanlon, 2011), and defining it only through its distinct functions serves to maintain social control of expertise that secures the profession's power (Eraut, 1994). Rather, we must account for socially constructed notions of a profession that promote its relationship with the larger world. Whereas in the past, expertise was an individually sought and university-controlled matter, we now produce expertise in multiactor networks that leads to co-constructed standards of practice (Palonen, Boshuizen, & Lehtinen, 2014).

Further situating our concept of the professional within postsecondary civic concerns, Novella Keith's work (2015) on border-crossing democratic civic professionals is especially instructive. Democratic civic professionals are mindful that they inhabit a multicultural and diverse world, and they prioritize personal responsibility, social responsibility, and inclusive practice (Keith, 2015, p. 84) to create social partnerships between the postsecondary and community spheres. They link civic work with democratic participation. Keith's concept is specifically focused on practitioners who understand their work as different from both the technocratic experts' (those who have the expertise necessary for problem-solving and who typically frame problems and potential solutions in isolation from diverse collaborators) and the social trustees' (those who, absent a democratic ideal, steward expertise and resources for the public good frequently in paternalistic ways). Rather, democratic civic professionals are aware of the ways they possibly promote hidden, exclusive assumptions about identity, knowledge, and practice within engagement. This awareness is gained through explicit consideration of our positionality, relationships with others, and the interdependencies we have and must maintain.

Taking these characterizations of profession into account, our project on the CEP now considers the four common aspects of a profession—(a) a distinct body of knowledge and practice, (b) a development of practice-scholar communities; (c) a shared professional identity; and (d) a shared set of ethical commitments (Bowman et al., 2004)—to make the case that CEPs share evolving notions of each of these elements and can, indeed, claim the identity of profession.

A Body of Knowledge and Practice

This literature review uses a big-tent framing of community engagement to encompass diverse methods of connecting postsecondary education and the larger publics of which it is a part. Within this framing, a variety of practice activities can be found: service-learning, student civic development, community-university partnership work, participatory research, advocacy and activist scholarship, and others. Though there are few empirical studies on CEPs (or staff or practitioners)—and none that empirically identifies the requisite knowledge, skills, and abilities of CEPs—we can draw upon the authors' experiences and a cursory review of the practice literature to determine the existence of a body of knowledge distinct from that of other academic professionals. Though the knowledge required to activate community-campus engagement builds upon some bodies of knowledge common to higher education professionals (e.g., college student development theory, organizational and institutional understanding, awareness of faculty work and reward structures, basic program development and administration knowledge, and critical reflection), it is uniquely focused on community-engaged pedagogical and research strategies, student civic development theory, engaged scholarship orientations, community development (and perhaps organizing), the mechanics of partnership development, and the concept of the engaged institution.

CEPs' practice environments are also unique and are often characterized by sitting betwixt and between boundaries. Of particular relevance to the CEPs' conception of practice is Whitchurch's work on blended (2009) and third-space professionals (2013) in higher education. In her comparative study of 54 blended professionals across the United States, the

United Kingdom, and Australia, Whitchurch (2009) developed a typology of blended professional identities and conducted extensive interviews with exemplars of each type. Whitchurch continued to evolve her blended professional work to acknowledge the presence of third-space environments (2013), which led to the conception of third-space professionals. According to Whitchurch (2009, 2013), as blended or third-space professionals, we leverage professional and academic expertise; straddle on- and off-campus environments; facilitate internal and external boundary-crossing projects; exert relational leadership that often activates networks rather than hierarchy; and maintain portfolios of work that include management, teaching, program administration, and research. Bartha and colleagues (2014) reinforce not just our occupation of third spaces but our role in creating them within their "A Manifesto From the Middle Ground of Campus-Community Partnerships." Calling to hybrid-hyphenateds, Bartha and colleagues suggest that there is no identifiable "we," or a singular job title that encapsulates the multitude of laborers who supply intermediary administrative work that is central to higher education's ability to be democratically and collaboratively engaged with the larger public. However, they acknowledge a shared concern among these laborers, which is the work of community engagement. Thus, the CEP's professional knowledge base builds upon postsecondary organizational expertise but particularly focuses on community-engagement-specific methods and theories and third-space practice environments.

A Practice-Scholar Community

Scholars such as Etzioni (1969) and Hoyle and John (1995) label a group with an emerging or evolving knowledge base as *semiprofessionals* or peripheral to a professional group. These groups, such as nurses or teachers—for whom preparation is largely centered on method or practice and usually does not include a proprietary theoretical grounding—have historically been categorized outside "true" professions (Scanlon, 2011). Yet, especially regarding teachers, vigorous arguments have been made to illustrate how sophisticated practice knowledge, which is necessarily a blending of theory and method, is a professional epistemology that also gives rise to a scholarly community (Shulman, 1987; Wenger, 1998). Similarly, CEPs have an evolving knowledge base that is a blending of sophisticated practice and theory. Our knowledge base is consistently critiqued, modified, and improved by those of us who operate as practitioner-scholars. Practitioner-scholars are concerned with systematic inquiry and reflective practice (Bringle, Clayton, & Hatcher, 2013). The notion of practitioner-scholars, or *pracademics* (Salipante & Aram, 2003; Van Til, 2000), has been briefly explored in relation to community engagement by scholars such as McReynolds and Clayton. McReynolds (2015) writes, "Practitioner-scholars have the unique ability to perceive deficiencies in current theories and practices. Their research and best pedagogical knowledge are needed to challenge and drive the development of a stronger academy" (p. 4).

By acknowledging, activating, and evolving our rich body of practice scholarship with others who share our identities, contexts, and commitments, we enact a professional epistemology. Doing so gives rise to claiming a professional status that is made manifest by having a practice-scholar community. There are multiple outlets for this practice-scholar community. On a local level, we critique and advance practice by sharing information within and across institutions. Many state-level Campus Compacts have provided convening spaces for professionals who are typically scripted in campus-based roles that support community service, service-learning, and engaged scholarship. At a national level, we see gathering spaces that welcome a wider assortment of CEPs, such as the Coalition of Urban and Metropolitan Universities, Imagining America, and Engagement Scholarship Consortium. We also see spaces that convene CEPs with particular foci, such as at the Practitioner-Scholar Forum of IARSLCE, the American Democracy Project, and the Bonner Foundation's directors' meetings. Within each of these venues, CEPs mutually critique and advance their practices and in many instances form practice-scholar communities.

A Shared Professional Identity

According to Palonen and colleagues (2014), professionals are characterized, in part, by maintaining a shared occupational identity that is co-constructed with others in the profession. Scanlon (2011) suggests that in a postmodern era, postmodern professionals eschew the cognitive and normative superiority traditionally espoused within professions, and instead embrace a reflexive and continual reconstruction of the self and role. This form of lifelong learning goes beyond the accumulation of formal degrees and credentials and is a holistic set of learning and practice experiences that advances a deepening identity. Drawing upon Schutz's "stranger" (1964), Wenger's "trajectories" (1998) , and Ibarra's "possible selves" (1999), Scanlon (2011) proposes that becoming a professional denotes the development of a sense of professional self. She suggests that this process of *becoming* goes beyond a continuum of end points from novice to expert, and instead points to lifelong, evolving professional learning. The reflexive and reflective development of professional identity that Scanlon suggests is particularly salient to the CEP and evokes a sense of depth and nuance rather than a sense of progression from one professional identity stage to the next. Bartha and colleagues (2014) reflect this nuanced identity in their portrait of administrative intermediaries who support public service:

> We labor within different institutional models and cultures and are rooted in different community identifications and networks. This does not trouble us: our work disposes us to productive alliances across differences. We share common experiences in campus-community partnerships and common commitments to bridge work. We recognize common good in making that work more generally visible and valued, where so much of it is obscured by academic hierarchies. (para. 3)

Our experience is that we are comfortable with each other *despite* the differences and we are comfortable in the in-between spaces. As such, our professional identity is associated with the purposes we serve rather than the job titles we occupy, and our journey of *becoming* (Scanlon, 2011) is focused on effecting increasingly deeper civic commitments through our administrative labor.

A Shared Set of Ethical Commitments

Typically, a profession espouses particular conduct norms that are values or ethics driven. Bowman and colleagues (2004) say that in addition to sharing technical skills (the ability to do things right), members of a profession share ethical skills ("the ability to do right things" [Bowman et al., p. xi]). Evetts's (2006) definition of *professionals* asserts that, in addition to other characteristics, they have a shared standard of ethical conduct. Scanlon (2011) proposes that in addition to having epistemological orientations (a knowledge base), professions have ontological orientations (or ways of being in the world). Taken together, these concepts sharpen our notion of a professional as someone who shares both the technical knowledge and the ethical principles of others in the profession. Bowman and colleagues (2004) provide a schema by which we understand the facets of professional work: technical expertise is the "how," ethics are the "why," and leadership is the "what." The previous sections described the source of our shared knowledge (the how) and described CEPs' shared professional identity as derived from the purposes we serve (the what), rather than the job titles we occupy. Fundamental to our commitment to the civic purposes of higher education is a belief that such a purpose is central and critical to a more just world. These commitments are the driving energy behind our work. They are the basis for developing a practice and technical knowledge of community engagement. Just as the other elements of a profession discussed here are co-constructed by members of that profession, so are ethical and leadership commitments. Whereas technical knowledge can be learned didactically, ethical commitments are refined through practice and depend on professional socialization (Bowman et al., 2004).

The picture of the community engagement profession we have painted here is one that is highly reflective, hybridized, purpose driven, and ethically principled. It rejects a narrow framing of specialized knowledge coming from one, singular preparatory pathway. Our understanding of profession is a socially constructed and collaboratively developed set of understandings and commitments; it would reject paths of professional development that are only didactic and do not facilitate reflection on practice and mentorship (of varying kinds). In the preceding sections, we confirmed through our experience as CEPs the elements of profession (a distinct body of knowledge and practice, development of practice-scholar communities, a shared professional identity, and a shared set of ethical commitments), and we offered reflection on the ways these elements can be seen in our practice and among CEPs generally. Each element is still arguably evolving, which is particularly fitting, given the conception of profession we advance within this project. Pointing to a finite canon of practice and knowledge, or endorsing only a select few practice-scholar communities, or homogenizing the titles of CEPs would oppose the socially constructed, democratic notion of their profession that we hope CEPs will maintain.

First-Generation Engagement Staff to Second-Generation Professionals

In addition to the four elements of profession outlined in the previous sections, an additional concept informs our notion of CEPs as professionals: attention to the second generation of engagement work (Welch & Saltmarsh, 2013). The authors of this chapter are administrative staff whose job is to support community engagement initiatives through our roles as engagement center directors. We see ourselves as active contributors to the field of community and civic engagement practice: We are active members and have held board of director positions within IARSLCE; participate deeply within Campus Compact well beyond this current research project, such as sitting on state advisory boards and conference planning committees; provide consultation or facilitate external program reviews of engagement initiatives for other institutions of higher education; sit on journal review and editorial boards; maintain active scholarship agendas; and routinely mentor emerging community engagement staff beyond our own institutions through formal mentorship programs, hosting student affairs interns, and being referred as mentors among our professional networks. Perhaps most poignant to the project at hand is that we both see ourselves as change agents who exert transformational leadership within specific institutions of higher education and within the field of community engagement more broadly.

As we reflect on the arc of our careers as CEPs we have seen a distinct progression from what used to be primarily instrumental responsibilities to more complex, transformational, democratic, and change-oriented work. The responsibilities we are addressing have not necessarily come with a new position, but more so with an evolving personal call, expectations of us by others within our institutions, and a greater professional awareness of the potential to deepen our institutions' civic commitments. While logistic responsibilities are still relevant to the work of a center, the potential to serve in a transformative or change-oriented role within the field seems to have burgeoned in the past 10 to 15 years.

The field of community engagement has evolved and experienced significant growth over the past generation of practice, research, and application. While a comprehensive review of the influential factors contributing to this evolution is not within this chapter's scope, a cursory outline of the areas and developments that have hastened the shift include

- the reframing of (or perhaps a realignment with) the historical purpose of higher education (Harkavy, 2015; Saltmarsh & Hartley, 2012);
- a clear demonstration of service-learning pedagogy's effectiveness and positive influence on empirically established outcomes (Ash & Clayton, 2005; Eyler & Giles, 1999; Eyler, Giles, Stenson, & Gray 2001);
- a bevy of national and international organizations calling for, advocating, and supporting the research, practice, and critique of service-learning and community engagement (e.g., IARSLCE, Campus Compact, Imagining America);
- informed calls for measuring and monitoring to transform the way community engagement is understood and facilitated (Gelmon, Holland, Driscoll, Spring, & Kerrigan, 2001; Holland, 1997; Perry, Farmer, Onder, Tanner, & Burton, 2015);
- the inclusion of service-learning as a high-impact practice for student engagement (Kuh, 2008, 2013), which equivocally serves

as a two-lane bridge between academic affairs (good teaching practices) and student affairs (good development practices);
- the development, implementation, and iterative refinement of the Carnegie Community Engagement Classification, which is the first national standard for institutionalized community engagement that prizes reciprocity, partnerships, and collaboration; and, most recently,
- landmark statements such as the *Campus Compact 30th-Anniversary Action Statement* (Campus Compact, 2016), which calls for solidarity around civic principles and campus action; *Democratic Engagement White Paper* (Saltmarsh, Hartley, & Clayton, 2009), which calls for our focus to move from disparate engagement activities to the civic processes that animate higher education; and *A Crucible Moment: College Learning and Democracy's Future* (National Task Force on Civic Learning and Democratic Engagement, 2012), which calls higher education to embed civic learning and democratic engagement in the educational experience.

These developments have produced an environment where an entire generation of students, faculty, staff, and community partners has thus created a new area of study, professional literature, and set of practices while shaping the design and architecture of community engagement structures on campus. Many campus centers originally designed to coordinate cocurricular volunteer service evolved into facilitating service-learning and are now expected to continue expanding in ways that also include new programming to promote civic forms of community engagement (Welch & Saltmarsh, 2013).

Since the early application and later integration of community engagement across campuses there has been an identifiable shift. This shift has been named and empirically documented by Welch and Saltmarsh (2013) as the shift from first- to second-generation community engagement. Within their investigation into the current practices and infrastructures of higher education centers and offices for community engagement, Welch and Saltmarsh initially conducted a review and analysis of extant literature and those successful applications from the 2010 Carnegie Foundation for Advancement of Teaching's elective Community Engagement Classification cycle. This thorough review uncovered "66 key characteristics at community engagement centers on college campuses.... These characteristics were categorized into six sections to assist in the organizational structure and format of a survey instrument" (Welch & Saltmarsh, 2013, pp. 28–29). The survey identified a range of empirical factors contributing to and demonstrating the complex and pivotal functions these spaces serve. The instrument was sent to 311 center directors, all from universities that had received a previous Carnegie Classification for Community Engagement, and received 147 responses.

The results from this investigation provided an overview of the infrastructural, operational, and programming responsibilities of centers or offices for community engagement associated with highly engaged institutions (as identified through the Carnegie Classification for Community Engagement process). These results illuminated the range of evident factors contributing to and demonstrating the complex and pivotal functions these spaces serve. For example, infrastructural data characterize these spaces as having primarily academic affairs reporting lines, budgeted institutional funds, and a clear indication of support in institutional strategic plans, and as being the centralized coordination sites for community engagement activities. Operationally, these spaces facilitate the measurement and monitoring of community engagement (e.g., student, faculty, community, and institutional impact); manage funding and resources to support faculty involvement; and deliver presentations to faculty, students, and other stakeholders to clarify institutional messaging associated with community engagement. Finally, the responsibility of programming for faculty, student, and community involvement is an essential element to a center's portfolio. This typically includes one-on-one consultation and development programs/funding for faculty; curricular/cocurricular programming, recognition, and leadership opportunities for students; and education opportunities on engaged pedagogy and site visits/meetings with community partners. These three areas, along with the specific examples underpinning each, have been determined by Welch and Saltmarsh (2013) as the most frequently identified responsibilities and duties of these spaces within the institution. These spaces, which across most campuses were primarily borne out of student affairs to coordinate cocurricular volunteer service, have now transformed to serve a "comprehensive and professional administrative role" responsible for coordinating and managing the community engagement initiatives and process across a campus and community (Welch & Saltmarsh, 2013, p. 48).

Salient to our goal in this book, the duties of these spaces within the institutional infrastructure and as a primary contributor to institutional strategic plans are clear. What needs to be further clarified and promoted is the nature, role, and perspective of the individuals who staff, lead, direct, and advance these spaces: CEPs. Liang and Sandmann (2015) articulate this explicitly in their recent call for ethnographic, exploratory research of informal and formal leaders involved in community engagement efforts.

It seems that the primary intention of an exploratory investigation of this nature would be to better understand the professionals responsible for these functions. This strongly supports our goal of identifying and articulating the components and competencies of a profession as complex and evolving as that of a CEP and, moreover, exploring the tenets of leadership associated within these spaces.

CEPs as Leaders

Contextualizing the leadership demands associated with community engagement in higher education, Baer, Duin, and Ramaley (2008) offer an explanation that supports a transformative approach:

> Boldly leading into an unknown future requires significant leadership skills and structural changes within the organization—a transformation of programs, services, practices, and policies. These include enabling future-orientation, flexible response tools as well as developing enterprise-wide intelligence systems for decision making and accountability. (p. 15)

Additionally, the larger purpose in identifying this call to leadership is to recognize the transformative impact that an approach can have on an institution and in particular spaces within institutions navigating shifts in purpose.

Much of the research exploring the role of leadership in promoting engagement has focused on the executive level such as chancellor, president, provost, and so on (Kezar, Gallant, & Lester, 2011; Liang & Sandmann, 2015; Plater, 2011; Sandmann & Plater, 2009, 2013). Much less is known about the operational or intermediary leadership level (e.g., directors, associate/assistant directors, other professional staff) and the competencies they need to thrive in second-generation conditions (see Welch & Saltmarsh, 2013), and how leadership influences that space. In their work on the conceptualization of distributed leadership as a model for mobilizing leadership from across an institution, Liang and Sandmann (2015) identify the reality of this situation. While the data they used to better understand leadership were primarily focused on executive leadership, they found the practice of leadership is multilayered through formal and informal roles across an institution. When it comes to the advancement and operationalizing of community engagement, the data underscore the importance of formal and informal leaders beyond the executive level. Liang and Sandmann (2015) identify the importance of executive leaders' rhetoric and the employment of "substantive strategies of financial support, personnel policy, strategic planning, and structural configuration" (p. 54) for the advancement of community engagement. As a manifestation of a distributed leadership approach, Harris (2008), cited in Liang and Sandmann (2015), calls for an *orchestration* in order for community engagement to become institutionalized.

In this, the question is as follows: At the day-to-day operational level, who conducts community engagement? We offer the following metaphor demonstrating the relationship between facilitating community engagement and creating music within an orchestra. The executive level of leadership (chancellor, provost, and deans) would serve the primary role of composer. Interestingly, the word *composer* actually comes from the Latin *com* and *pōnere*, literally meaning "one who puts together." In practice, this composition would manifest as strategic planning, rhetorical support, financial investment, and structural configuration for operationally embedding community engagement across an institution. The conductor, who has the key responsibility of unifying performers, setting the tempo, and listening critically to shape the sound (Kennedy & Kennedy, 2007), is equated to the director, lead administrator, or lead CEP for those units that facilitate community engagement within an institution. Within an orchestra there are various instruments (representing disciplines, fields, colleges, and nongovernmental organizations) and expert musicians (representing professors, support staff, community leaders, and students and student leaders) who are each playing their own respective pieces. Additionally, there is a certain level of interpretation at each point of communication and response. The conductor's interpretation of the composer's greater meaning sets the stage and direction for the musicians' response. When conducted with expertise (by the director, CEP, etc.), those musicians making the music create a harmony that every listener can appreciate.

While the institutional mission or vision plan is heavily shaped and crafted by executive or administrative leaders, the goals and initiatives associated with detailing, articulating, and operationalizing the plan are implemented farther down the organization chart—at the divisional or departmental levels. This level carries a high degree of importance because it is actually where community engagement becomes operationalized. Currently, the field seems to know more about the infrastructures (e.g., centers, offices, and spaces) responsible for managing community engagement than we do about the individuals working within these spaces. In the remaining sections of this chapter, we reflect on potential role characterizations of those individuals working on change-oriented civic engagement at the middle levels. In doing so, we hope to point CEPs toward leadership frameworks that they might emulate.

Characterizations: Tempered Radicals, Transformational Leaders, and Social Entrepreneurs

Leadership frameworks of the past that focused on a task-oriented leader existing within an explicitly defined, highly structured, and stratified system (Bensimon, Neumann, & Birnbaum, 1989) are not useful to the sort of second-generation CEP that is of concern to this project. The conception of leadership most germane to CEPs is one that is shared, relational, strategic, and oriented to complex processes (Avolio, Walumbwa, & Weber 2009; Yukl, 2010). It is a conception that liberates the transformational nature of this interpretation of leadership and its application (Northouse, 2013; Yukl, 2010) to community-campus engagement.

Kezar, Carducci, and Contreras-McGavin (2006) contextualize contemporary leadership within higher education by amalgamating three paradigms typically associated with approaches to inquiry: social constructivism, critical theory, and postmodernism. The synthesis of the three paradigms highlights the complexity and indeterminate components always at play within environments where leadership processes occur. These paradigms lean heavily into the idea that leadership is influenced by culture and local context, evolves continuously, is value bound and laden, and is simultaneously shaped by the subjective experience (relationship) of the leader/follower (Kezar et al., 2006). Kezar and colleagues (2006, as cited in Sandmann & Plater, 2013) suggest seeing leadership as a process that "allows scholars to embrace dynamic, process-oriented, collective, context bound, nonhierarchical perspectives of leadership focused on mutual power and influence that emphasize collaboration, cultural understanding, and social responsibility" (p. 514). A process-oriented form of leadership, such as that characterized by Kezar and colleagues, which is enacted on behalf of a democratic and institutionally transformative notion of community engagement implicates an array of change-oriented leadership approaches, such as those exhibited by tempered radicals, transformative leaders, and social entrepreneurs, which we explore in the following sections.

Tempered Radicals

CEPs can often find their value commitments at odds with the dominant ideology of their institution. Despite choosing to do our civic work from the postsecondary platform, we may face unsettling dissonance when our commitment to certain communities and ways of being in the world runs counter to the foci and norms of higher education. Meyerson and Scully (1995) use the term *tempered radicals* to describe those individuals who maintain multiple, often conflicting, commitments to their organizations as well as to their social justice ideals. Typically, tempered radicals fall into one of two categories: individuals whose social identities position them as outsiders within their institutions or those whose values are in conflict with the dominant values of the institution. The term *tempered radical* arises from the radical nature of challenging the status quo while remaining tempered, or incremental, in the approach to change. Further, Meyerson and Scully (1995) suggest we can interpret "tempered" in three ways: the first being a moderate approach, the second being toughened due to repeated phases of being heated and cooled, and the third being filled with temper or angered by the dissonance between our social justice commitments and those of our organizations. The notion of tempered radicals emerges from grassroots leadership theory (Kezar et al., 2011).

Tempered radicals challenge prevailing wisdom and incrementally nudge culture change in very localized ways focused on their immediate spheres of influence and work. They bring about change from inside a system or an organization (Meyerson, 2004). The theory of tempered radicalism embraces the continual evolution of organizations, leveraging small adjustments that position them to seize strategic opportunities for change when they arise (Meyerson, 2004). Using a spectrum of techniques ranging from disruptive self-expression, to taking small change-oriented actions that ultimately have a large impact, to strategically building alliances that build a critical mass of like-minded stakeholders (Meyerson, 2001), tempered radicals are acutely focused on changing organizational culture.

Transformational Leaders

Sandmann and Plater (2013) define *transformational leadership theory* as a process that occurs between leaders and followers where the focus is on identifying needed change within a system or an organization, collaboratively charting the course or steps for navigating the change, and determining in concert with others the purpose of empowerment or social change (Kezar et al., 2006). Essentially, transformative leadership is about transforming *with*, not transforming *for*, an individual or a community (McCloskey, n.d.). This delineation is an important one when contemplating transformative leadership as an actual process and not as an individual leader existing within an organizational or social vacuum.

Because transformational leadership is expressly concerned with facilitating change within a system or an organization, it is well suited for

CEPs who work in contexts where the second generation of engagement (Welch & Saltmarsh, 2013) is in process or could be hastened. Depending on the situation or context, various approaches to leadership could work effectively in maintaining the status quo (Bass, 1990; Chemers, 1997; Fiedler, Martin, & Mahar, 1994). Alternatively, through a mixed-methods study, Kirby, King, and Paradise (1992) identified that one of the consistent attributes associated with transformational leaders is their propensity to intentionally challenge the status quo. Fundamentally, democratic forms of civic engagement run counter to the status quo of higher education (Saltmarsh et al., 2009), and so require transformative leaders to steward their implementation.

Core to transformational leadership, particularly in times of transition, is the focus on identifying challenges and strengths, framing/reframing the strategic plan to align with identified challenges and strengths, collaboratively crafting initiatives that operationalize the plan, and bolstering support at all levels of an organization. The success of an organization is contingent on its ability to adapt and meet changes and challenges when they arise, and transformational leadership is the most effective approach to navigating shifting, changing, or evolving circumstances (Bass, 1990).

It should be noted that transformational leadership is not without its critics. Critics have identified that transformational leadership lacks conceptual clarity, has dimensions not clearly delimited, and overlaps with other similar conceptualizations of leadership, and at times frames the approach as an innate predisposition more than a learnable approach (Northouse, 2013). Conversely, research has consistently demonstrated the learnability associated with this approach to change and leadership (Bass, 1990). Moreover, the value associated with the transformational leadership paradigm, particularly in times of creating or managing changes, shifts, or evolutions, seems to outweigh the inadequacies associated with the approach.

Social Entrepreneurs

The demands of second-generation community engagement seem to call on a set of skills and attributes that are expressly articulated and appreciated within the realm of social entrepreneurship.[1] As a field and body of practice, social entrepreneurship was borne outside of higher education to the public or civic sector. Its roots are embedded in the fundamental idea that "levers of change can happen in business, public or nonprofit organizations, and hybrids of these approaches" (Enos, 2015, p. 9). Social entrepreneurs seek to deal in the currency of innovative solutions to communities' most pressing social problems with a scalable capacity for widespread change (Ashoka, n.d.). They have been recognized by their pattern-changing behaviors (Ashoka, n.d.), their forging and charting of new paths (Enos, 2015), and their commitment to pioneer innovations that benefit humanity (Skoll Foundation quoted in O'Heffernan, 2007). This process typically includes changing a system and, through the creative destruction and rebuilding of the system (versus accepting the status quo), moves communities in different directions (Ashoka, n.d.; Enos, 2015). The cases associated with effective social entrepreneurship focus on three key factors: the idea, the social entrepreneur, and the system or environment where it all exists (Bornstein, 2003). Social entrepreneurial attributes can be applied to the shift toward second-generation community engagement to help foster and influence an emergent system that is expressly concerned with civic renewal and social change.

According to Auerswald and Quadir (2007), social entrepreneurs seek to identify, refine, develop, and apply effective solutions to societal challenges with the greater purpose of changing the status quo that enables complacency in regard to societal issues. Like business entrepreneurs, social entrepreneurs primarily seek to redirect or realign resources "out of an area of lower and into an area of higher productivity and greater yield" (Baptiste Say cited in Dees, 1998), which in social entrepreneurship is characterized by the effectiveness of a solution to address a core challenge within a society.

The work of community engagement has always been about creative destruction. Whether it is reminding stakeholders of the original purpose of public higher education; dealing with issues of social justice, voting rights, or equal rights; serving as the critical conscience of society; breaking down hegemonic systems; or respiring life into a waning democracy, the field has always been about challenging and addressing the status quo. Social entrepreneurs do the same, and adopting their methods as CEPs provides a discourse that allows us to creatively destruct and reorient community engagement practices toward more civic and reciprocal ends. Adopting a social entrepreneurship lens may help us balance our focus on the higher education institutions in which we are embedded with an equally powerful focus on how we bring these institutions to their greater civic purposes, which is the project of social change.

Social entrepreneurship as an approach for managing innovation, connecting with social challenges, and disrupting the status quo is not intended to be framed as a panacea. As a practice for ideating and implementing "new approaches to meet social needs" (Enos, 2015, p. 53), social entrepreneurship is not without its critics, concerns, and questions. Social entrepreneurship has been criticized for its reliance and inherent dependence on individual approaches (Enos, 2015) and a disregard for or circumvention of the political system that influences our community's circumstances and opportunities (Enos, 2015; Giriharadas, 2011). Additionally, there are concerns of the limited, timely, and measurable impact that can be had within the nonprofit sector by aligning a focus on revenue building with a social focus. The focus on profits in contrast to the focus on real community impact can be problematic and lacking in the reciprocity demanded of social change (Jones, Warner, & Kiser, 2010). Finally, and perhaps the most salient critique of a social entrepreneurial approach, is the perceived lack of concern for a collaborative structure. This relies on an expert or "armchair activist" approach and propagates an attitude that lacks emic understanding or misses the attempt to fully understand the underlying histories, cultures, or nuances of a community prior to innovating and implementing an idea (Jones et al., 2010). These particular critiques are antithetical to many of the key criteria of community engagement.

These concerns are warranted, but we believe that much can be learned from the strengths of social entrepreneurship and the attributes of a social entrepreneur. We believe that an important difference is found at the very roots of social entrepreneurship and community engagement. Simply stated, community-campus engagement was born and raised within academia, and social entrepreneurship was born and raised within the wider community. They are like siblings separated at birth and raised by two different sets of parents. You can see similarities in the source code and the ultimate purpose and goal of bettering humanity, but the respective environments shaped them in different ways. We see entrepreneurship and community engagement complementing each other; the strengths of one can complement the other's gaps. One of these complementing strengths that is relevant to a CEP is found in Bornstein's (2003) work on the qualities of a social entrepreneur.

Through the facilitation and analysis of dozens of international and domestic case studies of social entrepreneurs, Bornstein (2003) illuminated six qualities that were associated with those who sought to not only implement an idea and vision but also catalyze a shift in a field, an industry, or a societal issue:

1. *"Willingness to self-correct.* Inclination to self-correct stems from the attachment to a goal rather than to a particular approach or plan" (pp. 238–239).

2. *"Willingness to share credit.* A willingness to share credit lies along the 'critical path' to success, simply because the more credit they share, the more people will want to help them" (p. 240).
3. *"Willingness to break free of established structures.* Entrepreneurs can gain the freedom to act and the distance to see beyond orthodoxy in their fields . . . [and] all innovation entails the ability to separate from the past" (p. 241).
4. *"Willingness to cross disciplinary boundaries.* Independence from established structures not only helps social entrepreneurs wrest free of prevailing assumptions it also gives them latitude to combine resources in new ways. This is identified as *social alchemy*" (p. 241).
5. *"Willingness to work quietly.* Many social entrepreneurs spend decades steadily advancing their ideas, influencing people in small groups or one-on-one" (p. 242).
6. *"Strong ethical impetus.* At some moment in their lives, social entrepreneurs get it into their heads that it is up to them to solve a particular problem" (p. 244).

These qualities, whether a person is an adopter of social entrepreneurship approaches or not, are critically valuable when navigating uncharted territory with the larger purpose of social change, development, and progress.

Conclusion

The conceptions of tempered radicals, transformational leaders, and social entrepreneurs discussed within the previous section may provide us with templates and vocabularies to explain the ways in which CEPs function as leaders on their campuses and within larger associations of civic workers. We believe that as the management of community engagement becomes more encompassing and the responsibilities become more complex, it is important that our notion of leadership within this work becomes more inclusive to acknowledge the integration of the whole orchestra: artists, patrons, conductors, and composers. It is equally important that those CEPs responsible for leading this work are better understood. What it takes to thrive in these conditions can help inform CEPs' practice, but more importantly it can help prepare the next generation of CEPs for the new level of expectation, purpose, and vision of post-second-generation community engagement. Moving our understanding of these positions from generic staff to defined professionals and leaders may be a way to signal the paradigm shift. We argue that claiming a professional identity allows us to retain the diverse foci and contexts we inhabit but still clarifies our shared bodies of practice and knowledge, scholarly community, identity as distinct from other academic workers, and ethical commitments.

The leadership frames we feel are most appropriate for understanding the CEP are not those that focus on the executive, but those that leave space for the intermediary, relational leader. We see tempered radicalism, transformational leadership, and social entrepreneurship as central to that conception. Gleaning insight from these leadership traditions may well position CEPs to lead and manage systemic shift within institutions of higher education, across blurred boundaries and third spaces, and within the greater sphere of democratic civic practice. It has been demonstrated that CEPs are part of a shift to the second generation of engagement, or what could be referred to as the *new frontier*. We are in a place to regroup as a collective, and more importantly as a profession. With respect to Ayn Rand (1952), instead of taking our next set of "first steps down new roads armed with nothing but [our] own vision" (p. 678), we can be equipped with an informed vision, a clearer understanding of responsibilities demanded by this new frontier, and the characteristics and approaches this environment will demand. In this, we will do what we do best: Organize ourselves; clarify purpose through professionalizing; and advance intentionally through dialogue, action, and reflection.

Note

1. For a thorough review of the historical underpinnings, alignment, challenges, and current state of affairs regarding social entrepreneurship and service-learning specifically as pedagogies, see Sandra Enos's (2015) critical yet appreciative review.

References

Ash, S., & Clayton, P. (2005). Generating, deepening, and documenting learning: The power of critical reflection in applied learning. *Journal of Applied Learning in Higher Education, 1,* 25–48.

Ashoka. (n.d.). *Ashoka innovators for the public good: About us.* Retrieved from www.ashoka.org/about

Auerswald, E. P., & Quadir, I. Z. (2007). *What is a social entrepreneur?* Retrieved from www.policyinnovations.org/ideas/commentary/data/social_entrepreneurs/:pf_printable

Avolio, B., Walumbwa, F., & Weber, T. J. (2009). Leadership: Current theories, research, and future directions. *Management Department Faculty Publications* 37. Lincoln: University of Nebraska.

Baer, L. L., Duin, A. H., & Ramaley, J. A. (2008). Smart change. *Planning for Higher Education, 36*(2), 5–16.

Bartha, M., Carney, M., Gale, S., Goodhue, E., & Howard, A. (2014). This bridge called my job: Translating, re-valuing, and leveraging intermediary administrative work. *Public: A Journal of Imagining America: Hybrid, Evolving, and Integrative Career Paths, 2*(2), Part 1: A Manifesto From the Middle Ground of Campus-Community Partnerships.

Bass, B. M. (1990). From transactional to transformational leadership: Learning to share the vision. *Organizational Dynamics, 18*(3), 19–31.

Bensimon, E., Neumann, A., & Birnbaum, R. (1989). *Making sense of administrative leadership: The "L" word in higher education.* ASHE-ERIC Higher Education Report Number 1. Washington, DC: School of Education and Human Development, George Washington University.

Bornstein, D. (2003). *How to change the world: Social entrepreneurs and the power of new ideas.* Oxford, England: Oxford University Press.

Bowman, J. S., West, J. P., Berman, E. M., & Van Wart, M. (2004). *The professional edge: Competencies in public service.* Armonk, NY: M. E. Sharpe.

Bringle, R. G., Clayton, P. H., & Hatcher, J. A. (2013). Research on service learning: An introduction. In P. H. Clayton, R. G. Bringle, & J. A. Hatcher (Eds.), *Research on service learning: Conceptual frameworks and assessment, IUPUI Series on Service Learning Research* (vol. 2A, pp. 3–26). Sterling, VA: Stylus.

Campus Compact. (2016). *Creating a great campus civic action plan.* Retrieved from http://compact.org/resource-posts/creating-a-great-campus-civic-action-plan/

Chemers, M. M. (1997). *An integrative theory of leadership.* Mahwah, NJ: Erlbaum.

Dees, J. G. (1998). *The meaning of "social entrepreneurship."* Durham, NC: Center for the Advancement of Social Entrepreneurship, Fuqua School of Business, Duke University.

Dingwall, R. (2008). *Essays on professions.* Ashgate classics in sociology. Burlington, VT: Aldershot.

Dostilio, L. D. (2016). The professionalization of community engagement: Associations and professional staff. In T. D. Mitchell, T. Eatman, & C. Dolgan (Eds.), *The Cambridge handbook of service learning and community engagement.* Cambridge, England: Cambridge University Press.

Dostilio, L. D., & McReynolds, M. (2015). Community engagement professionals in the circle of service-learning and the greater civic enterprise. *Michigan Journal of Community Service Learning, 22*(1), 113–117.

Enos, S. (2015). *Service-learning and social entrepreneurship in higher education: A pedagogy of social change.* New York, NY: Palgrave Macmillan.

Eraut, M. (1994). *Developing professional knowledge and competence.* Abingdon, England: Routledge.

Etzioni, A. (Ed.). (1969). *The semi-professions and their organization.* New York, NY: Free Press.

Evetts, J. (2006). Introduction: Trust and professionalism: Challenges and occupational changes. *Current Sociology, 54*(4), 515–531.

Eyler, J., & Giles, D. (1999). *Where's the learning in service-learning?* San Francisco, CA: Jossey-Bass.

Eyler, J., Giles, D., Stenson, C., & Gray, C. (2001). *At a glance: What we know about the effects of service-learning on college students, faculty, institutions and communities, 1993–2000* (3rd ed.). Washington, DC: Corporation for Learn and Serve America National Service Learning Clearinghouse.

Fiedler, F. F., Martin, M. M., & Mahar, L. (1994). *Improving leadership effectiveness: The leadership-match concept* (2nd ed.). New York, NY: Wiley.

Gelmon, S. B., Holland, B. A., Driscoll, A., Spring, A., & Kerrigan, S. (2001). *Assessing service-learning and civic engagement: Principles and techniques.* Providence, RI: Campus Compact, Brown University.

Giriharadas, A. (2011). *Real change requires politics.* Retrieved from www.nytimes.com/2011/07/16/us/16iht-currents16.html?_r=0

Harkavy, I. (2015, Winter/Spring). Creating the connected institution: Toward realizing Benjamin Franklin and Ernest Boyer's revolutionary vision for American higher education. *Liberal Education,* 38–47.

Harris, A. (2008). Distributed leadership: According to the evidence. *Journal of Educational Administration, 46*(2), 172–188.

Holland, B. (1997). Analyzing institutional commitment to service: A model of key organizational factors. *Michigan Journal of Community Service Learning, 4*(1), 30–41.

Hoyle, E., & John, P. D. (1995). *Professional knowledge and professional practice.* London: Cassell.

Ibarra, H. (1999). Provisional selves: Experimenting with image and identity in professional adaptation. *Administrative Science Quarterly, 44*(4), 764–791.

Jacoby, B., & Mutascio, P. (Eds.). (2010). *Looking in, reaching out: A reflective guide for community service learning professionals.* Boston, MA: Campus Compact.

Jones, L., Warner, B., & Kiser, P. M. (2010). Service-learning and social entrepreneurship: Finding the common ground. *Partnerships: A Journal of Service Learning and Civic Engagement, 1*(2), 1–15.

Keith, N. Z. (2015). *Engaging in social partnerships: Democratic practices for campus-community partnerships.* New York, NY: Routledge, Taylor & Francis Group.

Kennedy, M., & Kennedy, J. B. (2007). *Oxford concise dictionary of music* (5th ed.). Oxford, England: Oxford University Press.

Kezar, A. J., Carducci, R., & Contreras-McGavin, M. (2006). *Rethinking the "L" word in leadership: The revolution of research on leadership.* San Francisco, CA: Jossey-Bass.

Kezar, A. J., Gallant, T. B., & Lester, J. (2011). Everyday people making a difference on college campuses: The tempered grassroots leadership tactics of faculty and staff. *Studies in Higher Education, 36*(2), 129–151.

Kirby, P. C., King, M. I., & Paradise, L. V. (1992, May–June). Extraordinary leaders in education: Understanding transformational leadership. *Journal of Educational Research*, 303–311.

Kuh, G. (2008). *High-impact educational practices: What they are, who has access to them, and why they matter.* Washington, DC: Association of American Colleges & Universities.

Kuh, G. (2013). *Ensuring quality and taking high-impact practices to scale.* Washington, DC: Association of American Colleges & Universities.

Liang, J., & Sandmann, L. R. (2015). Leadership for community engagement: A distributed leadership perspective. *Journal of Higher Education Outreach and Engagement, 19*(1), 35–64.

McCloskey, M. W. (n.d.). *What is transformational leadership?* Retrieved from people.bethel.edu/~pferris/otcommon/TransformationalLeadership.pdf

McReynolds, M. (2015). The practice of engagement: Developing as a practitioner-scholar. In O. Delano-Oriaran, M. W. Penick-Parks, & S. Fondrie (Eds.). *Service-learning and civic engagement: A sourcebook.* Thousand Oaks, CA: SAGE.

McReynolds, M., & Shields, E. (Eds.). (2015). *Diving deep in community engagement: A model for professional development.* Des Moines, IA: Iowa Campus Compact.

Meyerson, D. E. (2001). Radical change, the quiet way. *Harvard Business Review, 79*(9), 92–104.

Meyerson, D. E. (2004). The tempered radicals: How employees push their companies little by little to be more socially responsible. *Stanford Social Innovation Review, 2*(2), 14–22.

Meyerson, D. E., & Scully, M. A (1995). Tempered radicalism and the politics of ambivalence and change. *Organization Science, 6*(5), 585–600.

National Task Force on Civic Learning and Democratic Engagement. (2012). *A crucible moment: College learning and democracy's future.* Washington, DC: Association of American Colleges & Universities.

Northouse, P. G. (2013). *Leadership: Theory and practice* (6th ed.). Thousand Oaks, CA: Sage.

O'Heffernan, P. (2007). *Defining social entrepreneurship.* Retrieved from archive.skoll.org/2007/07/10/defining-social-entrepreneurship/

Palonen, T., Boshuizen, H. P., & Lehtinen, E. (2014). How expertise is created in emerging professional fields. In S. Billett, T. Halttunen, & M. Koivisto (Eds.), *Promoting, assessing, recognizing and certifying lifelong learning* (pp. 131–149). New York, NY: Springer.

Perry, L., Farmer, B., Onder, D., Tanner, B., & Burton, B. (2015). A community-based activities survey: Determining the impact on and of faculty. *Metropolitan Journal, 26*(2), 25–45.

Plater, W. M. (2011). Collective leadership for engagement: Reclaiming the public purpose of higher education. In J. Saltmarsh & M. Hartley (Eds.), *"To serve a larger purpose": Engagement for democracy and the transformation of higher education* (pp. 102–129). Philadelphia, PA: Temple University Press.

Rand, A. (1952). *The fountainhead*. New York, NY: Signet Novel.

Salipante, P., & Aram, J. D. (2003). Managers as knowledge generators: The nature of practitioner-scholar research in the nonprofit sector. *Nonprofit Management and Leadership, 14*(2), 129–150.

Saltmarsh, J., & Hartley, M. (2012). *"To serve a larger purpose": Engagement for democracy and the transformation of higher education*. Philadelphia, PA: Temple University Press.

Saltmarsh, J., Hartley, M., & Clayton, P. (2009). *Democratic engagement white paper*. Boston, MA: New England Resource Center for Higher Education.

Sandmann, L. R., & Plater, W. M. (2009). Leading the engaged institution. In L. R. Sandmann, C. H. Thornton, & A. J. Jaeger (Eds.), *Institutionalizing community engagement in higher education: The first wave of Carnegie classified institutions*. New Directions for Higher Education, 147 (pp. 13–24). San Francisco, CA: Jossey-Bass.

Sandmann, L. R., & Plater, W. M. (2013). Research on institutional leadership for service learning. In P. Clayton, R. Bringle, & J. Hatcher (Eds.), *Research on service-learning: Conceptual frameworks and assessment* (pp. 505–535). Sterling, VA: Stylus.

Scanlon, L. (2011). "Becoming" a professional. In L. Scanlon (Ed.), *Becoming a professional: An interdisciplinary analysis of professional learning* (pp. 13–32). Dordrecht, Netherlands: Springer.

Schutz, A. (1964). The stranger. In *Collected papers II: Studies in social theory* (pp. 91–105). The Hague: Martinus Nijhoff.

Shulman, L. (1987). Knowledge and teaching: Foundations of the new reform. *Harvard Educational Review, 57*(1), 1–23.

Van Til, J. (2000, March). Executive education: What pracademics can teach nonprofit leaders. *Nonprofit Times*, 10–11.

Welch, M., & Saltmarsh, J. (2013). Current practice and infrastructures for campus centers of community engagement. *Journal of Higher Education Outreach and Engagement, 17*(4), 25–56.

Wenger, E. (1998). *Communities of practice: Learning, meaning, and identity*. New York, NY: Cambridge University Press.

Whitchurch, C. (2009). The rise of the blended professional in higher education: A comparison between the United Kingdom, Australia and the United States. *Higher Education, 58*(3), 407–418.

Whitchurch, C. (2013). *Reconstructing identities in higher education: The rise of "third space" professionals*. London: Routledge.

Yukl, G. (2010). *Leadership in organizations* (7th ed.). Englewood Cliffs, NJ: Prentice Hall.

Chapter Two

PLANNING A PATH FORWARD

Identifying the Knowledge, Skills, and Dispositions of Second-Generation Community Engagement Professionals

Lina D. Dostilio

This research, done as part of Campus Compact's Project on the Community Engagement Professional, seeks to identify the shared knowledge and practices of community engagement professionals (CEPs) (as described in Chapter 1) by looking to empirical practice literature. In doing so we identify the distinction between CEPs and the larger body of what Jencks and Riesman (1968) termed *academic professionals*. For those of us involved in this project, we feel there is a difference between how we, as CEPs, understand our work and how others involved in community-campus engagement might understand our work. We each have stories of others misunderstanding our roles, underappreciating or ascribing a limiting view of our potential contributions, or overendowing our abilities as something wholly unique to us as persons rather than characteristic of CEPs as a collective. Friedson (2001) concludes that the whole notion of professionalism is predicated on members of the profession possessing describable knowledge and competence that is different enough from what others possess such that those outside of the profession could not holistically evaluate work well done. This project does not intend to describe a profession that has only one professional preparation pathway, nor to develop a system of knowledge, skills, and attributes that are meant to be used in "policing" (à la Friedson, 2001) its own members. However, we believe that our work, knowledge, and attributes are distinct from other academic professionals *and distinct from other actors' within community-campus engagement* (e.g., faculty, community collaborators, or institutional executive leaders).

Typically, knowledge, skills, and attributes common among a particular group of workers are considered *competencies*. The literature on *competencies* is a rich body of work, and though the term remains one of the more recognizable ways to quickly capture a scheme of worker attributes, over time the concept has proven fuzzy (Boon & van der Klink, 2002). Because there are no strict definitional constraints on what key competencies are, they can be logically constructed but may not be able to be psychologically validated (Weinert, 2001). We recognize that describing the skills, knowledge, and qualities of CEPs as competencies may induce some concern that we are proposing a system of rigid, decontextual, and falsely distinct attributes. Despite this very real concern, we conclude that the word *competency* is a useful term to describe the common framework of qualities among CEPs. This chapter introduces the concept of competence and also presents a critique of competency frameworks that are instruments of efficiency or commodification. Approaching competency as a means to commodify labor or to prioritize efficiency undermines our ultimate goal of creating a knowledge base to enable us to construct theories of effective practice and to better inhabit roles as institutional change agents. Next I present the methods of a number of higher education professional groups that have sought to undertake similar projects. Finally, I describe the research that developed the "Preliminary Competency Model for Community Engagement Professionals"; (see Table 2.2); I discuss the research fellows who dedicated their time and expertise to the project as well as outline their approach, method of data collection, and findings. In closing, In closing, I offer the competency model in its entirety (see Table 2.2) and describe the next steps of the research project.

Competency Defined

Professional expertise is observed as high performance in a particular area of practice. High performance rests on using an established body of knowledge to address key aspects of a complex problem (Palonen, Boshuizen, & Lehtinen, 2014). Such expertise is made possible by acquiring discrete units of knowledge and skill and integrating them in such a manner as to transform our practice (Baartman & de Bruijn, 2011). Identifying and characterizing the discrete units within the practice of community-university engagement is vital if we are to understand how one becomes a CEP of the sort who supports a leadership or change agency orientation (see Chapter 1).

The discrete units combine to be known as *competencies* (coming from the Latin roots of *cognizance* and *responsibility* [Rychen & Salganik, 2001]), which are understood as integrated pieces of knowledge, skill, and attitude (Lizzio & Wilson, 2004). Typically, *knowledge* consists of knowing declarative facts, knowing particular procedures, or having awareness of a task or process itself; *skills* are concerned with manipulating, constructing, organizing, sequencing, directing action toward goals, or doing one's practice; *attitudes* or *dispositions* influence one's choice of actions, be they implicit or explicit, conscious or unconscious (Baartman & de Bruijn, 2011).

A number of benefits come from articulating a taxonomy of competencies for any given profession. These include identifying a threshold of knowledge that those coming into the practice ought to have; providing a road map for continued professional learning and development; devising, testing, and validating theories of effective practice; focusing reflective practice; developing curricula or professional development that is relevant to the profession; and directing mentorship efforts (Stevahn, King, Ghere, & Minnema, 2005). To this list we add one final benefit that is driven by the conception of professional we laid out in the previous chapter: Having an identified taxonomy of competencies for CEPs that promotes a relational, contextualized, reflective, and change-oriented practice professionalizes the field in a particular direction, moving from first-generation functions to second-generation civic concerns (Welch & Saltmarsh, 2013).

Critique of Competency Systems

In addition to offering benefits, articulating a model of competence carries significant concern. In particular, there is concern that establishing a list of competencies promotes an inflexible system of competence, which is often defined in a very particular cultural context and by those who are privileged to hold authority within a profession. This can be detrimental to those whose success is defined differently from the dominant worldview in which the competencies were developed or to those who are already marginalized within today's higher education environment (Jeris & Johnson, 2004). Another critique of competency models is that their rationalist approach creates "abstract, narrow, and over-simplified descriptions of competence that fail adequately to reflect the complexity of competence in work performance" (Delemare Le Deist & Winterton, 2005, p. 30). By fragmenting aspects of work, a false sense of concrete boundaries could be formed that prevent an artful, contextualized implementation of practice. Context is absolutely paramount to competence, and many view competence as a function of the context in which it is applied. (More discussion of how a competency frame can be problematic, particularly in a critical and contextualized view of practice, is included in Hernandez and Pasquesi's chapter on critical practice in this volume.)

Our goal in formulating a competency model is not to promote a singular worldview or advance a singular valuation of success, but to acknowledge that there is a threshold of knowledge and skill that CEPs have gained from the pioneers who came before them. Additionally, the practice of engagement has broadened from cocurricular service experiences and service-learning to innovative and nonstandardized forms of community-based learning, community-oriented research, and issue-based partnership development, as well as encompassing a host of community and economic development work. There is a need to articulate various components of knowledge, skill, ability, and dispositions. We do not believe that naming these qualities is problematic. Rather, the problem lies in how the idea of profession is conceptualized and how a competency model is applied. When the conception of profession endorses a model that is highly policed and exclusionary, relies only on didactic education, and is ascribed to those who have completed a literal or figurative checklist, the art and iterative development of excellent work is lost.

As explored in Chapter 1, our conception of profession is highly contextual, socially constructed, reflective, and relational. This description stands in opposition to the expert-informed, narrowly constructed, and highly policed forms of profession such as law or medicine. Our choice to include affective components as competency statements and to prioritize critical commitments as important to a variety of functional areas (but distinct from competencies) illustrates one of the ways in which our conception of profession influenced the development of the competency model. As for use of the competency model, our genuine hope is that the model is used as a formative and path-making device into iterative and reflexive professional development (rather than as a tool for hiring and firing). Though the exact ways in which it will be used are outside of our control, the ways in which our pilot respondents characterized its value (see the sections on pilot findings later in this chapter) bolster our belief that this step is a worthwhile and important one for CEPs.

Examples of Higher Education Professional Group Competency Identification

Other task groups within higher education have sought to identify the competencies necessary for their job roles. Each has taken a slightly different approach, yet all base their work on the idea that having an identified list of competencies provides benefits for those within the profession and discernable pathways for professional development. A number of academic specialty groups are presented here, and similarities and differences between each effort and our present CEP work are noted.

Training and Development Professionals

In 1976 the American Society for Training and Development (ASTD) undertook the identification of core competencies for training and development professionals, including those within higher education institutions found in human resource departments (Pinto & Walker, 1978). Their study began with cataloging the activities performed by ASTD members via self-report, reviewing the association's training and development handbook, and reviewing previous job role analyses. More than 1,000 items were listed across five activity categories; upon eliminating redundancies, the list was narrowed to 403 items, which was then simplified through feedback given by ASTD chapter members across a handful of states. The further-refined list of 105 items was included in a questionnaire that was sent to ASTD members across the United States ($N = 2,071$). Respondents were asked to rate frequency and importance of each item on a six-point scale. Median frequencies were used to determine the most and least important items. Based upon the results, 14 roles (and constituent competencies) were drafted for ASTD members that may occur in multiple combinations in any single training and development staff job. Each role then was viewed as a distinct module that could be used for professional development processes. Not all staff would occupy all 14 roles at any one time, nor are the acquisition of competencies linear in professional development. Rather, they provide a fluid model for the various areas of competence necessary for training and development professionals. The ASTD competency model has been revised a number of times, most recently in 2004 and 2013. Similar to the ASTD approach, the competency model for CEPs should be revised and updated as the work of community engagement evolves. Further, we do not propose that each CEP occupy all of the functional areas outlined at the same time or that their competency development would be linear.

Distance Education Professionals

Williams (2003) investigated the roles and competencies necessary for professionals to implement distance education in online environments. Like community engagement, at the time of the study, distance education had grown exponentially in higher education. Due to the ever-changing environment of technology, distance education staff must continually grow and develop to keep pace. Yet the competencies of the profession are not bound to the specific technological platform or tool available at that time. Williams used the Delphi method (a small group of geographically dispersed experts who provide anonymous input through multiple rounds of survey) to ask a panel of distance education experts to identify the roles and competencies of distance education professionals. The initial survey proposed 12 roles, each with embedded activities that were sourced from extant distance education literature. Over the course of four rounds, the list was refined and clarified. The results were 30 general competencies necessary in each of 13 roles of a distance education professional. The benefits of a Delphi model, designed to build consensus among diverse professionals, may not be appropriate for a competency model in which a democratic orientation is promoted. The reliance on experts or those known as experts may unintentionally marginalize the diversity of practice and emergent practice that could be found by surveying a wider number of CEPs.

Pro–Vice Chancellors

Spendlove (2007) conducted an "empirical scoping study" (p. 407) of the competencies needed for second-in-command leaders within UK higher education (at the level of pro–vice chancellor, rector, or principal). Noting that most research of UK higher education leadership had been conducted at the vice chancellor or presidential level, Spendlove addressed a knowledge gap by looking at the second level of leadership. The second level, abbreviated as the PVC (for pro–vice chancellor), is variously defined depending on the institutional context, and people who occupy the position may have academic or professional backgrounds or both. The study sought to identify competencies as a means to clarify paths of leadership development. Twelve PVCs participated in semistructured interviews that were thematically coded. The results were compared with Bartram's (2005) "Great Eight" competency model that outlines eight generic competencies:

1. leading and deciding,
2. supporting and cooperating,
3. interacting and presenting,

4. analyzing and interpreting,
5. creating and conceptualizing,
6. organizing and executing,
7. adapting and coping, and
8. enterprising and performing.

Unprompted themes that differed from the Great Eight were noted. The diversity among PVC positions is similar to the diversity within CEP positions in that their nature is affected by the institutional context and professional preparation of those who occupy them. However, the sheer number of CEPs requires a competency identification method that would gather a larger number of respondents. Interviewing a select few would not capture the complexity of the field or its practices.

Professional Evaluators

Professional evaluators have a role complexity similar to that of CEPs. Both have diversity within their position responsibilities, use various methods, and work with diverse stakeholders across diverse contexts. An exploratory study (King, Stevahn, Ghere, & Minnema, 2001) was conducted to determine the degree to which diverse practitioners reached agreement on a taxonomy of evaluator competencies that had been developed in 1999 (King, Minnema, Ghere, & Stevahn, 1999). A class of advanced graduate students used an assignment to devise the 1999 competencies. The 2001 exploratory study began by reviewing evaluation practice literature, standards for professional evaluation practice developed by the Joint Committee on Standards for Educational Evaluation in 1994, and the guiding principles publicized by the American Evaluation Association in 1995. King and colleagues (2001) then used the document review to create a draft of the *Essential Evaluator Competencies* and sought informal feedback from two experts in the field. The competencies (which included 4 domains of activity, 16 competency categories, and 49 competency items) were then validated using the multiattribute consensus reaching (MACR) method, an adaptation of the multiattribute consensus building process (Vanderwood & Erickson, 1994).

Small groups of respondents were convened. They individually rank-ordered the list of competencies using scores of 0–100, with 0 indicating little perceived importance and 100 indicating the highest perceived importance. Being sure to rank at least one competency item in each domain as 100, the respondents established anchor scores for each domain and its constituent competencies. Then the median scores and ranges for each item were shared with the group, and the group discussed their reasons for scoring items in the ways they had. The group was then encouraged to rerank those items for which there were wide ranges of scores, building toward agreement. The method provided systematically gathered quantitative (ranking) and qualitative (comments) data that were used to refine the list of competencies. The methods used for professional evaluators are particularly promising for developing CEP competencies. The systematic and inclusive data collection, starting point within relevant literature, and inclusion of graduate students as meaningful contributors are very similar to many of the conditions available to the CEP project.

Student Affairs Professionals

Professional standards for student affairs practitioners have been developed (Weiner, Bresciani, Oyler, & Felix, 2011) via document analysis of reports from the Student Affairs Administrators in Higher Education (NASPA), the American College Personnel Association (ACPA), and the Council for the Advancement of Standards (CAS). Although there have been many attempts to determine competencies for student affairs professionals (see Burkard, Cole, Ott, & Stoflet, 2005; Kuk, Cobb, & Forrest, 2007), the intention for the standards is to provide a benchmark of practice across the three main student affairs associations, which student affairs staff can use for professional development planning. The document analysis provided a list of competencies, which the authors chose to call *learning goals*, that provide structures for professional development opportunities and associated curriculum.

Weiner and colleagues (2011) reviewed 19 documents, consisting of officially sanctioned professional association reports. They began by circulating a list of documents for potential review to representatives of NASPA, ACPA, and CAS. The list of documents was expanded based upon representatives' suggested additions. Using line-by-line coding, the researchers identified shared themes and were able to produce eight learning goals for student affairs practitioners:

1. provide counseling, facilitation, and/or structures that support and enhance student learning and development;
2. develop and expand students' and colleagues' leadership skills and opportunities;
3. incorporate diversity into curricular and cocurricular experiences;
4. incorporate assessment, evaluation, and research into practice;
5. demonstrate organizational management and resource development, and promote fiscal responsibility;

6. accurately interpret and comply with laws and institutional policies;
7. commit to the guiding principles for ethical and collaborative professional practice; and
8. demonstrate sound supervision and conflict resolution skills. (p. 14)

The researchers also investigated differences within each of the eight learning goals for those just entering the profession versus those who were midlevel versus those who were longtime practitioners. Though this approach is intriguing, our conception of professional promoted within the CEP project advances Scanlon's (2011) idea of "becoming," which goes beyond a stage development from novice to expert, and instead promotes reflexive, evolving professional learning. CEPs have varied backgrounds; some come from bases of rich experience as community leaders, faculty, nonprofit executives, or student activists, and it would not be appropriate to consider them novices upon entering a CEP role.

Clarifying the Competencies of Community Engagement Professionals: Data Collection, Analysis, and Findings

The most pronounced difference between the Student Affairs Standards document review study (Weiner et al., 2011) and the CEP project is that it was built on many previous attempts to outline the skills, knowledge, attitudes, and practices of student affairs professionals, dating back to 1942. Presently, we have only one other attempt to identify a list of qualities or roles for CEPs:[1] *Diving Deep in Community Engagement: A Model for Professional Development* (McReynolds & Shields, 2015). Based on the reflections of 22 CEPs who experienced the Iowa Campus Compact Diving Deep Institute together, the book puts forward four categories of leadership roles—institutional strategic leader, organizational manager, field contributor, and community innovator—and 15 component activities. The model ties these together with the roles of communicator, reflector, and educator. Though the book describes the model as a competency model, the components are named in such a way as to present activities that are not explicitly linked with knowledge, skill, ability, and disposition. From this, we determined there was still a contribution to be made and that it could be done in a way that replicated the most promising and appropriate strategies from the other higher education competency development models described earlier in this chapter.

Given the diversity of positions and methods used within educational evaluation, and given the interest in receiving input from various evaluators (independent of their perceived expert status), the competency development method used among professional evaluators (King et al., 1999; King et al., 2001) appeared to be a very good model for the CEP project. Our method included the following phases: (a) development of a literature review from which a lengthy list of competencies was sourced, (b) pilot testing of the competency framework and review by prominent engagement leaders, and (c) the use of an open survey to collect a large response to the list of competencies.

Phase One: Literature Review

Fifteen research fellows were selected from across the country to assist in a large review of practice literature across seven areas: managing change within higher education, institutionalizing community engagement, faculty development, student civic development and learning, cultivating high-quality partnerships, critical practice, and program administration and evaluation. The fellows were predominantly staff who currently or previously supported community engagement practices within institutions of higher education. A few had stepped away from their professional work to pursue doctoral studies or had just completed their doctoral degrees.

Research fellows met almost weekly over a five-month period to create a shared learning community. During those meetings, the group learned about how to conduct a literature review and then learned about the nature of competencies. The group read, discussed, and often revisited Welch and Saltmarsh's (2013) study on community engagement centers and infrastructure. Their distinction between first-generation and second-generation engagement practice was a central frame for determining the skills, knowledge, and dispositions important to second-generation engagement. The research fellows split into pairs (and the occasional triad) and chose one of seven areas to guide their review of empirical literature dating from 1990 through the present. Each of the areas is presented as a chapter within this book, and the authors of each chapter describe their specific literature review method for that topic.

Due to the paucity of literature about CEPs (or staff or practitioners), very few studies explicitly listed knowledge, skills, abilities, or dispositions necessary for professionals. Rather, the research fellows observed the practice being promoted within the literature and inferred what qualities a CEP would need in order to support that practice effectively. During two of the weekly calls, the group reviewed a study and practiced inferring the knowledge, skills, abilities, and dispositions that CEPs might need to have to embody the practice. This practice of inferring competencies is directly dependent on the subjectivity of the research fellow, which, in this case, has a positive connotation. Scanlon (2011) points to the difference between knowledge *about* a profession and knowledge *of* a profession. The research fellows are all *of* the community engagement profession, and as such are well positioned to infer the competencies necessary to support the practices revealed in the literature.

Once the literature review was concluded, the distinct competencies within each functional area were pulled together in one list with duplicates excluded, with the exception of the commitments surfaced within the critical practice literature review. By their very nature, critical commitments cannot be positioned as competencies, as that would "reflect neoliberal character by eroding the nonmarket critical, ethical, and moral dimensions of practice" (Hernandez and Pasquesi, p. 58, this volume). A decision was made to list these commitments at the beginning of the competency list to call attention to their unique nature but also to assert their presence within the project. This was the first round of refining the competency model.

The competency list was formatted into a ranking tool so that the scoring system used in the MACR method (King et al., 2001) could be used to determine the degree to which CEPs perceive a particular competency as of high, moderate, or low importance. Slight wording changes were made to enhance the clarity of each item and to provide consistent verbiage: "Knowledge of . . ." to indicate an item of knowledge, "Able to . . ." to indicate skill or ability, and "Embrace . . ." to indicate a dispositional stance. After continued consideration, the critical commitments were then moved into each of the functional areas and listed alongside the other competencies. Though this might negate the stance that a critical commitment is not a competency, sidelining the commitments could have led respondents to assume they were something outside of normal practice and would have prevented us from knowing how CEPs ranked their importance in relation to other items within that functional area. In total, this led to 102 items across seven ares of focus.

Phase Two: Pilot Testing of the Model

Four professional association meetings were selected at which the competency ranking tool would be piloted, leading to the third round of refining the competency model. Participants were recruited from sessions advertised in the regular conference program. The sessions began with an overview of the project, including the definition of *community engagement professional*. Once informed consent procedures were explained, attendees were able to opt into or out of the pilot study and either remain in the session so that they could observe the discussion or leave and attend a different conference session. Participants then used either pen-and-pencil questionnaires or an online Qualtrics survey interface to answer demographic questions (see Table 2.1) and to rank each of the competency items using the scoring system described earlier. Following the rankings exercise, participants were reconvened in a focus group–styled conversation wherein five questions were explored:

1. What pieces of knowledge, skill, or disposition do you feel are missing?
2. What items were unclear?
3. Did the experience of ranking these items hold any value for you? If so, what?
4. What agendas of inquiry does this open up?
5. How might the refined list be used in practice?

Fifty-two completed survey responses (including demographic information) were collected. Two responses had some items for which there were rankings missing and so were excluded from the pilot data. In addition to the 52 completed surveys, four participants began the survey but did not finish, so their answers could not be included in the pilot data set. Eight people chose not to participate but to remain present for the discussion and so signed confidentiality agreements.

TABLE 2.1
Demographic Information

Years as staff within higher education	Supervision of other staff	Highest degree obtained
Years as a community engagement professional	Position title	Disciplinary affiliation
Type of institution	Unit location within the institution (reporting lines)	Faculty responsibilities in addition to administrative responsibilities
Gender	Race	Age
Primary area of functional responsibility	Previous professional development	Long-term professional career goal
Number of students enrolled of institution (under graduate and graduate)		

Pilot Participants

The 50 pilot respondents demonstrated a median number of six and a half years as community engagement staff, with the majority categorizing their primary area of function as comprehensive community engagement support, such as directing a center or otherwise occupying a campus-wide engagement position. Ninety-five percent held a graduate degree, and of those, 36% either held a doctorate or were presently pursuing one. The median age of pilot respondents was 36, with a range of 22 to 65 years of age. Of the 39 pilot respondents who chose to indicate a gender, 70% identified as female. Fifty-four percent supervised other engagement staff, with an average of nine staff members. Sixty-two percent expressed their primary area of function as comprehensive community engagement support, such as a center director or other campus-wide engagement position. Fourteen percent expressed their primary area of function as community partnership support, 10% as student development support, 6% as faculty development, and 4% as research or evaluation. Thirty-four percent of respondents (or 17) indicated they also had a faculty role, and of these, only 3 were tenure-track or tenured faculty. Of those respondents who indicated a long-term career objective, 23% hoped to become a hybrid administrator and faculty member; 18% hoped to become a university president; 17% wanted to be a community engagement unit director; 12% desired to move out of higher education to either a policy position, foundation work, nonprofit leadership, or state Campus Compact directorship; 12% hoped to become a vice president for community engagement; and 12% hoped to become tenured faculty.

Pilot Functional Area Findings

Respondents were asked to indicate how important they felt each functional area was based on *what they perceived a community engagement professional may need to know, do, and value in order to support change-oriented and civically oriented community engagement*. None of the functional areas received an average value score of less than 74, indicating that all of the functional areas were perceived as important.

Pilot Competency Findings

Respondents were then asked to indicate how important they felt *each* item *within* each functional area was based on the same criteria. Respondents used a 0- to 100-point ranking to indicate importance (0 being the least important and 100 being most important) and were instructed that at least one item in each functional area needed to be scored at 100 to establish an anchor score for each domain. As for the items within each functional area, those with an average value of 70 or below were cut from the competency model because they were not perceived as having high importance. Eight items were excluded from the model after the pilot round:

1. Leading change within higher education: Able to promote accountability
2. Leading change within higher education: Embrace an analytical perspective
3. Institutionalizing community engagement: Knowledge of risk management
4. Institutionalizing community engagement: Knowledge of organizational theory and models of institutionalization
5. Administrating community engagement programs: Knowledge of AmeriCorps, Work-Study, and other forms of student employment
6. Administrating community engagement programs: Able to develop and manage an international service experience
7. Facilitating faculty development and support: Able to manage distribution of calls for proposals, proposal review, fund distribution, and project management
8. Facilitating faculty development and support: Able to help faculty reflect on how they allot time to teaching, research, and community engagement

Pilot Missing Items/Functional Areas

Respondents were asked to describe items they felt were missing from the overall list, via the survey instrument and also during the focus groups held following the survey responses. Across these forums, only a few items came up repeatedly and could be considered as having shared support for their inclusion. These new items included the following:

- Administrating community engagement programs: Embrace community partners as coeducators
- Facilitating faculty development and support: Embrace multidisciplinary and interdisciplinary collaborations.

An additional functional area was identified as missing: community and economic development. Creating a functional area focused on community and economic development would require another cycle of development within the competency model including literature review, pilot testing, and then data collection. Presently, this round of development has not occurred, but it should be explored for inclusion in the competency model in the future.

Pilot Meaning-Making

During the focus group session following the ranking activity, respondents expressed a range of responses to the exercise. At each of the four sessions, multiple participants asked if they could have the competencies list to share with a supervisor, a supervisee, or an advisory group. When questioned about what value the competency list held, those requesting the tool described their hope to use the tool to *advocate* for themselves or for improved practice. As one person put it, "We do more than we give ourselves credit for; we do more than others credit us."

Some respondents expressed either being overwhelmed by the number of competencies or being surprised by how many of the competencies they feel they employ on a weekly or monthly basis. As one participant said, "This put words and conceptual framework around multidimensionality and explains why I am so tired at the end of the day." A number of participants shared variations of, "No wonder I'm tired," or, "I'm overwhelmed by this, but I'm often overwhelmed by the scope of my job."

At each session, quite a bit of discussion took place on whether the list of competencies could be reasonably applied to individuals or if it ought to be viewed as applicable to teams. Some insisted that a list of competencies of such number could only be exhibited across large teams and that the tool could assist them to reflect on the strengths and areas of team development. Other participants insisted they felt responsible for most of these functions individually, though perhaps not within a single day or season. At least one respondent in each session indicated he or she did not work in a team setting; one participant self-reported as an "office of one" and already felt pressure to support all functional areas alone. This could be linked to the sense of overwhelmedness or tiredness some participants expressed. Those respondents expressed validation in that they could show others the large scope of their work. Both groups agreed that the competency list provided clear directions for professional development, and one participant suggested, "Now I'll have a way to weigh my staff's requests for professional development experiences." Multiple participants thought they would use the competency model to structure professional goal-setting meetings, which typically occur as part of annual reviews, for themselves or for those they supervise.

The opportunity to reflect on one's practice was noted across the four sessions: "We talk about reflection all the time, but rarely do it. This was a real opportunity to take time to reflect on what I do and what I can do better." Another participant said, "[This exercise] made me reflect on [first] gen programs and why they no longer exist, and perceived importance of what we can negotiate, why roles are changing, why previous programs were not sustained." Interestingly, as participants reflected on why they ranked some items as more important than others, they expressed disagreement. Some felt that every competency on the list ought to be ranked at 100 (highly important) while others felt no draw to do so and enjoyed noting that some of the items were of very little importance in a second-generation frame.

Some participants provided feedback on the nature of the items, noting appreciation for the affective statements: "I appreciate that humility was included. It's like we're afraid to talk about the soft stuff." One participant recognized that the list provided statements that characterized both the "science" and the "art" of engagement work: "communicating with faculty is necessary, it's science; helping faculty to synergize the connections between engagement, their teaching and research is art." Another participant pointed to a similar dichotomy, saying,

> [This] clarifies for me, again, that there's content and instrumental capacity, but there's this whole piece of the self that I wonder if we spend enough time talking about, such as ambiguity, humility, critical consciousness, etc. These are things worth talking about. How do we do this in a way that has integrity and support each other more?

Phase Three: Second Round of Model Refinement

Upon completion of the pilot round, the model now had 93 distinct items of knowledge, skills and ability, and disposition as well as critical commitments within each area. After the number of competencies was reduced and some language clarified using the pilot findings, the competency model was reviewed with a group of engagement leaders whom Campus Compact convened. This gathering embedded the review of the competency model within a discussion of the value of creating a credential for engagement practitioners. The attendees included representatives from two state campus compacts, three large institutions recognized for their commitment to community engagement, the Association of American Colleges & Universities (AAC&U), the Coalition of Urban and Metropolitan Universities (CUMU), the American Association of

State Colleges and Universities (AASCU), Imagining America (IA), the New England Resource Center for Higher Education (NERCHE), and NASPA (Student Affairs Administrators in Higher Education). While general support with some concerns was expressed for a credential, those attending expressed unanimous support for the competency framework.

The final phase of data collection further refined the "Preliminary Competency Model for Community Engagement Professionals" through the use of survey procedures modeled after the MACR method (King et al., 2001). The survey replicated the rankings tool and open-ended questions used in the pilot study—revising for the updated number of competencies while retaining the demographic questions asked during the pilot phase and including two additional questions at the request of Campus Compact.

The survey link was distributed to all Campus Compact member institutions with a letter of introduction from the president of Campus Compact. It was also distributed through the networks of the engagement leaders who had attended the summit called by Campus Compact in which the model had been reviewed. The survey link was posted on the Higher Education Service-Learning Listserv. The research fellows, including the author of this chapter, e-mailed the link to CEPs within their professional networks. Finally, in hopes of attracting a robust respondent group from land-grant institutions, the author held a workshop with members of the Outreach and Engagement Professionals Network, a subgroup of the Engagement Scholarship Consortium. During that workshop, participants completed the survey.

Survey Respondents
There were a total of 414 respondents; 42% were unit leaders (e.g., center directors), 42.8% were unit staff (e.g., coordinators within larger offices), 6.42% were deans or division leaders, 5.2% were faculty leaders (e.g., faculty fellows or faculty who chaired advisory committees, but who did not have formal administrative responsibilities), and 3.67% were executive administrators. Respondents had an average number of 8.4 years as a CEP. The range of years of experience varied from 0.25 to 40. Of those who were considered unit staff, the mean number of years employed was 6; for unit leaders it was 10, for faculty leaders it was 13, for dean or division leaders it was 10.5, and for executive administrators it was 12.25.

Respondents indicated their primary area of functional responsibility. Fifty-eight percent were responsible for providing comprehensive support for community engagement, 21% for student development, 9%

for faculty development, 8% for community partnership support, and 4% other.

Thirty percent of respondents had a terminal degree. Thirty-two percent held faculty designations at their institutions. Of those, a little more than one-third were tenured or tenure track. Three hundred twenty-eight respondents indicated they had some teaching responsibilities and reported the percentage of their time spent teaching. Of these, 17% (or 56) spent 25% or more of their time teaching in any given year.

Three hundred fifteen respondents identified a gender. Of these, 80% (252) identified as female, and 20% (63) identified as male. Three hundred fifteen respondents also provided a description of their racial identity. The open-ended responses were highly varied in their description. Simple categories of White, non-White (for single-race identification), and multiple-race (for multiple-race identification) indicate that the majority of respondents were White (87%), whereas only 9% were non-White, Single Race, and 4% were non-White, multiple-race. Thus, the typical respondent was a White female.

Findings

Just as in the pilot, respondents were asked to rank each competency item on a scale of 0 to 100, with at least one item in each functional area receiving a 100 score to provide an anchor. A score between 80 and 100 indicated high importance.

Using an analysis of variance, there were no significant differences among the aggregated averages of the competencies within the functional areas when comparing respondents from the four primary areas of responsibility subgroups (those who are responsible for comprehensive support and those responsible for faculty, student, or partnership development). In other words, a respondent who was primarily responsible for a specific area of work (e.g., faculty development or student development) did not rank the competencies within that functional area in aggregate differently than did other respondents. This gives us confidence that there actually is a framework of knowledge, skill, disposition, and critical commitment that is found to be important across CEPs of various areas of responsibility.

Across all respondents, the following items averaged at or below a 75 score, given a 95% confidence interval, which is a five-point higher cutoff than for the previous round:

- Administering: Knowledge of curriculum development

- Partnerships: Knowledge of theories that guide partnership development
- Partnerships: Able to nurture a sense of closeness among partners
- Faculty development: Knowledge of various faculty career stages and ranks
- Faculty development: Able to articulate the pressures or "existential unease" of engagement without alienating or discouraging faculty

Four of the items—embrace the tension between charity and social change, knowledge of curriculum development, knowledge of various faculty career stages and ranks, and able to articulate the pressures or "existential unease" of engagement—were retained despite their mean survey scores due to the importance placed on these within the initial literature review.

There were 76 responses to one open-ended question: "Are there items missing from the previously identified areas of knowledge, skills, ability, and disposition that you feel are critical for a community engagement professional to possess?" Based upon themes within the responses, an additional 13 competencies were developed.

Resulting Competency Model
In total, the resulting competency model (see Table 2.2) contains 103 distinct areas of knowledge, skills and abilities, dispositions, and critical commitments across six functional areas. The three items that had mean scores of 75 or less but that were retained are noted, as are the 14 new competencies introduced as the result of open-ended suggestions.

Discussion and Next Steps

The primary goal of developing a list of competencies is to make it possible to create paths through which individuals gain competence. Without a systematic and empirical basis for a competency schema, our paths for competence development will be based in trial and error. In this way, we will continue the first generation's approach, which was to make it up as they went (Welch & Saltmarsh, 2013), rather than learn from, and perhaps be mentored by, those first-generation pioneers. An accompanying goal is to make visible the critical commitments that animate a second-generation orientation to supporting community engagement practice. It is only through naming and drawing attention to these critical commitments that we can, with concerted effort, socialize CEPs toward these ways of working.

TABLE 2.2
Preliminary Competency Model for Community Engagement Professionals, 2017

Development: The preliminary competency model was developed through an extensive literature review of community-engaged practice literature, piloted at a series of national meetings, refined, and then further refined through the survey responses of 414 community engagement professionals.

Uses: We envision a variety of applications for the CEP competency model, including professional development planning, learning community development, team development, structuring mentoring conversations, focusing research and theory development on effective practice, and socializing CEPs to the critical nature and change-oriented work of their positions.

Why "Preliminary"? We do not envision this framework to be fixed or static. It is typical for competency models to be revisited regularly as a field's practice evolves (e.g., see the evolution of the Student Affairs Educators Competencies, which are updated every four years).

Citation: L. D. Dostilio, J. Benenson, S. Chamberlin, S. Crossland, A. Farmer-Hanson, K. Hernandez, and colleagues (2016). *Preliminary Competency Model for Community Engagement Professionals.* In L. D. Dostilio (Ed.), *The Community Engagement Professional in Higher Education: A Competency Model for an Emerging Field.* Boston, MA: Campus Compact.

	Competencies		Dispositions	Critical Commitments
	Knowledge	*Skills and Abilities*		
Leading Change Within Higher Education	• Knowledge of democratic engagement and ability to encourage a democratic engagement orientation (participatory processes, cocreation of knowledge, coplanning, inclusivity, etc.) • Knowledge of change as a process that involves cultural and structural change • Knowledge of one's own personal agency as a change-maker	• Able to articulate connection between institutional mission and community engagement • Able to facilitate meetings and programs that are inclusive and participatory, and that promote reflective practice** • Able to integrate curricular and cocurricular pathways for student learning • Able to integrate goals and strategies of common initiatives	• Desire to participate fully in the institution (participating in governance, serving on committees, representing ethical concerns) • Embrace a proactive stance • Embrace innovation • Embrace perseverance	• *Embrace the tension between charity and social change** • Committed to developing critical consciousness through meaningful praxis (reflection, dialogue, and action) • Able to challenge problematic language use (e.g., paternalistic, dehumanizing, oppressive)

	• Knowledge of other initiatives that align with community engagement • Knowledge of the relevance of community engagement to other campus goals	• Able to manage conflict • Able to plan strategically • Able to tolerate ambiguity • Able to work in fluid environments • Able to work with rather than against administration (e.g., sharing information)	• *Embrace adaptability and risk taking*** • *Embrace diversity among collaborators and promote inclusion***	• Knowledge of ideologies and political, social and historical contexts underpinning higher education
Institutionalizing Community Engagement on a Campus	• Knowledge of institutional and program evaluation methods • *Knowledge of potential funders, grant seeking*** • *Knowledge of benchmarks or artifacts of institutionalization***	• Able to advocate for community engagement and communicate its value, vision, and goals in your context • Able to advocate for development of policies that support community engagement • Able to communicate an institution's brand of engagement (e.g., orientation and animating mission) • Able to conceive and implement institutional structures to support engagement • Able to cultivate a critical mass of supporters for engagement • Able to empower people within the institutions they serve and to hire and develop good staff	• Embrace respect for community perspectives	• Able to unveil, name, and challenge contradictions within practice • Able to work within the structural constraints of the institution toward social change

(Continues)

TABLE 2.2 (Continued)

	Competencies			Critical Commitments
	Knowledge	Skills and Abilities	Dispositions	
		• Able to leverage resources and advocate for community engagement as an institutional funding priority • Able to navigate the institution's political environment • Able to report data to strengthen institutional support • *Able to balance multiple priorities and to plan for short-term and long-term goals***		
Facilitating Students' Civic Learning and Development	• Knowledge of civic learning pedagogies (as potentially distinct from community-engaged pedagogies) • Knowledge of students' developmental trajectories and expression of civic learning and development • Knowledge of the ways in which students' identities inform and frame their community engagement experience, particularly those students from historically marginalized groups	• Able to facilitate peer-to-peer discussion that positively impacts student learning • *Able to construct solid learning outcome goals*** • *Able to collaborate with and support historically marginalized students***	• Embrace an asset-based mind-set that guides work with students • Embrace the value of contributing to the larger community as a role model for students	• Committed to cultivating authentic relationships with students • Committed to developing students' critical consciousness

Administering Community Engagement Programs	• Knowledge of assessment and evaluation methods; able to assess and evaluate impact of community engagement on its stakeholders (e.g., students, faculty, communities, institution) • Knowledge of civic skills • Knowledge of community-engaged pedagogies, including history, methods, underlying theories, and community challenges that may be addressed through community-engaged pedagogies • Knowledge of community-engaged scholarship, including history, methods, underlying theories, and community challenges that may be addressed through community-engaged scholarship • Knowledge of context: of self, of institution, of environments external to institution, of history of engagement	• Able to collaborate and work across role and disciplinary silos • Able to cultivate and maintain relationships • Able to cultivate and manage multiple funding streams and budgets • Able to develop and supervise staff • *Able to collect and analyze data*** • *Able to assess and evaluate impact of community engagement on its stakeholders*** • *Able to communicate effectively***	• Embrace critical thinking • Embrace visionary thinking • Embrace community partners as coeducators	• Committed to dialogue with communities • Able to unveil and disrupt unequal power structures • Able to recognize one's subject position in connection to privilege and oppression • Able to name injustices and power differentials

(*Continues*)

TABLE 2.2 (Continued)

	Competencies			Critical Commitments
	Knowledge	Skills and Abilities	Dispositions	
	• Knowledge of curriculum development* • Knowledge of institutional policies that may affect community engagement (e.g., faculty handbook, student handbook)			
Facilitating Faculty Development and Support	• Knowledge of how to approach differently motivated faculty using different strategies • Knowledge of how various departments or disciplines place value on categories of faculty work: teaching, research, and service • Knowledge of institutional constraints and possibilities that prevent or support faculty engagement • Knowledge of the logistics support needed to implement engaged teaching and research	• Able to articulate the pressures or "existential unease" of engagement without alienating or discouraging faculty* • Able to customize developmental training and support to fit each faculty member's needs and interests • Able to empathize with faculty and understand possibly conflicting demands on faculty time • Able to facilitate critical reflection wherein faculty encounter the limits of their own experience and value of leveraging community expertise	• Embrace humility • Embrace innovation/good at designing and implementing new programs • Embrace patience • Embrace persuasion • Embrace multidisciplinary and interdisciplinary collaborations	• Able to model effective communication to enhance co-construction of courses, research, and other collaborative enterprises between community partners and faculty • Understanding dynamics of power and privilege in faculty roles in moving toward emancipatory and democratic practices

Planning a Path Forward 51

	Knowledge	Skills	Dispositions
	• Knowledge of the needs, research interests, and areas of expertise of faculty engaging in CES • *Knowledge of various faculty career stages and ranks**	• Able to facilitate faculty learning from one another • Able to help faculty brainstorm how to incorporate community engagement into teaching and research • Able to help faculty synergize their teaching, research, and community engagement • *Able to model how to construct solid student learning outcome goals***	• Conscious of power relations inherent in partnerships • Committed to cultivating authentic relationships with communities
Cultivating High-Quality Partnerships	• Knowledge of self: self-awareness • *Knowledge of local community: history, strengths, assets, agendas, goals***	• Able to communicate across boundaries and roles, and between internal and external stakeholders • Able to connect campus and community assets • Able to initiate and maintain effective partnerships • Able to involve partnership members in reflection on and assessment of partnerships • Able to resolve conflict	• Embrace passion for and commitment to community engagement • *Desire to participate in the ongoing life of the community (participating in community-building events, serving on boards, being aware of and invested in community concerns)***

* Mean score of 75 or less, using a 95% confidence interval; **potential additions that were themes among open-ended "what is missing" responses.

Technical competence is developed through education, professional practice, mentorship, and professional development; ethical competence is developed through professional socialization and knowledge of and adherence to a code of ethics (Bowman, West, Berman, & van Wart, 2004). Within their literature review of vocational education, Baartman and de Bruijn (2011) investigated the processes by which competence is acquired. They determined there are three integration processes: low-road integration, which consists of learning automatization from repeated practice; high-road integration, which consists of coupling practice with reflection on the task; and transformative integration, which comes from critical self-reflection and openness to change. As Keith (2015) reminds us,

> Belonging to a profession is about more than having knowledge and skills that are relevant to a field of practice: it is about ways of seeing the world and of framing problems, assumptions, and value judgments. It is about personal disposition, ethical posture, and more. (p. 76)

Our hope is that the professional development pathways created in response to this project honor multiple forms of integration and balance didactic education with professional socialization, mentorship, experiential learning, and critical self-reflection.

With the exception of correlating primary areas of responsibility to the competency rankings, the findings shared here do not explore the insights gained by correlating the demographic information provided by respondents to their competency rankings. One of the immediate next steps of the project is to investigate if significant differences exist in the competency rankings among those with varying years employed, between gender or racial identity, between role types (unit staff, unit leaders, faculty leaders, or executive leaders), with varying percentages of time spent teaching, and on different reporting lines. It is also important to begin to drill down more exhaustively into subsets of competencies. For example, understanding how items are integrated to develop greater competence in conflict resolution, assessment and evaluation, relationship development, and so on is vital to carving out professional development pathways.

Finally, and perhaps most importantly, revisiting this competency framework periodically in a systematic way (similar to how the student affairs competency model is periodically revised) is vital to refining and pushing forward our practice. The 414 respondents to the final survey were predominantly female and White. Developing a more robust respondent group that is more representative of the diversity now found among CEPs is absolutely critical to this continued refinement. And, of course, developing more diversity within the ranks of CEPs moving forward is paramount to this effort.

Tremendous credit is due to the research fellows who worked so diligently to develop the literature review that informed this competency model. Our work is a first attempt that must be revisited and refined. It is making visible a catalog of work and capacities that we understand to be our trade but that until now were largely invisible and unnamed to those who were not involved in the work of supporting community-campus engagement.

Note

1. Competencies have been identified for faculty who pursue community-engaged scholarship (Blanchard et al., 2009; Jordan et al., 2012) and for civic engagement as a field of study (Brammer et al., 2012) but none have been identified for staff or what we call community engagement professionals.

References

Baartman, L. K., & de Bruijn, E. (2011). Integrating knowledge, skills and attitudes: Conceptualising learning processes towards vocational competence. *Educational Research Review, 6*(2), 125–134.

Bartram, D. (2005). The great eight competencies: A criterion-centric approach to validation. *Journal of Applied Psychology, 90*(6), 1185–1203.

Blanchard, L. W., Hanssmann, C., Strauss, R. P., Belliard, J., Krichbaum, C., Waters, E., & Seifer, S. (2009, August). Models for faculty development: What does it take to be a community-engaged scholar? *Metropolitan Universities, 20*, 47–65.

Boon, J., & van der Klink, M. (2002). Competencies: The triumph of a fuzzy concept. In *Proceedings of Academy of Human Resource Development Annual Conference*, Honolulu, HI, February 27–March 3, 1:327–334.

Bowman, J. S., West, J. P., Berman, E. M., & van Wart, M. (2004). *The professional edge: Competencies in public service*. Armonk, NY: M. E. Sharpe.

Brammer, L., Dumlao, R., Falk, A., Hollander, E., Knutson, E., Poehnert, J., . . . Werner, V. (2012). *Core competencies in civic engagement*. North Andover, MA; Center for Engaged Democracy Policy Paper Series, Merrimack College.

Burkard, A. W., Cole, D. C., Ott, M., & Stoflet, T. (2005). Entry-level competencies of new student affairs professionals: A Delphi study. *Journal of Student Affairs Research and Practice, 42*(3), 545–571.

Delemare Le Deist, F., & Winterton, J. (2005). What is competence? *Human Resource Development International, 8*(1), 27–46.

Friedson, E. (2001). *Professionalism: The third logic*. Chicago, IL: University of Chicago Press.

Jencks, C., & Riesman, D. (1968). *The academic revolution*. New York, NY: Doubleday.

Jeris, L., & Johnson, K. (2004). Speaking of competence: Toward a cross-translation for human resource development (HRD) and continuing professional education. In *Proceedings of Academy of Human Resource Development Annual Conference*, Austin, TX, March 4–7, 2:1103–1110.

Jordan, C., Doherty, W., Jones-Webb, R., Cook, N., Dubrow, G., & Mendenhall, T J. (2012). Competency-based faculty development in community-engaged scholarship: A diffusion of innovation approach. *Journal of Higher Education Outreach and Engagement, 16*(1), 65–96.

Keith, N. (2015). *Engaging in social partnerships: Democratic practices for campus-community partnerships*. New York, NY: Routledge Taylor Francis Group.

King, J. A., Minnema, J. E., Ghere, G., & Stevahn, L. (1999). *Essential evaluator competencies*. Minneapolis, MN: Program Evaluation Studies, University of Minnesota.

King, J. A., Stevahn, L., Ghere, G., & Minnema, J. (2001). Toward a taxonomy of essential evaluator competencies. *American Journal of Evaluation, 22*(2), 229–247.

Kuk, L., Cobb, B., & Forrest, C. (2007). Perceptions of competencies of entry-level practitioners in student affairs. *NASPA Journal, 44*(4), 664–691.

Lizzio, A., & Wilson, K. (2004). Action learning in higher education: An investigation of its potential to develop professional capability. *Studies in Higher Education, 29*(4), 469–488.

McReynolds, M., & Shields, E. (Eds.). (2015). *Diving deep in community engagement: A model for professional development*. Des Moines, IA: Iowa Campus Compact.

Palonen, T., Boshuizen, H. P., & Lehtinen, E. (2014). How expertise is created in emerging professional fields. In S. Billett, T. Halttunen, & M. Koivisto (Eds.), *Promoting, assessing, recognizing and certifying lifelong learning* (pp. 131–149). New York, NY: Springer.

Pinto, P. R., & Walker, J. W. (1978). What do training and development professionals really do? *Training and Development Journal, 32*(7), 58–64.

Rychen, D. S., & Salganik, L. H. (2001). *Defining and selecting key competencies*. Cambridge, MA: Hogrefe & Huber.

Scanlon, L. (2011). "Becoming" a professional. In I. Scanlon (Ed.), *Becoming a professional: An interdisciplinary analysis of professional learning* (pp. 13–32). Dordrecht, Netherlands: Springer.

Spendlove, M. (2007). Competencies for effective leadership in higher education. *International Journal of Educational Management, 21*(5), 407–417.

Stevahn, L., King, J. A., Ghere, G., & Minnema, J. (2005). Establishing essential competencies for program evaluators. *American Journal of Evaluation, 26*(1), 43–59.

Vanderwood, M. L., & Erickson, R. (1994). Consensus building. *Educational Outcomes for Students With Disabilities, 2*, 99.

Weiner, L., Bresciani, M. J., Oyler, J., & Felix, E. (2011). Developing and implementing professional standards for student affairs practitioners. *Journal of Student Affairs, 20*, 86–93.

Weinert, F. E. (2001). Concept of competence: A conceptual clarification. In D. S. Rychen & L. H. Salganik (Eds.), *Defining and selecting key competencies* (pp. 45–65). Seattle, WA: Hogrefe & Huber.

Welch, M., & Saltmarsh, J. (2013). Current practice and infrastructures for campus centers of community engagement. *Journal of Higher Education Outreach and Engagement, 17*(4), 25–56.

Williams, P. E. (2003). Roles and competencies for distance education programs in higher education institutions. *American Journal of Distance Education, 17*(1), 45–57.

Chapter Three

CRITICAL PERSPECTIVES AND COMMITMENTS DESERVING ATTENTION FROM COMMUNITY ENGAGEMENT PROFESSIONALS

Kortney Hernandez and Kira Pasquesi

Since the 1990s the community engagement movement has navigated an enduring tension in centralizing political and democratic dimensions within the overall mission of higher education (Saltmarsh, 1996). Bowker (2012) contended that while higher education continues to embrace "the building of social capital," critical thought "as community extrication and community resistance" may not yet be a popular reality (p. 107). Meanwhile, studies like Bellah's (1985) *Habits of the Heart* and Putnam's (2001) *Bowling Alone* point to fundamental political and social challenges plaguing our nation, all rooted in endemic individualism (Bowker, 2012). Conscious-minded scholars and educators engage the political and democratic dimensions of higher education through critical orientations to community engagement practice and research.

Higher education literature drawing from critical theory and pedagogy in community engagement, civic engagement, and service-learning reflects an increasing focus on critical perspectives (e.g., Daigre, 2000; d'Arlach, Sanchez, & Feuer, 2009; Hart, 2006; Marullo, 1999; Masucci & Renner, 2000; Mitchell, 2005, 2008, 2013; Porfilio & Hickman, 2011; Schensul, Berg, & Brase, 2002; Seedat, 2012; Webster & Coffey, 2011). Notably, Rhoads (1997), Masucci and Renner (2000), and Rosenberger (2000) articulated critical orientations to community engagement through "critical community service" and "critical service-learning." Following their advocacy, Tania Mitchell (2008) identified social change, the redistribution of power, and development and maintenance of authentic relationships as central tenets of critical community-based practice. Community engagement professionals (CEPs) operating from a critical, and therefore political, stance strive to work collectively *with* communities (Porfilio & Hickman, 2011) as they challenge, problematize, and navigate systemic injustices (Mitchell, 2008) in collective struggle (Darder, 2015).

This chapter builds upon Mitchell's (2008) seminal work on critical service-learning and draws from extant literature on critical approaches to community engagement, civic engagement, and service-learning. We reviewed literature from the 1990s to the present day,[1] as this has been widely considered the boom period for service-learning in higher education (Jacoby, 1996). From this initial search, we isolated literature that reflected elements of critical practice for CEPs in higher education and used reference lists from key sources to identify further reading. An interesting finding from the search of key literature was that critical community engagement and critical civic engagement yielded very few results as compared to the more widely known notion of critical service-learning. Thus, we drew from literature on community engagement in higher education that reflected elements of critical practice to infer the principles of CEPs presented in this chapter.

As authors, we identify as critical CEPs and scholars who are committed to the process of political clarity through our work (Darder, 2015; Freire, 1970; Masucci & Renner, 2000). Like Darder (2015), we embrace that "critical dialogue *and praxis* [provide] a collective space in which our ambiguities and contradiction can be expressed, critiqued and transformed, through a spirit of solidarity" (p. 112, emphasis added). Our writing and political work stem from the complexities of our social identities and collective struggles in navigating critical practice. In reviewing the literature, we recognize the importance of critical practice as a political project, a commitment to the elimination of oppressive structures, with a move toward social justice. As such, if this critical commitment is honored, it can reflect revolutionary and emancipatory possibilities (Porfilio & Hickman, 2011). We also view critique as necessary to engage the critical dimensions of community engagement, problematize taken-for-granted knowledge, and create space for alternative ways of knowing (Stewart & Webster, 2011). Consequently, a review of the critical practice literature on community engagement would be incomplete without a critique of the term *competency*.

Here we briefly address critiques of competency models that informed our decision to present critical principles instead of competencies for CEPs in higher education. We then outline critical principles of social change, power, and authenticity for CEPs. We close with a brief discussion of implications for research and community engagement practice.

Critical Principles for Community Engagement Professionals

Critiques of competency models call attention to an underlying positivistic framework (Chappell, Gonczi, & Hager, 2000) that superficially breaks down complex tasks into discrete fragments (J. S. Bell & Mitchell, 2000). Van Velsor and Quinn (2012) noted that competencies can suggest that the same universal skills apply to all groups or situations regardless of context. This framing reinforces individualistic notions of work that contradict critical commitments to social and political contexts. Competency models can also reflect neoliberal character by eroding the nonmarket critical, ethical, and moral dimensions of practice (Rossiter & Heron, 2011). Kliewer (2013) warned that if neoliberalism is not acknowledged or engaged, higher education will continue to educate citizens who are socialized, defined, and consumed as products of a market society. Additional critiques of the term *competency* point to discourses of economic rationalism, hegemonic or dominant group influence, and the systematic devaluing of social power distribution (Chappell et al., 2000; McKay, 2004). It is also important to note that competencies, or skills and behaviors that people and organizations aspire to do, are notably distinct from observable practices or action (Van Velsor & Quinn, 2012).

The use of the term *competency* is a rare occurrence in the critical community engagement literature reviewed. In fact, we identified just a single article on the critical pedagogy model of civic competence through service-learning (Stokamer, 2013). Thus, we advocate that the use of the term *competency* is inadequate for our current discussion of CEPs engaging in critical practice. Therefore, we draw on the work of critical pedagogues to assist in systematically positing a "set of principles tied to the radical belief in the historical possibility of transformation [that] can be tentatively fleshed out for the purpose of teaching and to better understand what is implied by a critical perspective of education, society, and the world" (Darder, Baltodano, & Torres, 2009, p. 9). Further, Darder and colleagues (2009) asserted that radical principles, beliefs, and practices are needed to engage critically with the historical realities for disenfranchised populations who are at the mercy of capitalism, racialization, and various forms of oppression.

This chapter reviews literature on critical practice in college and university community engagement as a means to articulate emergent critical principles for CEPs in three areas: social change, power, and authenticity. We put forth these critical principles with an understanding that "even carefully crafted guidelines for practice can do damage if they are not placed in the context of social realities, namely different and competing interests as well as outright conflict . . . for example, class, race, gender and even nationality" (Cruz, 1990, p. 322).

Critical Principles of Social Change

CEPs who engage in critical practice are deeply committed to the revolutionary possibility of social change through an understanding and commitment to work *with* communities. Moore (1990) contended that experiential or service-learning educators could "represent one of the few paths to creating a critical pedagogy—a form of discourse in which teachers and students conduct an unfettered investigation of social institutions, power relations, and value commitments" (p. 273). Crucial to this assertion is the recognition that Moore (1990), focusing on educators, does not mention how communities play a part in this investigation and creation of a critical pedagogy. Thus, analyses of social change need to be reflective of the creation of a critical pedagogy *with* communities in which empowerment plays a key role for people who have been marginalized (Webster & Coffey, 2011).

Stewart and Webster (2011) posited that challenging the field, holding authors accountable for the conclusions they reach, presenting other perspectives, and disrupting the status quo can lead to social change. Yet awareness of cultural differences does not automatically grant the critical understanding or ability to question inequalities that are a result of structural realities, often leading to the perpetuation of oppressive social structures (Kinefuchi, 2010). As such, fostering social change is no easy task (Diemer, Voight, & Mark, 2010), as CEPs engaging in critical practice must become "*believers* in and not . . . *resisters* of social change" (Wu & Dahlgren, 2011, p. 291). Mitchell (2008) built upon this reality through an examination that the borders of institutions and society may not openly invite social change, yet the ethical implications and obligations are inherent to critical practice.

This section addresses three critical principles for CEPs emerging from a review of critical practice literature on social change: an understanding of the dialectics of social change, the development of critical consciousness through praxis, and a commitment to collective labor and struggle.

Understanding the Dialectics of Social Change

Engaging in social change work is difficult and also political. As such, CEPs "may need to work outside of traditional non-profit and community-based organizations to partner with groups actively working to change systems and structures (in contrast to 'simply' offering services)" (Mitchell, 2008, p. 54). Critical literature with an emphasis on social change at times juxtaposes social change with its contradictory counterpart: charity (Endres & Gould, 2009; Hill-Jackson & Lewis, 2011; Livingston, 2011; Marr, 2014; Marullo & Edwards, 2000; Ward & Wolf-Wendel, 2000). Morton (1995) typologically examines this juxtaposition as a reflection of the manner in which service can be conceptualized as a continuum that represents a move from charity to social change. Moreover, Endres and Gould (2009) suggested that the conflation of charity work and social change can be linked to institutional racism and White privilege, reifying rather than challenging the system of White privilege. Seedat (2012) critically noted that the dialectical interconnectedness of community engagement as informed by social forces, liberatory intellectual thinking, and traditions is reflective of a complex and messy process. The overarching theme of charity as an oppositional force for social change inherently reflects this *dialecticity* (Davis & Freire, 1981) of social change. According to Freire (1970), dialectical thought is when "world and action are intimately interdependent" (p. 53).

As CEPs navigate the dialectical nature of social change and the contradictions that are at work in regard to community engagement, one must disrupt dichotomies. For example, Sperling (2007) noted that the dichotomizing of the world into the needy and the privileged undermines social change. Hicks-Peterson (2009) rejected the false binary between service and social justice, arguing that critical engagement can lead to involvement for students in political activism and social change. Kinefuchi (2010) examined the way in which the critical practice literature often expresses a critical orientation over and against the more traditional conception of a charity approach. Astutely noting the dialectical at work, Kinefuchi (2010) also recognized that a course may include elements of both approaches and asked, "Are 'critical' and 'charitable' mutually exclusive?" (p. 78). Deeply embedded within this understanding of the dialectical nature of social change and the dichotomies and contradictions that exist is the recognition and move toward the unity of one's words and actions as reflective of a deep, true commitment to social justice and change. For CEPs, this requires the move beyond mere rhetorical engagements toward actions that reflect a grounded, critically conscious commitment to collectively struggle *with* communities (Darder, 2015).

Development of Critical Consciousness Through Praxis

The writings of Brazilian educator and philosopher Paulo Freire have conceptually and pedagogically anchored critical approaches to community engagement (e.g., Diemer et al., 2010; Kajner, Chovanec, Underwood, & Mian, 2013; Marr, 2014; Masucci & Renner, 2000; Porfilio & Hickman, 2011; Rosenberger, 2000; Webster & Coffey, 2011; Wu & Dahlgren, 2011) through "his conception of praxis, dialogic education, a liberationist educational paradigm, and a redefined role of teaching" (Saltmarsh, 1996, p. 14). One of Freire's (1970) most influential works, *Pedagogy of the Oppressed*, has grounded critical educators, scholars, community members, students, and CEPs through an articulation of oppressive structures, praxis, and emphasis on the development of critical consciousness (Deans, 1999). While Freire is often in line with and cited in the critical community engagement and service-learning literature for what the spirit of his work embodies, it is also important to note that in more traditional forms of this literature (e.g., Hatcher & Bringle, 1997; Ross & Boyle, 2007; Stanton, 1994) the reflection/action process (also known as Kolb's experiential learning cycle) is often cited, whereas Freire's "action-reflection dialectic of praxis" (Deans, 1999, p. 15) is not.

According to Freire (1970), action reflects authentic praxis "only if its consequences become the object of critical reflection" (p. 66), and to achieve this praxis, one must trust in the oppressed. Thus, liberation embodies praxis, as it is the action and reflection of men and women upon their world in order to change it (Freire, 1970). Freire's radical engagement of praxis in relation to Kolb's experiential learning cycle might best be viewed through what Aronowitz (1993) feared as a consequence of

Freire's (and Dewey's) political stance—the watering down of Freire's pedagogical praxis for more "depoliticized teaching methods" (Deans, 1999, p. 19). Thus, despite the influences of Dewey, who was a valued proponent of democratic schooling, critical CEPs must move past the tendency to engage Freire's work as just another "version of the experiential learning cycle which he called praxis" (Kolb, 2015, p. 342).

As a consequence, CEPs must be critically and astutely aware of the historical, philosophical, political, social, economic, and systematic ways in which antipolitical, acritical, benevolent forms of community engagement are at work so that they may oppose the "watered down" (Deans, 1999, p. 19) forms of critical practice. The social change principle of developing critical consciousness through praxis is drawn from the community engagement literature with an explicit understanding that Freire's work and critical pedagogy embody what CEPs engaging in critical practice should seek to espouse wholeheartedly. Thus, for CEPs, community members, students, and all involved, "their critical discourse is indicative of their praxis, which suggests that *the collective* could counter the coercive power dynamics and create social change" (Wu & Dahlgren, 2011, p. 271, emphasis added). Seedat (2012) asserted that "community engagement is a dynamic, shifting and complex process" as well as "a form of action, liberatory thought and praxis" (p. 489). For critical CEPs their praxis should lead to further development of their critical consciousness.

In line with a Freirean perspective, Kinefuchi (2010) defined *critical consciousness* as "authentic, dialogic relationships based on acknowledgment of power difference, mutuality, and deliberative collaborative effort" (p. 79). Critical consciousness reflects engaging with taken-for-granted assumptions, in addition to analyzing power relations and the move toward more authentic relationships (Kinefuchi, 2010). For CEPs, engagement with power and assumptions includes an understanding of dominant discourse and practices that disempower communities despite the appearance of helpfulness or apoliticism. Thus, a critical perspective counters the notion that the community is a problem that must be solved by the students—who represent the problem solvers (Kinefuchi, 2010). While critical consciousness is a crucial principle for CEPs, it is important to also recognize that the depth and focus of consciousness will vary across individuals.

Commitment to Collective Labor and Struggle

Drawing upon Freire's commitment to a revolutionary praxis, in order to challenge dehumanization and unveil contradictions within our practices through an ongoing political process, CEPs must engage in collective labor. As Darder (2015) writes, collective labor is "a labor born of love, but deeply anchored in an unceasing commitment to know, through both theory and practice, the nature of the beast that preys on our humanity" (p. 7). Stemming from the societal phenomenon of individualism (Bellah, 1985; Putnam, 2001), Bowker (2012) illuminates the reality that the destruction of the collective "will lead to a future in which society is purchased" by powerful ideological forces that individuals will not be able to resist (p. 114). Thus, Bowker (2012) astutely points out that what we must take note of is the reality that the neoliberal forces leading to the destruction of the collective are themselves a collective phenomenon. Moreover, Kecskes (2006) notes that "egalitarian ideas of limiting professionalism and maximizing collective citizen participation in the production of public service are long-established" (p. 8). A commitment to collective labor and struggle must remain at the forefront of CEPs who engage in critical practice.

Critical Principles of Power

CEPs who engage in critical practice recognize and address issues of power. The act of community building lays bare the power relationships that influence all facets of engagement, including resource allocation, governance, decision-making, leadership opportunities, and evaluation (Potapchuk, Leiderman, Bivens, & Major, 2005). In this section, we offer a brief review of power from critical theory literature in an attempt to highlight the varied and complex approaches to analyzing power. We then introduce two critical principles of power for CEPs inferred from the community engagement literature: consciousness of power relations and unveiling and disrupting unequal power structures.

Power is an integral component of critical practice in community engagement, yet our literature review revealed that what we mean by *power* is often vague or unacknowledged in discussions of community engagement. *Power* can be defined as a product, or commodity, that can be given, received, transferred, or taken away (Bloome, Power Carter, Christian, Otto, & Shuart-Fairs, 2005). It can also be viewed as a process or a set of relations between people and institutions embedded in social and cultural practices. For example, *hegemony* refers to the pervasive and invisible social control of dominant groups over subordinate groups that appears both legitimate and natural (Gramsci, 1971; Hebdige, 1979). From a feminist perspective, power is also characterized in terms of caring relationships with the potential to bring people together for mutual benefit (Bloome et al., 2005). Power can therefore be *used* for social good and *abused* as a means of social control over one group by another (van Dijk, 2008).

Consciousness of Power Relations

Foucault (2000) reminds us that one can never escape power or truth regimes in social relations and institutions. Critical literature on power in community engagement offers examples of power relations in community engagement, including oppressive institutional structures and norms (Verjee, 2012) that subvert community-based partnerships (Sandmann & Kliewer, 2012), abstractions of community as homogeneous units (Dempsey, 2010), paternalistic or "othering" language (Seider & Hillman, 2011; Veloria, 2015), and discourses that privilege institutions of higher education (Bortolin, 2011). Scholars have also pointed to power relations perpetuating the underside or limits of service-learning (Butin, 2006; Eby, 1998; Jones, Gilbride-Brown, & Gasiorski, 2005), including binaries of privileged service providers and underprivileged service recipients (Henry, 2005), cultural deficit thinking (Sperling, 2007; Veloria, 2015), and the invisibility or silencing of identities (Gent, 2011). Using a critical race counterstory, Cann and McCloskey (2015) highlighted the White savior and "poverty pimpin' project" of outreach work while examining the intersections of racism and ableism.

A critically conscious CEP has an understanding of asymmetrical power relations. CEPs can equip themselves to develop a nuanced consciousness of power dynamics with an understanding of theoretical concepts and historical context underpinning power struggles in community engagement. For example, neoliberal ideology manifests in higher education through market-driven approaches to campus operations, a focus on efficiency, valuing of the individual over collective action, and the privatization of public services (Kecskes & Foster, 2013). Kliewer (2013) explained that "recognizing structural governance or organizing mechanisms of neoliberal ideology can help civic education scholars and practitioners understand mechanisms that have the effect of limiting the movement's efforts to achieve democratic and justice aims" (p. 74). Mechanisms of Western power and knowledge regimes can limit attempts at intercultural relationships, such as collaborations with Indigenous peoples and tribal nations (Steinman, 2011). Highlighting histories of colonialism and collective struggles of decolonization is a necessary step in decentering Eurocentric approaches to community engagement (Dean, 2015).

Unveiling and Disrupting Unequal Power Structures

CEPs not only recognize power relations but also name injustices and work to redistribute power inside and outside of the academy (Mitchell, 2013). Unveiling unequal power structures requires recognition of one's subject position in connection to privilege and oppression. Privilege is a sociopolitical construct that recognizes how individuals with dominant cultural identities in our society are afforded more benefits and experience fewer obstacles due to their social group membership (Johnson, 2006). Various forms of oppression, such as racism, classism, sexism, heterosexism, ableism, and trans oppression, are interconnected yet distinctive in a system of power and privilege (L. Bell, 2007). Scholars have called for exploration of unearned privileges (e.g., Madsen Camacho, 2004; Mitchell, 2008) and the disruption of assumptions about knowledge, power, and identity (Butin, 2005). An understanding of privilege is essential in naming power differentials, examining root causes of social problems, and engaging critical approaches to subjectivity (Catlett & Proweller, 2011; Dunlap, Scoggin, Green, & Davi, 2007; Madsen Camacho, 2004). With this consciousness, CEPs are better equipped to support others in examinations of power, privilege, and oppression in the context of community engagement efforts.

CEPs can unveil power differentials by disrupting problematic language use. For example, Dempsey (2010) challenged abstract discussions of community engagement that position notions of community as homogeneous units and negate a plurality of experiences, identities, and perspectives. Further, Seider and Hillman (2011) observed paternalistic and "othering" language invoked by White or affluent students in their study of service-learning courses. Veloria (2015) also identified student discursive practices of deficit thinking and color-blind ideologies in a study of sensemaking about race in the context of a service-learning project. Ambiguities surrounding portrayals of community and deficit or paternalistic language can dehumanize those with whom we seek to build authentic relationships in community engagement. Freire (1970) expressed that "dehumanization, which marks not only those whose humanity has been stolen, but also . . . those who have stolen it, is a distortion of the vocation of becoming more fully human" (p. 28). CEPs, therefore, must explicitly challenge assumptions revealed through language, discursive practices, and abstractions as a means to disrupt unequal power dynamics in conflicted spaces.

The work of unveiling power structures must also take into account the ability of higher education to change internally as we tackle not only the systemic injustices facing our communities but also the many forms of injustices embedded within the academy (Maurrasse, 2001). Rooted in counterstories from women of color in academe, Verjee (2012) called for institutional accountability through the transformation of hegemonic structures prior to forming respectful, trusting, and authentic relationships. Moreover, Dempsey (2010) challenged the ways that metaphors of campus and community divisions absolve colleges and universities of wrongdoing in their entangled historical, political, and economic relationships with surrounding communities. These complex and sometimes painful relationships encompass such issues ranging from employment, land use, and police enforcement (Ostrander, 2004) to complicity in gentrification and segregation (Sullivan et al., 2001). In seeking to develop and maintain authentic relationships, CEPs must see themselves as members of a community and understand the contexts in which they are laboring (Hart, 2006).

Critical Principles of Authenticity

We turn next to critical principles of authenticity for CEPs in higher education. It is important to note that while discussions of authenticity are common in the community engagement literature (e.g., Mitchell, 2008; Noel, 2011), some critical scholars contest claims of authenticity as rational, superior, and implying a fixed *truth* rooted in dominant perspectives (e.g., Subedi, 2008). We use the term in our discussion of critical principles while continuing to interrogate its connections to power and authority in Western discourse. In this section we explore two critical principles of authenticity for CEPs: navigating identity politics and developing and maintaining authentic relationships.

Navigating Identity Politics

One's identity as a CEP is intertwined with the complexities of one's social identities. In other words, how we identify in terms of race, ethnicity, gender identity and expression, sexual orientation, social class, religion, and ability status, among other facets of identity, influences approaches to community engagement and how they are received (Mueller & Pickett, 2015). CEPs navigate identity politics on a daily basis, stemming from perceptions of their intersecting identities. For instance, Harden (2009) shared his experiences as a Black man teaching service-learning grounded in critical race theory at a predominantly White institution. He narrated complex relationships with the university, community, other faculty, and students that inform how he situates himself as an educator. Further, Mitchell, Donahue, and Young-Law (2012) examined the prevalence, and therefore invisibility, of Whiteness in service-learning pedagogy. They argued that the absence of a critical focus on race in service-learning can normalize White privilege and perpetuate White supremacy in teaching and learning practices. While additional researchers acknowledge the positions from which they write (e.g., Langseth, 2000; Veloria, 2015), the gaze of community engagement literature in large part focuses outward toward students.

CEPs who navigate identity politics recognize that students and the community experience community engagement in qualitatively different ways. As Butin (2003) reminds us, service-learning can serve as a "site of identity, construction, deconstruction, and reconstruction" (p. 1684). Gent (2011), for instance, examined disability as a sociopolitical construct that perpetuates an oppressive culture of ableism in community engagement. Evans, Taylor, Dunlap, and Miller (2009) edited a collection centering race in community engagement by highlighting the voices and experiences of African Americans. Additional scholarship has explored issues of social class (Dacheux, 2005; Henry, 2005; Yeh, 2010), intersections of race and class (Novick, Seider, & Huguley, 2011), racial identity development (Simons et al., 2011), and Whiteness or White privilege specifically (e.g., Dunlap et al., 2007; Endres & Gould, 2009; Green, 2001; Mitchell et al., 2012). In navigating identity politics, Langseth (2000) reminds CEPs to invest in the same ongoing personal and professional development that we ask of students.

Developing and Maintaining Authentic Relationships

While literature on best practices for partnerships in community engagement abounds (e.g., Bringle & Hatcher, 2002; Clayton, Bringle, Senor, Huq, & Morrison, 2010; Jacoby & Associates, 2003; Maurrasse, 2001; Torres, 2000), literature on how to develop and maintain authentic relationships is less expansive (Rosenberger, 2000). Therefore, CEPs must be intentional about their personal approach to forming collaborative relationships rooted in a sense of belonging and human connection. One such approach is what Sturm, Eatman, Saltmarsh, and Bush (2011) called *full participation*, meaning practices that "enable people, whatever their identity, background, or institutional position, to thrive, realize their capabilities, engage meaningfully in institutional life, and contribute to the flourishing of others" (p. 3). Relationships based on connections acknowledge and address power and difference, affirm interdependence and mutual trust, and develop common goals (Mitchell, 2008). This was illustrated by d'Arlach and colleagues (2009) finding that community members in a language exchange program felt more equal in the service relationships as they began to humanize "the other," or college student participants. However, it is essential to note that the discourse of "humanizing the other" is problematic in that, as Freire (1970) would suggest, it implies *false generosity*. Freire (1970) critically noted that the humanizing of "the other" in the oppressor consciousness is subversion, and thus not the pursuit of full humanity or authentic relationships.

CEPs who develop and maintain authentic relationships listen and make space to form connections. In his Deweyan theory of democratic listening, Garrison (1996) emphasized the vulnerability required to listen in ways that create new understandings when challenged with alternative insights and ways of being in the world. He described the act of dialoguing across difference as inherently dangerous in the disturbed equilibrium that disturbs habitual ways of feeling, thinking, and acting. Listening is an essential component of being with others with whom we seek to build relationships as we form new connections. Steinman (2011) recommended an alternative approach to collaborations with tribal nations based on Regan's (2010) notion of making space. Making space for marginalized community knowledge, perspectives, and voices serves as a way to decenter dominant perspectives and to explore social locations in relation to inequalities. Authenticity, therefore, relies on dialogue and connection (Mitchell, 2008).

Mitchell (2008) posited that authentic relationships demand attention to social change as well as an analysis of power. For CEPs who seek to engage authentically in relationships, they must continually examine themselves with a commitment to the people they are working alongside of in community (Freire, 1970). As such, CEPs seeking to develop and cultivate authentic relationships must be mindful of cultural inauthenticity and invasion (Freire, 1970). Cultural inauthenticity and invasion disrespect the potential of communities as invaders infiltrate the cultural context, which constitutes not only an act of domination but also an act of violence. Authentic relationships must be built in communion with others and must constantly be reexamined to understand the tensions that exist in relations of power and progress toward social change.

Summary and Implications

We identified critical principles for CEPs in the areas of social change, power, and authenticity through a review of the extant literature on community engagement. The critical principles of social change included understanding the dialectics of social change, the development of critical consciousness through praxis, and a commitment to collective labor and struggle. Critical principles of power were consciousness of power relations and unveiling and disrupting unequal power structures. Principles of authenticity involved navigating identity politics and developing and maintaining authentic relationships.

Our process of inferring critical principles for CEPs points to gaps in current literature with implications for research. For example, we recognized a dearth of research on queering community engagement and limited exploration of ability/disability (e.g., Gent, 2011) and national origin or nationality (e.g., Madsen Camacho, 2004; Wu & Dahlgren, 2011). We also noted scant research on the social identities or positionality of CEPs influencing approaches to practice (e.g., Harden, 2009). Similar to higher education research at large (see Harper, 2012), a limited subset of scholarship on racial and ethnic difference in community engagement named the prevalence of White supremacy or racism in institutional norms (e.g., Boyle-Baise & Binford, 2005; Cann & McCloskey, 2015; Endres & Gould, 2009; Harden, 2009; Mitchell & Donahue, 2009; Simons et al., 2011; Veloria, 2015; Verjee, 2012). Furthermore, Sperling (2007) stressed that

> so far, no researcher has asked the truly difficult questions such as how it feels to be a parent of an 'underachieving' child who is being tutored by an anonymous 19-year-old. . . . Or, for that matter, whether most parents would agree that it is their child's responsibility to convince White college students not to be racist? (p. 314)

His sentiments reinforce investigating diverse, and often silenced, perspectives through critical inquiry.

An examination of critical principles for CEPs also contributes to an evolving understanding of community engagement practice. This review of literature calls CEPs to examine their practice in the context of movement building, solidarity, and engaging in a collective struggle for a more just world. We are left thinking about the connections (or disconnections) between community engagement and multicultural, diversity, or inclusion efforts in higher education (Association of American Colleges & Universities, 1995; Boyle-Baise, 2002; Cipolle, 2010; Hurtado, 2007; O'Grady, 2000; Roper, 2012). Sanchez (2005) urged that we must begin by making colleges and universities more equitable and inclusive; otherwise, social change efforts aimed outside of our campuses will not be taken seriously. CEPs can participate in groups with communities around critical questions and engage in difficult dialogues with each other about our profession's future. Such questions could include: What narratives do we tell about our role as CEPs or cultural workers (Freire, 1998), and what interests are served by these narratives? How can we create spaces, disrupt structures, change policies, and critique practices that allow all people to thrive and become more fully human through a collective process of engagement? How can CEPs participate in centralizing the community as well as engaging issues of diversity and social justice in college and university community engagement?

Conclusion

The distinguishing factor of critical practice is that no formulaic or universal implementation exists, constituting its critical nature (Darder et al., 2009). Given this philosophical heterogeneity, CEPs must be committed to the struggle for the liberation of oppressed populations. This includes a deeper examination of the way in which community engagement is constructed within higher education and carried out in communities, so as not to reflect a unidirectional form of practice that dismisses the power of the collective struggle. As such, we close the review of critical literature with more questions, conflicts, and tensions than when we started. Hart (2006) articulated a dilemma in "knowing something you so wholeheartedly believe in as good for the future of our society may, simultaneously, at best mask the issues, continue the silence of the marginalized, and perpetuate the *status quo*; or at worst, pose the risk of causing more harm to already oppressed and marginalized populations through silence and indoctrination" (p. 29). The critical principles of social change, power, and authenticity allow CEPs to labor and struggle collectively with communities toward social change and emancipatory practices.

Note

1. As a starting point for this literature review, we searched approximately 30 key terms, which included some variations and combinations of the following words: *community, engagement, service-learning, critical, practice, professional, pedagogy, multicultural, social justice, social change, power, authenticity, praxis, critical consciousness, competency*. We also searched for words that reflect a critical stance tied to critical pedagogy and theory. From the initial search of these key terms, we isolated the literature that reflected a critical stance and practices in relation to *community engagement, civic engagement*, and *service-learning*.

References

Aronowitz, S. (1993). Paulo Freire's radical democratic humanism: The fetish of method. In P. McLaren & P. Leonard (Eds.), *Paulo Freire: A critical encounter* (pp. 8-24). New York, NY: Routledge.

Association of American Colleges & Universities. (1995). *The drama of diversity and democracy: Higher education and American commitments.* Washington, DC: Author.

Bell, J. S., & Mitchell, R. (2000). Competency-based versus traditional cohort-based technical education: A comparison of students' perceptions. *Journal of Career and Technical Information, 17*(1), 5–22.

Bell, L. (2007). Theoretical foundations for social justice education. In M. Adams, L. A. Bell, & P. Griffin (Eds.), *Teaching for diversity and social justice* (2nd ed., pp. 1–14). New York, NY: Routledge.

Bellah, R. N. (1985). *Habits of the heart: Individualism and commitment in American life.* Berkeley, CA: University of California Press.

Bloome, D., Power Carter, S., Christian, B. M., Otto, S., & Shuart-Fairs, N. (2005). *Discourse analysis and the study of classroom literacy and literacy events: A microethnographic perspective.* Mahwah, NJ: Lawrence Erlbaum Associates.

Bortolin, K. (2011). Serving ourselves: How the discourse on community engagement privileges the university over the community. *Michigan Journal of Community Service Learning, 18*(1), 49–60.

Bowker, M. H. (2012). Defending the ivory tower: Toward critical community engagement. *Thought and Action: The NEA Higher Education Journal, 28*(1), 106–117.

Boyle-Baise, M. (2002). *Multicultural service learning: Educating teachers in diverse communities.* New York, NY: Teachers College Press.

Boyle-Baise, M., & Binford, P. (2005). "No one has stepped there before": Learning about racism in our town. In D. W. Butin (Ed.), *Service-learning in higher education: Critical issues and directions* (pp. 139–156). New York, NY: Palgrave Macmillan.

Bringle, R. G., & Hatcher, J. A. (2002). Campus-community partnerships: The terms of engagement. *Journal of Social Issues, 58*(3), 503–516.

Butin, D. (2003). Of what use is it? Multiple conceptualizations of service learning within education. *Teachers College Record, 105*(9), 1674–1692.

Butin, D. W. (2005). Preface: Disturbing normalizations of service-learning. In D. W. Butin (Ed.), *Service-learning in higher education: Critical issues and directions* (pp. vii–xx). New York, NY: Palgrave Macmillan.

Butin, D. W. (2006). The limits of service-learning in higher education. *The Review of Higher Education, 29*(4), 473–498.

Cann, C. N., & McCloskey, E. (2015). The poverty pimpin' project: How Whiteness profits from Black and Brown bodies in community service programs. *Race Ethnicity and Education,* 1–15. Retrieved from www.tandfonline.com/doi/abs/10.1080/13613324.2015.1096769

Catlett, B. S., & Proweller, A. (2011). College students' negotiation of privilege in a community-based violence prevention project. *Michigan Journal of Community Service Learning, 18*(1), 34–48.

Chappell, C., Gonczi, A., & Hager, P. (2000). Competency-based education. In G. Foley (Ed.), *Understanding adult education and training* (2nd ed., pp. 191–205). St. Leonards, New South Wales: Allen & Unwin.

Cipolle, S. B. (2010). *Service-learning and social justice: Engaging students in social change.* Lanham, MD: Rowman & Littlefield.

Clayton, P. H., Bringle, R. G., Senor, B., Huq, J., & Morrison, M. (2010). Differentiating and assessing relationships in service-learning and civic engagement: Exploitative, transactional, or transformational. *Michigan Journal of Community Service Learning, 16*(2), 5–22.

Cruz, N. (1990). A challenge to the notion of service. In J. Kendall (Ed.), *Combining service and learning: A resource book for community and public service* (Vol. 1, pp. 321–323). Raleigh, NC: National Society for Internships and Experiential Education.

Dacheux, T. (2005). Beyond a world of binaries: My views on service-learning. In D. W. Butin (Ed.), *Service-learning in higher education: Critical issues and directions* (pp. 67–70). New York, NY: Palgrave Macmillan.

Daigre, E. (2000). Toward a critical service-learning pedagogy: A Freirean approach to civic literacy. *Academic Exchange Quarterly, 4*(4), 1–10.

Darder, A. (2015). *Freire and education.* New York, NY: Routledge.

Darder, A., Baltodano, M., & Torres, R. D. (2009). *Critical pedagogy reader: Theory and practice* (2nd ed.). New York, NY: Routledge.

d'Arlach, L., Sanchez, B., & Feuer, R. (2009). Voices from the community: A case for reciprocity in service-learning. *Michigan Journal of Community Service Learning, 16*(1), 5–16.

Davis, R., & Freire, P. (1981). Education for awareness: A talk with Paulo Freire. In R. Mackie (Ed.), *Literacy and revolution: The pedagogy of Paulo Freire* (pp. 57–69). New York, NY: Continuum.

Dean, A. (2015). Colonialism, neoliberalism, and university-community engagement. In C. Janzen, D. Jeffrey, & K. Smith (Eds.), *Unravelling encounters: Ethics, knowledge, and resistance under neoliberalism* (pp. 175–194). Waterloo, Ontario: Wilfrid Laurier University Press.

Deans, T. (1999). Service-learning in two keys: Paulo Freire's critical pedagogy in relation to John Dewey's pragmatism. *Michigan Journal of Community Service Learning, 6*(1), 15–29.

Dempsey, S. E. (2010). Critiquing community engagement. *Management Communication Quarterly, 24*(3), 1–32.

Diemer, M., Voight, A., & Mark, C. (2010). Youth development in traditional and transformational service learning programs. In T. Stewart & N. Webster (Eds.), *Problematizing service-learning: Critical reflections for development and action* (pp. 155–174). Charlotte, NC: Information Age Publishing.

Dunlap, M., Scoggin, J., Green, P., & Davi, A. (2007). White students' experiences of privilege and socioeconomic disparities: Toward a theoretical model. *Michigan Journal of Community Service Learning, 13*(2), 19–30.

Eby, J. W. (1998). *Why service-learning is bad.* Retrieved from glennblalock.org/

Endres, D., & Gould, M. (2009). "I am also in the position to use my whiteness to help them out": The communication of Whiteness in service learning. *Western Journal of Communication, 73*(4), 418–436.

Evans, S. Y., Taylor, C. M., Dunlap, M. R., & Miller, D. S. (Eds.). (2009). *African Americans and community engagement in higher education: Community service, service-learning, and community-based research*. Albany, NY: State University of New York Press.

Foucault, M. (2000). *Power*. New York, NY: New Press.

Freire, P. (1970). *Pedagogy of the oppressed*. New York, NY: Seabury Press.

Freire, P. (1998). *Teachers as cultural workers: Letters to those who dare teach*. Boulder, CO: Westview Press.

Garrison, J. (1996). A Deweyan theory of democratic listening. *Educational Theory, 46*(4), 429–451.

Gent, P. J. (2011). Service-learning and the culture of ableism. In T. Stewart & N. Webster (Eds.), *Problematizing service-learning: Critical reflections for development and action* (pp. 223–243). Charlotte, NC: Information Age Publishing.

Gramsci, A. (1971). *Prison notebooks*. New York: International Publishers.

Green, A. E. (2001). "But you aren't White": Racial perceptions and service-learning. *Michigan Journal of Community Service Learning, 8*(1), 18–26.

Harden, T. (2009). A service or a commitment? A Black man teaching service-learning at a predominantly White institution. In S. Y. Evans, C. M. Taylor, M. R. Dunlap, & D. S. Miller (Eds.), *African Americans and community engagement in higher education: Community service, service-learning, and community-based research* (pp. 105–118). Albany, NY: State University of New York Press.

Harper, S. R. (2012). Race without racism: How higher education researchers minimize racist institutional norms. *The Review of Higher Education, 36*(1), 9–29.

Hart, S. (2006). Breaking literacy boundaries through critical service-learning: Education for the silenced and marginalized. *Mentoring and Tutoring, 14*(1), 17–32.

Hatcher, J. A., & Bringle, R. G. (1997). Reflection: Bridging the gap between service and learning. *College Teaching, 45*(4), 153–158.

Hebdige, D. (1979). *Subculture: The meaning of style*. London: Routledge.

Henry, S. H. (2005). "I can never turn my back on that": Liminality and the impact of class on service-learning experiences. In D. W. Butin (Ed.), *Service-learning in higher education: Critical issues and directions* (pp. 45–66). New York, NY: Palgrave Macmillan.

Hicks-Peterson, T. (2009). Engaged scholarship: Reflections and research on the pedagogy of social change. *Teaching in Higher Education, 14*(5), 541–552.

Hill-Jackson, V., & Lewis, C. W. (2011). Service *loitering*: White pre-service teachers preparing for diversity in an underserved community. In T. Stewart & N. Webster (Eds.), *Problematizing service-learning: Critical reflections for development and action* (pp. 295–324). Charlotte, NC: Information Age Publishing.

Hurtado, S. (2007). Linking diversity with the educational and civic missions of higher education. *The Review of Higher Education, 30*(2), 185–196.

Jacoby, B. (1996). *Service-learning in higher education: Concepts and practices*. San Francisco, CA: Jossey-Bass.

Jacoby, B., & Associates (Eds.). (2003). *Building partnerships for service-learning*. San Francisco, CA: Jossey-Bass.

Johnson, A. G. (2006). *Privilege, power, and difference* (2nd ed.). Boston, MA: McGraw-Hill.

Jones, S., Gilbride-Brown, J., & Gasiorski, A. (2005). Getting inside the "underside" of service-learning: Student resistance and possibilities. In D. W. Butin (Ed.), *Service-learning in higher education: Critical issues and directions* (pp. 3–24). New York, NY: Palgrave Macmillan.

Kajner, T., Chovanec, D., Underwood, M., & Mian, A. (2013). Critical community service learning: Combining critical classroom pedagogy with activist community placements. *Michigan Journal of Community Service Learning, 19*(2), 36–48.

Kecskes, K. (2006). Behind the rhetoric: Applying a cultural theory lens to community-campus partnership development. *Michigan Journal of Community Service Learning, 12*(2), 5–14.

Kecskes, K., & Foster, K. M. (2013). Three questions for community engagement at the crossroads. *Journal of Public Scholarship in Higher Education, 3*, 7–17.

Kinefuchi, E. (2010). Critical consciousness and critical service-learning at the intersection of the personal and the structural. *Journal of Applied Learning in Higher Education, 2*, 81–97.

Kliewer, B. (2013). Why the civic engagement movement cannot achieve democratic and justice aims. *Michigan Journal of Community Service Learning, 19*(2), 72–79.

Kolb, D. A. (2015). *Experiential learning: Experience as the source of learning and development* (2nd ed.). Saddle River, NJ: Pearson Education.

Langseth, M. (2000). Maximizing impact, minimizing harm: Why service-learning must more fully integrate multicultural education. In C. O'Grady (Ed.), *Integrating service learning and multicultural education in colleges and universities* (pp. 247–262). Mahwah, NJ: Lawrence Erlbaum Associates.

Livingston, S. M. (2011). Virtual adoption of service learning through controlled discourse. In T. Stewart & N. Webster (Eds.), *Problematizing service-learning: Critical reflections for development and action* (pp. xiii–xxi). Charlotte, NC: Information Age Publishing.

Madsen Camacho, M. (2004). Power and privilege: Community service learning in Tijuana. *Michigan Journal of Community Service Learning, 10*(3), 31–42.

Marr, V. L. (2014). *Growing "homeplace" in critical service-learning: An urban womanist pedagogy* (Unpublished doctoral dissertation). Wayne State University, Detroit, MI, available at digitalcommons.wayne.edu/cgi/viewcontent.cgi?article=1901&context=oa_dissertations

Marullo, S. (1999). Sociology's essential role: Promoting critical analysis in service-learning. In J. Ostrow, G. Hesser, & S. Enos (Eds.), *Cultivating the sociological imagination: Concepts and models for service-learning in sociology* (pp. 11–28). Washington, DC: American Association of Higher Education.

Marullo, S., & Edwards, B. (2000). From charity to justice: The potential of university-community collaboration for social change. *American Behavioral Scientist, 43*(5), 895–912.

Masucci, M., & Renner, A. (2000). Reading the lives of others: The Winton Homes Library project—A cultural studies analysis of critical service learning for education. *High School Journal, 84*(1), 36–47.

Maurrasse, D. J. (2001). *Beyond the campus: How colleges and universities form partnerships with their communities.* New York, NY: Routledge.

McKay, H. (2004). Locating the fault line: The intersection of internationalisation and competency-based training. *International Education Journal, 4*(4), 203–211.

Mitchell, T. D. (2005). *Service-learning and social justice: Making connections, making commitments* (Unpublished doctoral dissertation). University of Massachusetts–Amherst.

Mitchell, T. D. (2008). Traditional vs. critical service-learning: Engaging the literature to differentiate two models. *Michigan Journal of Community Service Learning, 14*(2), 50–65.

Mitchell, T. D. (2013). Critical service-learning as a philosophy for deepening community engagement. In A. Hoy & M. Johnson (Eds.), *Deepening community engagement in higher education: Forging new pathways* (pp. 263–269). New York, NY: Palgrave Macmillan.

Mitchell, T. D., & Donahue, D. M. (2009). "I do more service in this class than I ever do at my site": Paying attention to the reflections of students of color in service-learning. In J. Strait & M. Lima (Eds.), *The future of service-learning: New solutions for sustaining and improving practice* (pp. 172–190). Sterling, VA: Stylus.

Mitchell, T. D., Donahue, D. M., & Young-Law, C. (2012). Service learning as a pedagogy of whiteness. *Equity and Excellence in Education, 45*(4), 612–629.

Moore, D. (1990). Experiential education as critical discourse. In J. Kendall (Ed.), *Combining service and learning: A resource book for community and public service* (Vol. 1, pp. 273–283). Raleigh, NC: National Society for Internships and Experiential Education.

Morton, K. (1995). The irony of service: Charity, project, and social change in service-learning. *Michigan Journal of Community Service Learning, 2*(1), 19–32.

Mueller, J. A., & Pickett, C. S. (2015). Politics of intersecting identities. In S. K. Watt (Ed.), *Designing transformative multicultural initiatives: Theoretical foundations, practical applications, and facilitator considerations* (pp. 193–207). Sterling, VA: Stylus.

Noel, J. (2011). Striving for authentic community engagement: A process model from urban teacher education. *Journal of Higher Education Outreach and Engagement, 15*(1), 31–52.

Novick, S., Seider, S. C., & Huguley, J. (2011). Engaging college students from diverse backgrounds in community service learning. *Journal of College and Character, 12*(1), 1–8.

O'Grady, C. (2000). Integrating service learning and multicultural education: An overview. In C. O'Grady (Ed.), *Integrating service learning and multicultural education in colleges and universities* (pp. 1–19). Mahwah, NJ: Lawrence Erlbaum Associates.

Ostrander, S. A. (2004). Democracy, civic participation, and the university: A comparative study of civic engagement on five campuses. *Nonprofit and Voluntary Sector Quarterly, 33*, 74–93.

Porfilio, B. J., & Hickman, H. (2011). *Critical service-learning as revolutionary pedagogy: A project of student agency in action*. Charlotte, NC: Information Age Publishing.

Potapchuk, M., Leiderman, S., Bivens, D., & Major, B. (2005). *Flipping the script: White privilege and community building*. Silver Spring, MD: MP Associates and the Center for Assessment and Policy Development.

Putnam, R. D. (2001). *Bowling alone: The collapse and revival of American community*. New York, NY: Simon & Schuster.

Regan, P. Y. L. (2010). *Unsettling the settler within: Canada's peacemaker myth, recolonization, and transformative pathways to decolonization* (Unpublished doctoral dissertation). University of Victoria, Victoria, British Columbia.

Rhoads, R. A. (1997). *Community service and higher learning: Explorations of the caring self*. Albany, NY: State University of New York Press.

Roper, L. D. (2012). Strengthening the connection between community service and diversity. *Journal of College and Character, 13*(1), 1–3.

Rosenberger, C. (2000). Beyond empathy: Developing critical consciousness through service learning. In C. O'Grady (Ed.), *Integrating service learning and multicultural education in colleges and universities* (pp. 23–43). Mahwah, NJ: Lawrence Erlbaum Associates.

Ross, L., & Boyle, M. E. (2007). Transitioning from high school service to college service-learning in a first-year seminar. *Michigan Journal of Community Service Learning, 14*(1), 53–64.

Rossiter, A., & Heron, B. (2011). Neoliberalism, competencies, and the devaluing of social work practice. *Canadian Social Work Review, 28*, 305–309.

Saltmarsh, J. (1996). Education for critical citizenship: John Dewey's contribution to the pedagogy of community service learning. *Michigan Journal of Community Service Learning, 3*(1), 13–21.

Sanchez, G. (2005). *Crossing Figueroa: The tangled web of diversity and democracy*. Foreseeable Futures Number 4. Syracuse, NY: Imagining America.

Sandmann, L. R., & Kliewer, B. W. (2012). Theoretical and applied perspectives on power: Recognizing processes that undermine effective community-university partnerships. *Journal of Community Engagement and Scholarship, 5*(2), 20–28.

Schensul, J., Berg, M., & Brase, M. (2002). Theories guiding outcomes for action research for service-learning. In A. Furco & S. H. Billig (Eds.), *Service-learning: The essence of the pedagogy* (pp. 125–146). Greenwich, CT: Information Age Publishing.

Seedat, M. (2012). Community engagement as liberal performance, as critical intellectualism and as praxis. *Journal of Psychology in Africa, 22*(4), 489–498.

Seider, S. C., & Hillman, A. (2011). Challenging privileged college students' othering language in community service learning. *Journal of College and Character, 12*(3), 1–7.

Simons, L., Fehr, L., Black, N., Hogerwerff, F., Georganas, D., & Russell, B. (2011). The application of racial identity development in academic-based service learning. *International Journal of Teaching and Learning in Higher Education, 23*(1), 72–83.

Sperling, R. (2007). Service-learning as a method of teaching multiculturalism to white college students. *Journal of Latinos and Education, 6*(4), 309–322.

Stanton, T. K. (1994). The experience of faculty participants in an instructional development seminar on service-learning. *Michigan Journal of Community Service Learning, 1*(1), 7–20.

Steinman, E. (2011). "Making space": Lessons from collaborations with tribal nations. *Michigan Journal of Community Service Learning, 18*(1), 5–18.

Stewart, T., & Webster, N. (2011). Preface: Why problematize service-learning and why now? In T. Stewart & N. Webster (Eds.), *Problematizing service-learning: Critical reflections for development and action* (pp. xiii–xxi). Charlotte, NC: Information Age Publishing.

Stokamer, S. (2013). Pedagogical catalysts of civic competence: The development of a critical epistemological model for community-based learning. *Journal of Higher Education Outreach and Engagement, 17*(1), 113–121.

Sturm, S., Eatman, T., Saltmarsh, J., & Bush, A. (2011). *Full participation: Building the architecture for diversity and public engagement in higher education*. White paper. New York, NY: Columbia University Law School: Center for Institutional and Social Change.

Subedi, B. (2008). Contesting racialization: Asian immigrant teachers' critiques and claims of teacher authenticity. *Race Ethnicity and Education, 11*(1), 57–70.

Sullivan, M., Kone, A., Senturia, K., Chrisman, N. J., Ciske, S. J., & Krieger, J. W. (2001). Researcher and researched-community perspectives: Toward bridging the gap. *Health Education and Behavior, 28,* 130–149.

Torres, J. (Ed.). (2000). *Benchmarks for campus/community partnerships*. Providence, RI: Campus Compact.

van Dijk, T. A. (2008). *Discourse and power*. New York, NY: Palgrave Macmillan.

Van Velsor, E., & Quinn, L. (2012). Leadership and environmental sustainability. In S. E. Jackson, D. Ones, & S. Dilchert (Eds.), *Managing human resources for environmental sustainability* (pp. 241–262). San Francisco, CA: Jossey-Bass.

Veloria, C. N. (2015). "Maybe this is because of society?" Disrupting and engaging discourses of race in the context of a service-learning project. *Humanity and Society, 39*(2), 135–155.

Verjee, B. (2012). Critical race feminism: A transformative vision for service-learning engagement. *Journal of Community Engagement and Scholarship, 5*(1), 57–69.

Ward, K., & Wolf-Wendel, L. (2000). Community-centered service learning: Moving from doing for to doing with. *American Behavioral Scientist, 43*(5), 767–780.

Webster, N., & Coffey, H. (2011). A critical connection between service-learning and urban communities: Using critical pedagogy to frame the context. In T.

Stewart & N. Webster (Eds.), *Problematizing service-learning: Critical reflections for development and action*. Charlotte, NC: Information Age Publishing.

Wu, C., & Dahlgren, R. L. (2011). Discourse of advocacy: Student learners' critical reflections on working with Spanish-speaking immigrant students. In T. Stewart & N. Webster (Eds.), *Problematizing service-learning: Critical reflections for development and action* (pp. 263–294). Charlotte, NC: Information Age Publishing.

Yeh, T. L. (2010). Service-learning and persistence of low-income, first-generation college students: An exploratory study. *Michigan Journal of Community Service Learning, 16*(2), 50–65.

Chapter Four

PROGRAM ADMINISTRATION AND EVALUATION

Ashley J. Farmer-Hanson

Community engagement professionals (CEPs) are called upon to orchestrate civic engagement practices among multiple stakeholders, and this orchestration often occurs through the direction of programs—or administration. Within Welch and Saltmarsh's (2013) study of more than 100 centers at Carnegie-classified institutions, they found two generations of community engagement practice: The first-generation CEPs had to "make it up as they went" (Welch & Saltmarsh, 2013, p. 1) and were often primarily concerned with the implementation of cocurricular volunteer service. Second-generation CEPs now learn the basics of practice from others and from empirical literature; their responsibilities are concerned with more comprehensive community engagement programming for the whole campus. CEPs are responsible for "overseeing campus-wide community engagement requirements" (Welch & Saltmarsh, p. 1), which includes being a resource clearinghouse on community engagement materials and developing and implementing policies and procedures for risk management and transportation, along with assessment, evaluation, and research. Along with multiple administrative duties, respondents to the survey stated that they spend a large portion of their time consulting with faculty and community partners on projects and grants. The research also found that CEPs are deeply invested in student learning and development and ensuring that students' leadership skills and voice were a high priority in the work they coordinate. In short, second-generation CEPs continue to support the tasks related to cocurricular volunteer service, but the majority of their work is spent administrating and evaluating broad community engagement programs that support and involve multiple stakeholders. This kind of second-generation administration and evaluation is the subject of this literature review.

The community engagement trend in higher education continues to grow, but as found in this literature review and other resources, such as *Diving Deep in Community Engagement* by McReynolds and Shields (2015), very little information is available specifically about the CEP. To grow the field and the work, research must be conducted to understand CEPs' specific roles, and a key piece of this research is on program administration and evaluation. Programs must have a visionary director to lead the institution in community engagement, which is why this literature review is so important.

Over 50 articles, books, and journals were reviewed to create the framework for the competencies expressed as knowledge, skills, personal attributes, and abilities. Resources for this review were collected from multiple online databases. A special emphasis was given to scholarly literature in the past 20 years. The following databases were used: Academic Search Complete, SAGE, Education Resources Information Center (ERIC), Google Scholar, and ProQuest. The literature review began by searching the terms *community engagement* and *civic engagement administration*. These terms provided the most results while searching databases. Based on articles found, the search terms and phrases were refined and included *service-learning risk management, service-learning evaluation, assessing civic knowledge, civic engagement outcomes, service-learning coordinator, civic engagement, student affairs, service-learning advising,* and *service-learning mentoring*. Terms such as *fund-raising, measuring,* and *monitoring* were also used but did not provide results pertinent to this literature review.

Framework of Competencies

Community engagement work is a very broad form of administrative work that relies on specificity and an array of academic and community knowledge. For example, with the service-learning boom in the late 1990s more coordinator and director roles were created (Welch & Saltmarsh, 2013). With currently no specific graduate degrees or certificate programs for CEPs it can be a challenge to identify a shared knowledge base, but foregrounded

Program Administration and Evaluation 81

TABLE 4.1
Summary of Program Administration Competencies

Knowledge	Skills	Abilities	Personal Attributes
• Institutional policy • Risk management • Pedagogy and curriculum development • Awareness of intercultural differences • Awareness of oppression	• Program design/structure • Development of international service opportunities • Assessment/evaluation	• Networking • Marketing	• Critical thinker • Visionary

in 40 years of practice, the literature review provided the following trends in the areas in which CEPs must have knowledge to effectively support program administration and evaluation: institutional policy, risk management, pedagogy and curriculum development, intercultural differences and oppressed populations, and community partner structure and knowledge (see Table 4.1). While this list appears long, it was evident from the literature that CEPs are expected to be competent in a variety of skills, abilities, and personal attributes and possess a large knowledge base.

Knowledge

The literature review found that a CEP should have a knowledge base that includes information on institutional policy, risk management, pedagogy and curriculum development, and intercultural differences and oppressed populations.

Institutional Policy

CEPs must develop familiarity with their institution's policies governing faculty and student teaching, learning, and activity. There are often formal and informal rules to establishing relationships with individuals; tenure and promotion policies, risk management policies, and employee and student handbook knowledge must be developed. The CEP should also have an understanding of institutional policy on areas including developing formal relationships with outside donors and nonprofits (Jacoby

& Mutascio, 2010; McReynolds & Shields, 2015). By networking with faculty and other staff, CEPs can develop an understanding of the political atmosphere and be able to navigate the campus culture.

Much attention has been paid to changes within tenure and promotion policies to legitimize community-engaged scholarship within faculty teaching and research. Embedded within this concern is CEPs' familiarity with tenure and promotion policy so that they are able to flag areas of potential risk for faculty and support faculty as they consider and seek to change these policies. Imagining America convened the Tenure Team Initiative in 2005 to investigate changes to tenure and promotion policy that would make community-engaged scholarship possible. Their work produced a literature review, survey research, and peer feedback of the state of affairs in 2005 at Imagining America member institutions and resulting strategies for change (Ellison & Eatman, 2008). Navigating faculty policies to promote public scholarship was also a focus within the New Times Demand New Scholarship reports (I and II) produced by the TRUCEN network of Campus Compact (Stanton, 2008). Within these reports, repeated calls were made for tenure and promotion policy revision.

Biddix, Somers, and Polman (2009) developed a case study on democratic engagement and civic engagement learning outcomes of campus protest in which they conducted multiple interviews and analyzed archival documentation. The university of interest had a history of campus activism and a mission set on developing students with skills to be engaged in society. In their study Biddix and colleagues (2009) found that effective student protest conducted within existing institutional policy promoted deep student civic learning and also effectively changed institutional policy such that greater community benefit was achieved. Students must be taught how to be active in their communities, but written rules often dictate how to properly execute their democratic rights.

The student handbook comes into use when students are demonstrating or exercising their democratic rights on campus. For example, the CEP should teach and show students how to access the policy and also work with the administration to allow exercise of students' rights. With this informal educating comes knowledge in student development theory. CEPs must be able to understand how students develop, which plays a part in how they interpret and understand the student handbook. A director must value the variety of perspectives and somehow create an environment that is accepting of campus activism, which allows students to "participate in a democratic society" (Biddix et al., 2009, p. 143). CEPs also need to know how to hold students accountable according to institutional policy when students make poor decisions that violate policy.

Risk Management

Risk management is a key piece of a CEP's role. CEPs are often responsible for coordinating training and educational sessions for staff, faculty, and students in regard to community engagement so that risk can be minimized. CEPs should work within the institution to develop guidelines and parameters for risk management (McReynolds & Shields, 2015; Oates & Leavitt, 2003). Without a policy the institution is open to litigation. As found in Dostilio and Molchan's (2015) case study, many organizations rely on the Volunteer Protection Act of 1997 as the only risk management strategy for the agency, which does not fully protect an organization from litigation. A full risk management strategy should be developed.

In this review, it was often difficult to find research within the last 5 to 10 years that focused on specific risk management strategies for CEPs. The 2008 Risk Management Fact Sheet published by the National Service-Learning Clearinghouse (2008) outlined key areas that CEPs should include in a risk management manual. The areas range from risk management policies and procedures to forms, waivers, and background checks.

CEPs should be able to develop a risk management plan (in conjunction with risk management and counsel administrative associates) and actively educate their constituents on the risk management policy and plan. This can be particularly vital at institutions that don't have a formal risk management policy in place and where that "burden of enacting risk management strategies tends to fall on the shoulders of faculty and administrators" (Dostilio & Molchan, 2015, p. 5). Through conversations, training, and networking, the institution will have a better possibility of keeping everyone safe and lower their liability. Most of the activities that CEPs sponsor or are involved in coordinating are conducted off campus. The CEP needs to understand the risk management policy in transportation, volunteering with vulnerable populations, and any specific training that volunteers should have prior to their service.

Pedagogy and Curriculum Development

CEPs serve as a resource provider, and one of the areas in which they are asked to assist is curriculum development. Oates and Leavitt (2003) developed their publication to provide best practices on service-learning and to serve as a resource for individuals who are providing service-learning opportunities to students. Oates and Leavitt's research (2003) focused on four models of integrating service-learning into learning communities. A key element of their findings is that an effective service-learning program takes advantage of the expertise of faculty, student affairs professionals, and community partners. To do this well, no matter where the CEP is housed, he or she must be knowledgeable in best practices for community engagement and its integration with learning, and also have an understanding of pedagogy and curriculum development. The CEP is often seen as the primary resource when an instructor is in need of assistance, but may also serve a valuable role for curriculum development bodies within an institution. A knowledge base in this area provides not only faculty with the tools they need to support student learning but also CEPs with the opportunity to teach best practices and create reciprocal relationships with community partners. (Additional information on this can be found in Chapter 9.)

Intercultural Differences and Oppressed Populations

With the wide variety of populations CEPs work with on their campuses, they must have a knowledge base in intercultural differences and awareness of how groups of people are oppressed. Sandmann, Kliewer, Kim, and Omerikwa's (2010) study focused on reciprocal relationships and how to have successful relationships with community partners. The authors determined that a CEP must first have an understanding of the variety of forms of power that exist. Their analysis produced the relational engagement framework grounded in three theoretical perspectives on power: Freire, Foucault, and Rawls. CEPs should have knowledge of their power in relationships and recognize it, but not abuse the innate power that they have because of the resources they control. By recognizing their power and educating faculty and staff about oppressed populations and sharing knowledge of intercultural differences, CEPs can begin to build relationships. Students should also have training in cultural difference and become aware of their own privileges. Confronting these issues and exposing various populations to the very visible and invisible issues can enhance the experience. The CEP has to know and understand the populations that community partners are serving and how the partnership with the university can build capacity and solve problems within the community. The understanding of power and oppression is often explored in critical race theory and within critical practice literature. (More information related to critical practice appears in Chapter 3.)

Skills and Abilities

The skills required of a CEP are varied and broad. The practice literature suggests that these skills would include program design and structure (which includes staff development, relationship building, communicating, and providing resources), developing international service opportunities and travel accommodations, assessment and evaluation, networking, and marketing.

Training Development of Center Staff

Welch and Saltmarsh (2013) found that most CEPs are responsible for an average of three professional staff members, who often include assistant directors, graduate assistants, and VISTA service members. In Massey and Gouthro's (2011) case study they analyzed a community outreach center that was a part of Queen's University in Kingston, Ontario, Canada. In their study they assessed the effectiveness of the center to university students and community partners. They concluded that Queen's was not meeting the needs of the constituents because not all of the center staff were well trained and versed in the services that are available. To be an effective resource CEPs must provide training and development to their staff, but also firsthand opportunities to understand the needs and agendas of the community. A CEP should invest time into not only training the staff but also developing them and handling any human resource management issue that may arise (McReynolds & Shields, 2015). From managing volunteers to managing staff, people management is a large piece of what CEPs do. They have to ensure that people have the skills and capability to develop into effective and efficient staff members. CEPs often play the role of mentor to paid and unpaid staff along with holding people accountable and providing praise for a job well done. The CEP should have the ability to lead the sustained process of the department, which starts with the staff (Plater, 2011).

Community Partnerships

Without community partnerships and established relationships with nonprofit agencies, a significant piece of the CEP's work does not exist (Jones & Palmerton, 2010). Jones and Palmerton (2010) stress that a CEP's role should be grounded in principles of partnership development and working toward "designing the relationship" (p. 166) to meet the needs of both parties. Developing partnerships with community partners is an important piece for CEPs to do. In Bringle and Hatcher's (2002) study about campus-community partnerships, the focus was on the phases of a relationship; we can infer how CEPs play an integral role from the initial development of a relationship to maintaining that relationship and dissolution. When establishing and maintaining relationships with community partners, it is critical for the CEP to understand the implications of a clear mission, an accessible campus clearinghouse (central unit on campus), compatibility, effective communication, and a skilled staff. These implications reinforce the need for a CEP to be institutionally knowledgeable, strategic, and capable as a leader or member of a team responsible for engaged work. (Additional information about partnership development can be found in Chapter 8.)

Partnerships With Students

Developing relationships is very important for a CEP (Jacoby & Associates, 2003; Jacoby & Mutascio, 2010). Students are a key element to the work that is conducted. To plan programs and develop community engagement opportunities, a relationship must be established with students first (Biddix et al., 2009). Students can be an excellent resource on advisory boards, but board service can also be an element of leadership development. Through serving on boards, students are developing their leadership skills in a safe environment that will eventually prepare them for the workforce. A study conducted by Zlotkowski (2006) found that academics and student affairs must be connected to develop a holistic student. The student voice is a significant element of community engagement, and opportunities to allow their voices to be heard should be provided.

The director must be aware of civic skills: "organization, communication, collective decision making, and critical thinking" (Hatcher, 2011, p. 85). CEPs should have a grasp on what a civic identity entails and how to foster within students civic growth and development. (More about students' civic learning and development can be found in Chapter 7.) Many CEPs provide community-based work-study programs out of their office, which create long-term relationships with community partners (Jacoby & Associates, 2003; Zlotkowski, 2006). Often, paired with work-study are AmeriCorps programs. CEPs must have knowledge about the application to, implementation of, and tracking of the state's AmeriCorps program (Hoy & Meisel, 2008). While managing these programs the CEP is responsible for matching students with community partners. This task can be difficult, but is something that benefits both parties (Hynes & Nykiel, 2004). Understanding the motivation of the student and the nonprofit can be vital to assisting with developing a relationship and placing the student volunteer and continuing to stay in compliance with the federal work-study program and AmeriCorps.

Internally, institutions can create programs that foster the student voice. Zlotkowski (2006) found that scholarship programs, intentional training, treating students as colleagues, developing student and faculty relationships, and creating opportunities for students to serve as entrepreneurs are all ways to foster community engagement on campus. Supporting students can be done in a variety of ways, but as people who are connected through national and state networks, such as Campus Compact, CEPs have a great opportunity to connect students with those organizations as well (Jacoby & Associates, 2003; McReynolds & Shields, 2015). CEPs should have the ability to work with higher education associations to promote engaged scholarship (Gibson, 2006). The students can build a network with peers similar to them and gain development from others outside of the university.

Resource Provider

Resources can be defined in multiple ways, and the CEP and the institution must define what resources will be available to and through the CEP's department. Through the literature review we found that the CEP should provide multiple resources to a variety of constituents, including students, faculty, staff, administrators, and community partners (Jacoby & Associates, 2003; Moely, Billig, & Holland, 2009). Specific items that should be available to faculty include syllabi, reflection materials, evaluations, and learning contracts (Jacoby & Associates, 2003; McReynolds & Shields, 2015; Moely et al., 2009; Oates & Leavitt, 2003). The CEP should develop a website or an easily accessible cloud storage that provides all of these examples electronically for faculty to have at their disposal. Faculty may want a training session or professional development opportunity to become educated on these specific areas (Jacoby & Associates, 2003; Moely et al., 2009). In this case, the CEP must demonstrate that he or she is an in-house expert and be prepared to answer questions and develop curriculum for areas that he or she may not have personally studied.

Engstrom (2003) found that the CEP is looked to when a faculty member is in search of grant funding to support a community engagement project. As a result, the CEP needs to be knowledgeable in grant writing and have the skill set to teach others how to complete a successful grant application. Providing financial support for projects and educational opportunities is often a large need, and some CEPs have access to additional resources (Moely et al., 2009). They need to identify what resources are needed to develop or maintain the program and identify where those resources will come from (Jacoby & Mutascio, 2010; McReynolds & Shields, 2015). An established relationship with institutional advancement will provide an avenue to a variety of funding sources and endowments, which can provide sustainable funding over time. The CEP should have the ability to garner resources and support through her or his network and beyond (Kezar, Gallant, & Lester, 2011).

International Service Opportunities

Ibrahim's (2012) "International Service-Learning as a Path to Global Citizenship" demonstrates that as globalization is expanding, institutions are taking on a more global purpose. International service opportunities provide students with large learning opportunities, and structured programs provide students with the tools to become productive global citizens. The institution may look to the CEP to assist with developing or managing an international service program. This includes travel logistics, partnership research, housing, health care, orientation development, and budget development and management (Curtin, Martins, Schuartz-Barcott, DiMaria, & Ogando, 2013; Jacoby & Associates, 2003). The CEP also needs to work on a risk management plan if an emergency happens while traveling abroad.

As stated previously, networking is a huge asset for a CEP, but especially in service-learning abroad because the CEP has the ability to bring faculty together to discuss their service-learning experiences. CEPs also have the ability to network with other institutions and national organizations such as Break Away to share best practices and to gather documents or information about community partners. Beyond logistics the CEP should have a knowledge base in reflection and conducting pretrip learning meetings or class sessions that focus on "history, politics, language, culture, and specific area being studied" (Curtin et al., 2013, p. 550). They should teach other staff, faculty, and student leaders how to conduct these sessions with their participants and students.

Just as CEPs working locally need to have an understanding of power and oppression, CEPs working globally must be aware of the ethical dilemmas that global community engagement presents. Particularly in the pre–health sciences professions, much has been written about the potential damage caused by well-meaning preprofessional health students who provide services beyond their expertise or in settings that are detrimental to the very people whom students (and their institutions) are hoping to help (Wallace, 2012). Working groups such as GASP (Global Activities by Students at Pre-Health Levels) and Better Volunteering, Better Care (an interagency initiative) investigate best practices within service provision globally and produce ethical guidelines with which CEPs should be familiar. In addition to potential harm done in communities, CEPs also ought to be familiar with unintended distress experienced by students who participate in global community engagement. Students transitioning home from an experience in developing nations may experience significant distress, often characterized as *transformation*, that needs attention. In his work on intercultural service-learning, Kiely (2004) explores the *chameleon complex*, or students "learning how to translate their emerging global perspective . . . into action upon reentry into the United States. Chameleon complex represents the internal struggle between conforming to, and resisting, dominant norms, rituals, and practices in the United States" (p. 15).

Assessment and Evaluation

Documenting the effectiveness of one's community engagement work and guiding others to do the same entails a system of *tracking, documenting, assessing*, and *evaluating*. Though the terms are frequently used interchangeably, there are distinctions between and among them. CEPs must know when tracking and documenting needs to occur (e.g., tracking outputs of community engagement, like numbers of people involved, numbers of hours served, or numbers of projects completed), versus when assessment of student learning needs to take place (e.g., determining the degree to which student learning outcomes can be demonstrated), versus when institutional or unit-level community engagement initiatives need to be evaluated (e.g., the effectiveness of an anchor institution strategy or the outcomes of a community-based writing program).

Knowing how to measure community engagement efforts, how to involve others in that measurement, and how to leverage the results is vital for CEPs—yet the area is one of struggle. Within his study of reciprocity as sustainability within a community-campus partnership, Bloomgarden (2013) declared, "Engagement office staff and community partners alike face persistent challenges to accessing, prioritizing, and implementing assessment resources and strategies from inside and beyond their organizations" (p. 140). One of the most recognizable frameworks for measuring an institution's commitments to community engagement is the Carnegie Classification for Community Engagement. Among the 2006 and 2008 community engagement classification applications, one consistent weakness was a lack of a comprehensive assessment plan for community engagement as well as specific assessment of the impact of community engagement on various constituencies: students, faculty, community, and so on (Driscoll, 2008).

As drivers of institutional community engagement strategies, CEPs need to know how to evaluate the institution's progress and how to collaborate with others to do so. One model that may be helpful is the development of an assessment committee that can plan how to assess and measure community engagement across campus (McReynolds & Shields, 2015).

A variety of tools have been produced to help institutions measure the progress they've made toward deepening or institutionalizing forms of engagement: the self-assessment rubric for the institutionalization of service-learning (Furco, 1999), a matrix for levels of commitment to service (Holland, 1997), and the anchor institution dashboard (Dubb, McKinley, & Howard, 2013).

Conducting student learning assessment can be a challenge for CEPs because they often use assessment tools that allow the student to self-report learning, rather than evaluate the student's learning directly (Bringle & Hatcher, 2009; Keshen, Holland, & Moely, 2010). Civic development and learning can happen across multiple environments and can include cocurricular volunteer experiences, club activities, service-learning opportunities, student protest, community-based research, and more. These opportunities can happen in formal and informal areas; a CEP should be aware of all of the opportunities available and have a knowledge base of how to assess student growth and learning in all of them. Much work has been done to identify civic learning outcomes that might be assessed at the course or student experience level (Gelmon, Holland, Driscoll, Spring, & Kerrigan, 2001; Hatcher, 2011; National Task Force on Civic Learning and Democratic Engagement, 2012; Norris, Siemers, Clayton, Weiss, & Edwards, forthcoming).

In regard to partnerships, tools exist that range from measuring the outcomes of the single partnership—Comprehensive Model for Assessing Service-Learning and Community-University Partnerships (Holland, 2001)—to working across sectors and institutions to measure a group's collective impact on a particular civic issue (Hanleybrown, Kania, & Kramer, 2012). However, community engagement doesn't take place alone, and neither does assessment. Gelmon's (2003) research focused on ensuring that assessment was conducted with community partners. She found that campus partners often don't involve the community partner in the research, or they create an atmosphere that is not conducive for them to provide feedback and input in the project that often has a large impact on their daily work. It was suggested that a plan be established with the community partner while developing the initial relationship or study. Throughout the process the campus partner should be mindful of where meetings and discussions are established to provide a space that is not intimidating and allows the partner to be a part of the process. The community partner voice in the assessment process is key to ensure that both parties' needs are being met (Hatcher & Bringle, 2012; McReynolds & Shields, 2015; Oates & Leavitt, 2003). To be treated and considered cofacilitators, their voice must be included in this process (Hatcher & Bringle, 2012). Having an established relationship and identifiable goals at the beginning of the relationship is key to sustainability and reciprocity (Gelmon, 2003). Once findings are established, Gelmon suggests that they be shared with the institution's internal and external audiences, such as community partners, donors, and funders.

Networking and Communicating

Networking with a variety of populations is often a key responsibility of a CEP. Engstrom (2003) and Jacoby and Mutascio (2010) emphasize in their publications that the CEP should have the ability to network with staff in academic affairs and student affairs. This connection is essential because both areas of campus are often involved in coordinating and working with community partners. Both parties often have the same goal of building community partnerships, but they sometimes do not work together. Many community engagement opportunities take place all around an institution, and bridging the gap between academic affairs and student affairs leverages the work that is being done. As indicated in this chapter, the CEP should network with faculty, staff, students, institutional advancement, and research. Attending events within and outside of the university is vital for a CEP to lead a successful program.

Pigza and Troppe (2003) focused a large portion of their campus infrastructure models on communication. Their *integrated model* provides a few key units with the responsibility of coordinating service in collaboration with community partners, rather than a *fragmented model*, where multiple people are sending information out, or even a *concentrated model*, where one person is sending information out and not allowing a true partnership to take place. At most institutions, the CEP is expected to be the primary individual who will communicate with community partners or take the lead in an *integrated model*. They are responsible for serving as the face of not only the office but also the university. These CEPs are also in a role where they need to communicate frequently with the campus community about the community needs and vice versa (Moely et al., 2009). As CEPs, they need to have advanced communication skills and the ability to change their method of delivery based on the audience and the particular model that the institution has adopted.

Budgeting and Grant Management

According to the 2004 Campus Compact annual survey, 46% of campuses had centers or offices with a budget less than $20,000. In the 2015 survey, 60% had budgets in excess of $100,000, with the largest category of respondents (33%) having budgets of more than $250,000 (Campus

Compact, 2015). Managing the fiscal resources available to support community engagement is seen as one of the core aspects of building institutional capacity for community engagement among institutionally focused engagement advocates (Weerts & Sandmann, 2010). The marked growth in fiscal allocations between 2004 and 2014 indicates growth in responsibility for CEPs to manage and cultivate such funding. Community engagement requires human and financial capital. Pigza and Troppe (2003) found that while establishing a community engagement department, an infrastructure should be established, which requires the skills to manage the department budget, while also managing and tracking grant and endowment funding. Gibson (2006) found that research universities should invest in seven areas to advance civic engagement at their institution; one of them was sustainable funding and support for grant programs.

Weerts has developed a body of work that ties financial support for community engagement and fund-raising strategies based upon community engagement to the strength of an institution's commitment to community engagement (Sandmann & Weerts, 2008; Weerts, 2007a, 2007b; Weerts & Hudson, 2009). In particular, service-learning or other forms of curricular engagement are consistently a starting point for insisting that engagement be a funding priority; research institutions carry larger and more complex engagement budgets, and internal seed grants are typically used to incentivize and support engagement (Weerts & Hudson, 2009). The ability to raise, manage, and disperse funds for community-based projects and as resources for faculty and student engagement is part and parcel of the CEP's job.

Marketing

Programs can exist, but if they are not marketed, people within and outside of the institution may not know about them. As referenced in other sections, marketing is a key piece of assessment and fund-raising. As found in Massey and Gouthro's (2011) research, getting the campus community and community of the region to understand where the community engagement office is and what services are provided can be an essential piece to serving both populations. Constituents who are not fully aware of what services are available will not utilize them. A CEP must know the audience and essentially develop a brand for the department. Knowledge of social media and other marketing tools is vital to reaching a wide variety of audience members. Marketing should include sharing success stories and progress with the community (McReynolds & Shields, 2015; Oates & Leavitt, 2003). This might spur interest in the program and interest more partnerships. A CEP should have skill sets in relationship building and networking.

Personal Attributes

Personal attributes can be difficult to teach, but to be successful a CEP should have critical thinking and visionary skills to expand and develop the department to its full potential and to build partnerships on and off campus.

Critical Thinking and Visionary Skills

A CEP works with multiple constituents inside and outside of the institution. CEPs are asked to think about a broad scope of issues of administration and evaluation among the many other things they must accomplish in their role. To do this they must have critical thinking and visionary skills. In the review of literature it was found that to have a successful department the individual must be a visionary (Jacoby & Associates, 2003; Jacoby & Mutascio, 2010; Oates & Leavitt, 2003). They must be able to analyze the current conditions of the department, identify the ways in which to move it forward, and develop a plan to implement the changes. Long-term goals and initiatives keep the department moving forward and provide a way to ensure the best practices are being conducted (McReynolds & Shields, 2015). CEPs should have the ability to move beyond an emphasis on service-delivery and informational or programmatic approaches toward catalytic approaches that foster citizen professionalism and civic agency and thereby "create sustained cultures of civic life" with multiplier effects (Boyte, 2008, 2009, p. 25). By doing so, this will prevent initiatives from being considered "special"—that is, removed from the culture and structure of the institution (Gibson, 2006; Saltmarsh & Hartley, 2011). They should have the ability to advocate for centers and engage in interdisciplinary work that focuses on addressing public issues (Gibson, 2006). Many people often use assessment tools such as the Carnegie Classification in Community Engagement as a way to gather and collect data that support their work and advocate for their center (McReynolds & Shields, 2015). A CEP must be aware of Carnegie Classification in community engagement and have an established understanding of the prestige that the classification has within higher education (Hatcher, 2011).

Implications for Future Research

As McReynolds and Shields (2015) found, there is very little research on the CEP. Much of the research pertinent to this chapter was dedicated to faculty, staff, and students without reference to the individual who would be leading the initiatives in program administration and evaluation. More research should be conducted on the CEP's role in institutional policy, risk management, pedagogy and curriculum development, intercultural differences and oppressed populations, and community partner structure and knowledge. The research that was found stated, for example, that faculty should have training in service-learning or have resources available, but most of the time it was also implied that the CEP was the one providing that information or conducting the training. Assessment and evaluation are key aspects of a CEP's role, but an evaluation of effective CEP practice is not available and would provide a better understanding of the multiple roles CEPs play on college campuses and in communities.

References

Biddix, J. P., Somers, P. A., & Polman, J. L. (2009). Protest reconsidered: Identifying democratic and civic engagement learning outcomes. *Innovative Higher Education, 33*, 133–147.

Bloomgarden, A. (2013). Reciprocity as sustainability in campus-community partnership. *Journal of Public Scholarship in Higher Education, 3*, 129–145.

Boyte, H. C. (2008). Public work: Civic populism versus technocracy in higher education. In D. W. Brown & D. Witte (Eds.), *Agents of democracy: Higher education and the HEX journey* (pp. 79–102). Dayton, OH: Kettering Foundation.

Boyte, H. C. (2009). *Civic agency and the cult of the expert*. Dayton, OH: Kettering Foundation.

Bringle, R. G., & Hatcher, J. A. (2002). Campus-community partnerships: The terms of engagement. *Journal of Social Issues, 58*, 503–516.

Bringle, R. G., & Hatcher, J. A. (2009). Innovative practices in service-learning and curricular engagement. *New Directions for Higher Education, 147*, 37–46.

Campus Compact. (2015). *Preparing to accelerate change: Understanding our starting line, 2015 Annual Member Survey*. Boston, MA: Campus Compact.

Curtin, A. J., Martins, D. C., Schuartz-Barcott, D., DiMaria, L., & Ogando, B. (2013). Development and evaluation of an international service learning program for nursing students. *Public Health Nursing, 30*(6), 549–556.

Dostilio, L., & Molchan, K. (2015). Relational approach to co-constructed risk management. In O. Delano-Oriaran, M. W. Penick-Parks, & S. Fondrie (Eds.), *The SAGE sourcebook of service-learning and civic engagement* (pp. 435–443). Thousand Oaks, CA: SAGE.

Driscoll, A. (2008). Carnegie's community-engagement classification: Intentions and insights. *Change: The Magazine of Higher Learning, 40*(1), 38–41.

Dubb, S., McKinley, S., & Howard, T. (2013). *The anchor dashboard: Aligning institutional practices to meet low-income community needs*. Takoma Park, MD: Democracy Collaborative.

Ellison, J., & Eatman, T. K. (2008). *Scholarship in action: Knowledge creation and tenure policy in the engaged university.* Syracuse, NY: Imagining America.

Engstrom, C. M. (2003). Developing collaborative student affairs–academic affairs partnerships for service-learning. In B. Jacoby & Associates (Eds.), *Building partnerships for service learning* (pp. 65–84). San Francisco, CA: John Wiley & Sons.

Furco, A. (1999). *Self-assessment rubric for the institutionalization of service-learning in higher education.* Berkeley: University of California Press.

Gelmon, S. B. (2003). Assessment as a means of building service-learning partnerships. In B. Jacoby & Associates (Eds.), *Building partnerships for service learning* (pp. 42–64). San Francisco, CA: John Wiley & Sons.

Gelmon, S. B., Holland, B. A., Driscoll, A., Spring, A., & Kerrigan, S. (2001). *Assessing service-learning and civic engagement: Principles and techniques.* Providence, RI: Campus Compact, Brown University.

Gibson, C. M. (2006). *New times demand new scholarship: Research universities and civic engagement—a leadership agenda.* Medford, MA: Tufts University and Campus Compact.

Hanleybrown, F., Kania, J., & Kramer, M. (2012). Channeling change: Making collective impact work. *Stanford Social Innovation Review, 20*, 1–8.

Hatcher, J. (2011). Assessing civic knowledge and engagement. *New Directions for Higher Education, 149*, 81–92.

Hatcher, J. A., & Bringle, R. G. (Eds.). (2012). *Understanding service-learning and community engagement: Crossing boundaries through research.* Charlotte, NC: Information Age Publishing.

Holland, B. (1997). Analyzing institutional commitment to service: A model of key organizational factors. *Michigan Journal of Community Service Learning, 4*(1), 30–41.

Holland, B. A. (2001). A comprehensive model for assessing service-learning and community-university partnerships. *New Directions for Higher Education, 2001*(114), 51–60.

Hoy, A., & Meisel, W. (2008). *Civic engagement at the center: Building democracy through integrated cocurricular and curricular experience.* Washington, DC: Association of American Colleges & Universities.

Hynes, R. A., & Nykiel, A. L. (2004). Maximizing outcomes of volunteer programs through a functional approach to motivation. *Journal of College and Character, 5*(9).

Ibrahim, B. L. (2012). International service-learning as a path to global citizenship. In J. A. Hatcher & R. G. Bringle (Eds.), *Understanding service-learning and community engagement: Crossing boundaries through research* (pp. 11–24). Charlotte, NC: Information Age Publishing.

Jacoby, B., & Associates (Eds.). (2003). *Building partnerships for service learning.* San Francisco, CA: John Wiley & Sons.

Jacoby, B., & Mutascio, P. (Eds.). (2010). *Looking in, reaching out: A reflective guide for community service-learning professionals.* Boston, MA: Campus Compact.

Jones, S. R., & Palmerton, A. (2010). How to develop campus community partnerships. In B. Jacoby & P. Mutascio (Eds.), *Looking in, reaching out: A reflective guide for community service-learning professionals* (pp. 163–184). Boston, MA: Campus Compact.

Keshen, J., Holland, B. A., & Moely, B. E. (Eds.). (2010) *Research for what? Making engaged scholarship matter*. Charlotte, NC: Information Age Publishing.

Kezar, A., Gallant, T., & Lester, J. (2011). Everyday people making a difference on college campuses: The tempered grassroots leadership tactics of faculty and staff. *Studies in Higher Education, 36*(2), 129–151.

Kiely, R. (2004). A chameleon with a complex: Searching for transformation in international service-learning. *Michigan Journal of Community Service Learning, 10*(2), 5–20.

Massey, J., & Gouthro, K. (2011). Community outreach: Assessment and program planning for off-campus students. *Assessment Update, 23*(1), 6–8.

McReynolds, M., & Shields, E. (2015). *Diving deep in community engagement: A model for professional development*. Des Moines, IA: Iowa Campus Compact.

Moely, B. E., Billig, S. H., & Holland, B. (Eds.). (2009). *Creating our identities in service-learning and community engagement*. Charlotte, NC: Information Age Publishing.

National Service-Learning Clearinghouse (2008). *Fact sheet: Risk management and liability in higher education service-learning*. Washington, DC: Learn and Serve America's National Service-Learning Clearinghouse.

National Task Force on Civic Learning and Democratic Engagement. (2012). *A crucible moment: College learning and democracy's future*. Washington, DC: Association of American Colleges & Universities.

Norris, K. E., Siemers, C., Clayton, P. H., Weiss, H. A., & Edwards, K. E. (in press). Critical reflection and civic mindedness: Expanding conceptualizations and practices. In T. D. Mitchell, T. Eatman, & C. Dolgan (Eds.), *Cambridge handbook for service learning and community engagement*. Oxford, England: Oxford University Press.

Oates, K. K. & Leavitt, L. H. (2003). *Service-learning and learning communities: Tools for integration and assessment*. Washington, DC: Association of American Colleges & Universities.

Pigza, J. M., & Troppe, M. L. (2003). Developing an infrastructure for service-learning and community engagement. In B. Jacoby & Associates (Eds.), *Building partnerships for service learning* (pp. 106–130). San Francisco, CA: John Wiley & Sons.

Plater, W. M. (2011). Collective leadership for engagement: Reclaiming the public purpose of higher education. In J. A. Saltmarsh & M. Hartley (Eds.), *"To serve a larger purpose": Engagement for democracy and the transformation of higher education* (pp. 102–129). Philadelphia, PA: Temple University Press.

Saltmarsh, J., & Hartley, M. (2011). Conclusion: Creating the democratically engaged university—possibilities for constructive action. In J. A. Saltmarsh & M. Hartley (Eds.), *"To serve a larger purpose": Engagement for democracy and the transformation of higher education* (pp. 289–299). Philadelphia, PA: Temple University Press.

Sandmann, L. R., Kliewer, B. W., Kim, J., & Omerikwa, A. (2010). Toward understanding reciprocity in community-university partnerships: An analysis of select theories of power. In J. Keshen, B. A. Holland, & B. E. Moely (Eds.), *Research for what? Making engaged scholarship matter* (pp. 3–23). Charlotte, NC: Information Age Publishing.

Sandmann, L. R., & Weerts, D. J. (2008). Reshaping institutional boundaries to accommodate an engagement agenda. *Innovative Higher Education, 33*(3), 181–196.

Stanton, T. K. (2008). New times demand new scholarship: Opportunities and challenges for civic engagement at research universities. *Education, Citizenship and Social Justice, 3*(1), 19–42.

Wallace, L. J. (2012). Does pre-medical 'voluntourism' improve the health of communities abroad? *Journal of Global Health Perspectives, 1*, 1–6.

Weerts, D. (2007a). Public engagement and emerging roles for institutional advancement. *International Journal of Educational Advancement, 7*(2), 75–78.

Weerts, D. J. (2007b). Toward an engagement model of institutional advancement at public colleges and universities. *International Journal of Educational Advancement, 7*(2), 79–103.

Weerts, D., & Hudson, E. (2009). Engagement and institutional advancement. *New Directions for Higher Education, 2009*(147), 65–74.

Weerts, D. J., & Sandmann, L. R. (2010). Community engagement and boundary-spanning roles at research universities. *Journal of Higher Education, 81*(6), 702–727.

Welch, M., & Saltmarsh, J. (2013). Current practice and infrastructures for campus centers of community engagement. *Journal of Higher Education Outreach and Engagement, 17*(4), 25–56.

Zlotkowski, E. (2006). *Students as colleagues*. Providence, RI: Campus Compact.

Chapter Five

ENVISIONING, LEADING, AND ENACTING INSTITUTIONAL CHANGE FOR THE PUBLIC GOOD

The Role of Community Engagement Professionals

Romy Hübler and Melissa Quan

The literature on institutional change in higher education is vast, and many approaches to change exist. Scholars recognize community engagement as an important tool for change that meets the needs of learners and society at large (Ramaley, 2006). Much of the literature on community engagement has focused on best practice as well as institutionalization. Welch and Saltmarsh (2013) argue that the field of community engagement is transitioning from its first generation of development into its second generation, which is marked by an evolution of campus centers coordinating service and volunteering opportunities to now creating programming that promotes community-engaged teaching, scholarship, and leadership development. In this new phase, scholars are looking to better understand community engagement as a tool for institutional and cultural change to enable higher education to achieve its public purpose (Saltmarsh & Hartley, 2011; Saltmarsh, Hartley, & Clayton, 2009).

The literature review in this chapter is informed and shaped by our professional experiences and standpoint, as we ourselves are community engagement professionals (CEPs). We arrived at our current CEP roles via different paths: Melissa was inspired by her involvement in postgraduate service and nonprofit work and has followed a path of learning on the job, while Romy was inspired during graduate studies and international experiences and has sought out formal learning experiences such as a fellowship with Imagining America and a leadership role in University of Maryland, Baltimore County's (UMBC) BreakingGround initiative. Romy also pursues research projects on civic engagement, engaged pedagogies, public scholarship, and institutional change. Though we each occupy stages in our careers different from the other's, we are both committed to building institutional structures that support democratic community engagement and identify with the characteristics of boundary spanners, third-space professionals, and grassroots change agents.

The first step in conducting this literature review involved the identification of key search terms, including *higher education* and *institutional change* or *culture change* or *organizational change*, *higher education* and *systemic change*, *higher education* and *public good*, *higher education capacity building*, *democracy* and *institutional change*, *civic agency* and *institutional change*, *community engagement* and *institutional change* or *organizational change*, *Carnegie Community Engagement Classification* and *institutional change*, *the engaged institution*, *higher education* and *leadership*, *higher education* and *leadership for change*, and *leadership* and *change* or *institutional change*. The primary tools for the search were Google Scholar and WorldCat UMBC. We also used citations from key articles to identify additional resources. Finally, we each relied heavily upon our own compilation of key articles, built over time through doctoral research and work in the field. We excluded articles that focused on the institutionalization of community engagement and rather focused on articles that addressed change process that met the characteristics of *democratic engagement* and *second-order changes* as defined in the following sections.

Assumptions

This literature review outlines competencies CEPs need to support institutional change for democratic community engagement in higher education. A set of assumptions underlying this literature review includes

- the purpose of higher education is to promote democracy and civic engagement (Boyer, 1996; Boyte & Mehaffy, 2008; Gibson, 2006; Hartley, 2011),
- community engagement is essential to fulfill this purpose (Finley, 2011; Fisher, Fabricant, & Simmons, 2004; Goettel & Haft, 2010), and
- community engagement runs counter to the dominant norms of higher education (Boyte, 2000; Eatman, 2012; Mathews, 2011; Rice, 2003; Snyder, 2008).

Therefore, institutional and cultural change are necessary to achieve the public purpose of higher education. Before discussing the competencies that CEPs need to effect such change, we define the term *change* relative to higher education and community engagement.

Defining Change

Throughout our literature review, we look deeply at Adriana Kezar's extensive scholarship on higher education leadership and change. Decades of research on institutional change in higher education frame Kezar's 2014 book, *How Colleges Change: Understanding, Leading, and Enacting Change*, in which she suggests that change can occur based on external factors (adaptation), unintentional mimicking (isomorphism), or intentional implementation of new initiatives or practices (innovation or reform). Kezar (2014) and Kezar and Eckel (2002b) argue that comprehensive changes affect values, beliefs, and structures of the entire enterprise. They conclude that change is a multifaceted concept that can focus on content, scope, level, or focus and each facet requires distinct approaches. Kezar laments that this complexity has often been overlooked in existing literature. Little is known about the processes involved in transformational or large-scale change in higher education, which Kezar and Eckel (2002b) attribute to a dearth of empirical studies on the topic, generalizations about change strategies, a presentation of strategies in isolation, atheoretical approaches to the study of institutional change, and incomplete methodologies. Further, Kezar, Gallant, and Lester (2011) explain that scholars tend to focus on senior leadership, resulting in little knowledge about the roles of faculty and staff in the process. Building on Kezar's work, we define *institutional change* as a complex process that can be led by people with or without positional authority that results in deep cultural transformation of existing norms.

A Case for Change

To contextualize the competencies CEPs need to support institutional change, it is important to identify the norms and traditions that community engagement leaders endeavor to transform in higher education. They include disciplinary and structural silos (Boyte, 2009; Boyte & Fretz, 2011; Checkoway, 2001; Gibson, 2006; Saltmarsh et al., 2009), detached research practices (Boyer, 1990, 1996; Boyte, 2000), one-way pedagogies (Boyte, 2008), lip-service approaches (American Association of State Colleges and Universities, 2002), reward systems that do not value community-engaged teaching and scholarship (Gibson, 2006), and isolation from communities (Gibson, 2006).

Through change, community engagement leaders hope to create the *engaged institution*, which utilizes its intellectual and institutional resources to address the multiple crises of contemporary society (Checkoway, 2001). The engaged institution is further characterized by public engagement, that is, partnerships between institutions of higher education and the public that are place related, interactive, mutually beneficial, and integrated (American Association of State Colleges and Universities, 2002). An institution with this focus democratizes knowledge by supporting individuals in becoming "producers of public goods and co-creators of civic life" (Boyte, 2008, p. 87).

Role of CEPs: Tempered Through Context and Networks

CEPs can play an important role in achieving transformational change and creating the engaged institution. In the following sections, we outline competencies, identified or inferred from a review of institutional change literature, that CEPs need to effectively participate in and support this process. We present these competencies in three categories: envisioning change, leading change, and enacting change. As we explain in more detail in the section on envisioning change, these competencies do not represent a fixed list, but must rather be contextualized and adjusted based on the institutional setting. While we propose that CEPs need to possess or be familiar with these competencies, they may not use every competency as their relevance depends on where the CEPs' institutions are located within the change process and the CEPs' distinct roles within their institutions. Additionally, as Kezar (2014) notes, individual campus leaders, practitioners, scholars, faculty, and staff may not possess all the characteristics necessary to shepherd change and thus embed their work in larger networks of people seeking change. Kezar (2014) suggests that "in order to have the human capital required for advancing the change effort, additional stakeholders with a broad set of change capabilities across all skill areas—political, cultural, planning and relationship-building—should be assembled to enhance the process" (p. 109).

Review of Literature

Envisioning Change

A review of higher education institutional change literature indicates the importance of not only understanding "what is" but also envisioning "what can be." As we will illustrate in this section, envisioning change requires understanding change as a process, acknowledging context, and articulating a shared vision.

Understanding Change as a Process

Change must be understood as a process. In their book on transformational change in higher education, Eckel, Hill, and Green (1998) examine debates of change and their own experiences based on their work with 26 universities and colleges that took part in the ACE Project on Leadership and Institutional Transformation. The authors explain that institutional change is a process that "(a) alters the culture of the institution by changing select underlying assumptions and institutional behaviors, processes, and products; (b) is deep and pervasive, affecting the whole institution; (c) is intentional; and (d) occurs over time" (p. 3). Aligned with second-order changes as described by Cuban (1988), this process "introduce[s] new goals, structures, and roles that transform familiar ways of doing things into new ways of solving persistent problems" (p. 342). Because an institution's "underlying character can be dramatically altered" (Kezar, 2014, p. 92) in this process, institutional change requires a slow and careful response from stakeholders.

Envisioning pervasive change demands that CEPs know that it occurs over time. They must further know strategic planning strategies, including the setting of goals and objectives, and the use of data, benchmarks, and concrete goals to take incremental steps toward larger-impact results (Plater, 2011). Identifying strategies to renew the civic mission of research universities, Checkoway (2001)—in an article based on his LeFrak Lecture at the University of Maryland, his earlier works, and the Wingspread Declaration on Renewing the Civic Mission of the American Research University—provides further insights into the skills CEPs need to navigate this process. He argues that change agents need to be strategic and "think ahead, anticipate alternatives, and achieve results over time" (Checkoway, 2001, p. 142). This strategy, which is also important in leading and enacting change, is essential in envisioning change as it lays the basis for future steps. Complementary *personal attributes* include being strategic, forward looking, and able to adjust.

Acknowledging Context
Envisioning change requires a consideration of context in order to identify what type of change to pursue, what approaches to select, and what needs to meet (Kezar, 2014). Eckel and colleagues (1998) speak to the importance of continuous evaluation of context as "colleges and universities need the ability to assess their environments, to decide whether, when, and how to act, and to change accordingly" (p. 1). Multiple levels of context require our attention: self, institution, and external to the institution.

Context of self. When envisioning institutional change, the context of self is important. As Kezar (2014) notes, change agents need to "understand that different tools are accessible to them and that these resources vary based on their position within the institutional leadership" (p. 117). At the same time, Boyte (2009) explains—in an essay based on his earlier writings, his organizing experiences, and Kettering Foundation reports—that when people organize, they become cocreators and coproducers. In this role, it may be possible to surpass existing available resources and create new ones that are more suitable to institutional change efforts.

CEPs must know their level of agency and align their strategies with their resources when envisioning change in order to determine necessary skills, abilities, and attributes, and to identify and recruit other stakeholders (Kezar, 2014). It is essential that CEPs be able to reflect on their agency and identify available resources. Being strategic, proactive, and self-reflective are essential personal attributes for CEPs in this role (Kezar, 2014).

Context of the institution. Understanding the context of the respective institution is essential to institutional change. Institutions of higher education constitute "living communities and dynamic cultures" (Boyte, 2009, p. 3), requiring an ongoing examination of context to ensure that the vision for change remains relevant. Without articulating the purpose of change and taking into account the needs and desires of institutional stakeholders, new structures may emerge but transformational change will be unlikely to occur (Eckel & Kezar, 2003). Too often, Kezar (2014) argues, change agents ignore the context, resulting in "a lack of analysis of the organization, its readiness for change, an initiative's fit or suitability, and alterations that may be necessary in order for a plan to work well within a specific context" (p. xiv).

To achieve institutional change, CEPs must know the context in which their institutions operate and adopt appropriate strategies (Kezar, 2014; Kezar & Eckel, 2002a). To strengthen these strategies, CEPs must also develop knowledge of relevant initiatives and efforts on campus that align with their change vision—such as efforts to create change around diversity—and possess the skills to integrate or collaboratively carry out these initiatives (Checkoway, 2001; Kezar, 2014; Sturm, Eatman, Saltmarsh, & Bush, 2011). CEPs must further have the *skill* to reevaluate their change vision based on potential shifts in context. *Personal attributes* that may aid CEPs in these tasks include being collaborative, analytical, and innovative.

Context external to the institution. The external context further represents an important sphere. As Boyte (2009) explains, "The university is intricately embedded in systems and cultures across the world" (p. 29). When pursuing institutional change, Kezar (2014) suggests considering the following external factors: (a) greater calls for accountability and transparency as a result of decreased trust from external stakeholders; (b) a larger impact of social and economic realities on institutions of higher education, which diminishes their independence; and (c) the need to work with fewer resources and achieve more because of financial constraints stemming from the recession. She adds that these contexts are dynamic, resulting in the contemporary context of leading change being different than in the past.

In addition, it is important to consider the broader history of the higher education community engagement movement. Scholars recognize the tremendous progress that has taken place through the creation of coordinating centers, the proliferation of service-learning, and increased engagement in public scholarship (Saltmarsh et al., 2009). However, Saltmarsh and Hartley (2011) argue that transformative institutional change in higher education has stalled. They explain that the existence of centers and larger numbers of service-learning courses does not necessarily represent institutional change, and community engagement efforts continue to be compartmentalized and episodic. They thus advocate utilizing Cuban's (1988) second-order changes to deeply integrate democratic civic engagement into higher education.

Envisioning institutional change requires that CEPs *know* external contexts and currents of the broader civic engagement movement. They need to have the *skills* to address accountability and transparency concerns of external stakeholders, incorporate social and economic realities into their vision for institutional change, and use limited resources wisely. As Kezar (2014) proposes, CEPs need to be skilled in social media and emerging technology to communicate their vision and engage stakeholders. We infer that the *personal attributes* of being adaptable, analytical, articulate, and resourceful would support CEPs in this work.

Articulating a Shared Vision
To effect institutional change, it is paramount to articulate a shared vision that guides approaches and actions. As Kezar (2014) explains, a vision, along with creating a network and support structures, is an important aspect in determining an institution's readiness for change and in garnering support from top-level leadership.

Community engagement scholars provide insights into the potential content of such a vision. While Boyte (2009) does not explicitly discuss the articulation of a vision, he suggests "explor[ing] the public dimensions of professions, disciplines, and individual faculty experiences" (p. 28) to achieve culture change. Such an exploration may be particularly useful in articulating what a shared vision may look like across roles, departments, and experiences. Similarly, Checkoway (2001) proposes strategies to renew the civic mission of higher education, particularly at research universities. These strategies include strengthening student learning, involving faculty, and increasing institutional capacity for civic renewal. Paying attention to these strategies when articulating a shared vision for institutional change may be important as they illustrate the significance of community engagement in multiple spheres of higher education.

To articulate a shared vision, it can be inferred that CEPs need to know about the importance of illustrating the relevance of community engagement across roles, departments, and experiences. CEPs must thus be able to generate a vision and criteria for success in partnership with numerous stakeholders to foster meaningful impact throughout the university (American Association of State Colleges and Universities, 2002; Gibson, 2006). Moreover, CEPs have to be able to discern common language to interpret and convey the institution's stance toward community engagement and "ensure that learning outcomes for the institution as a whole include some form of engagement" (Plater, 2011, p. 118). In addition, CEPs should be able to communicate ways in which engagement can occur in scholarship, teaching, and service (Gibson, 2006; Kellogg Commission, 1999). It can be inferred that CEPs need *personal attributes* that support collaboration, communication, and innovation.

Leading Change

Institutional change literature also points to the importance of leadership. It is not, however, only top-level leadership that is required for institutional change. Kezar (2014) argues, "As it has become more conventional to define *leadership* as facilitating or creating change, leaders have been found to exist at all levels of organizations" (p. 110; emphasis added). In her landmark work on grassroots leaders, Meyerson (2003) interviewed 182 people from business organizations and 56 self-identified change agents to illustrate their experiences navigating "being different" and "fitting in" while utilizing their differences to positively change their institutions. She illustrates that "bottom-up" change agents who are not in positions of authority often take leadership roles. Such "tempered radicals," Meyerson and Scully (1995) argue, do not silence themselves and their identities or opt to depart from their organizations, but rather temper their actions to achieve change from within their organizations. Despite this type of grassroots leadership, Kezar (2014) states that much emphasis has been placed on *leadership* defined as positions of authority, but "leadership is not synonymous with authority" (p. 110). She instead advocates for a reconceptualization of leadership as being much broader and inclusive.

Such reconceptualization is particularly useful for CEPs who occupy a range of positions within any one institution of higher education's hierarchical organization. Typically, they are found within a unit of engagement or as a staff within an academic department tasked with stewarding that department's community engagement efforts, in which case their change efforts occur on the grassroots level. But many CEPs are also third-space professionals who are less bounded, are equipped with mixed portfolios and backgrounds, and cross long-standing professional and academic boundaries (Whitchurch, 2013). Bartha, Carney, Gale, Goodhue, and Howard (2014) refer to such CEPs as "hybrid-hyphenateds," as they are "working in or aspiring to para-academic, intermediary, coordinating, and administering positions at the interface of campus-community partnership development and in the interspaces of the university" (para. 1).

In this section, we outline competencies that CEPs need to lead change. They include embracing democratic principles and practices, navigating complex structures, utilizing cocreative organizing methods, and working with administration.

Embracing Democratic Principles and Practices

Scholars have identified democratic principles and practices as essential in leading institutions to value the civic purpose of higher education. Saltmarsh and colleagues' (2009) white paper on democratic engagement summarizes a 2008 meeting at the Kettering Foundation in which 33 academic leaders identified strategies to promote transformative community engagement and democratic citizenship in higher education. The authors emphasize the need to go beyond activities and to focus on the process and purpose of democratic engagement. They call for reciprocity, collaboration, mutual construction of knowledge, inclusion, and approaches that are asset based, relational, and problem oriented. Reflecting on civic engagement work in higher education, Saltmarsh and Hartley (2011) similarly provide recommendations for constructive action in order to create democratically engaged universities. They recommend modeling democratic values through active and collaborative leadership, which requires the elimination of hierarchies, the promotion of dialogue, the authentic incorporation of multiple experiences and perspectives in decision processes, and the treatment of students and community members as full participants.

To lead institutional change based on democratic principles and practices, CEPs must have the ability to develop and practice relational habits of democracy (Boyte, 2008, 2009; Boyte & Fretz, 2011), tolerate ambiguity and act without predetermined outcomes (Boyte, 2009), and engage critics (Kezar & Eckel, 2002b). CEPs must also be able to collaborate (Kezar & Eckel, 2002b; Plater, 2011) by working across roles (American Association of State Colleges and Universities, 2002; Kezar & Eckel, 2002b) and disciplinary silos (Gibson, 2006). They need to have the skills to strive for inclusivity in order to understand everyone's stories and motivations and meet their expectations (American Association of State Colleges and Universities, 2002; Boyte, 2009). Personal attributes that support CEPs in this role are being collaborative (Plater, 2011; Saltmarsh et al., 2009) and inclusive (Saltmarsh et al., 2009).

Navigating Complex Structures
Institutions of higher education are complex systems held together by institutional culture. Eckel and colleagues (1998) explain that this culture consists of a "common set of beliefs and values that creates a shared interpretation and understanding of events and actions" (p. 3). Eckel and colleagues (1998) argue that institutional culture is not monolithic but rather comprises various subcultures. To transform institutional culture, the authors add that change must be deep and pervasive, encouraging people across the institution to think and act differently. Because dominant structures often do not align with the agenda of the civic engagement movement, such changes must normalize approaches that may at first seem counternormative, such as "the capacity to learn in the company

of others and not to rely solely on the expertise of the academy" (Saltmarsh et al., 2009, p. 7).

CEPs who are leading change need to know that intentional culture change serves as a precursor to addressing structural change (Boyte, 2008, 2009). To achieve such culture change, they need to be able to confront some of the academy's norms and traditions (Boyte & Fretz, 2011) and temper change strategies based on their cultural context (Kezar et al., 2011). CEPs must also be able to balance interlinked and simultaneous strategies (Kezar & Eckel, 2002b). In addition, they need to be able to identify the various facets of change. As Kezar (2014) explains, change agents "are responsible for watching out for isomorphism, leading as thoughtfully as possible through adaptation processes, carefully choosing innovations and reforms, and considering how all these various types of change tax the organization and its human and financial resources" (p. xii).

Utilizing Cocreative Organizing Methods
Cocreative organizing methods can be useful to change agents who navigate these structures. Harry Boyte, who has authored nine books on the topic of citizenship, democracy, and community organizing, and published more than 100 articles, essays, reports, and commentaries in academic and nonacademic outlets, provides two such cocreative approaches: everyday politics and constructive politics. Boyte (2004) understands *politics* as "the way a society as a whole negotiates, argues about, and understands its past and creates its present and its future" (p. 1). He explains that everyday politics occurs when the broad citizenry engages in this participatory process. Utilizing the concept of constructive politics, Boyte (2011) explains that democracies require a participatory process in which diverse citizens are cocreators who build and shape society. Everyday politics and constructive politics thus denote a participatory process in which the citizenry engages in public work as cocreators of democracy.

These cocreative organizing methods are applicable to institutional change in higher education. Boyte (2009) explains that change agents need to fully understand technocracy and its implications, which requires conceiving of institutions as "living human communities, capable of reconstruction through organizing" (p. 16). This type of organizing, he adds, does not call for mobilizing, but rather fostering civic agency to be accountable, to learn to negotiate and compromise, and to deal positively with conflict. Democratizing knowledge-based institutions, such as colleges and universities, further requires that change agents investigate the production of knowledge and culture as a form of power. Taking a public-work approach in this investigation, Boyte (2009) adds, it "rejects the conventional model of college cultures as aggregations of discrete units in competition with each other; instead, it conceives of college cultures as living wholes, calling particular attention to the public dimensions of such cultures" (p. 29).

It can thus be inferred that CEPs have to know about and be familiar with organizing methods that understand large-scale change as possible. CEPs need to be able to identify power dynamics and work collaboratively to alter complex institutional structures. Being courageous and not shying away from taking risks are personal attributes that support CEPs in this work, as change "will not be led by the faint of heart" (Kellogg Commission, 1999, p. 11). Additional personal attributes include perseverance, flexibility, and patience.

Working With Administration
Grassroots change leaders need to work with people in positions of authority and power. While several layers may be "separating them from the senior leadership of the college or university in which they are playing boundary-spanning roles" (Ramaley, 2014, p. 17), institutional change requires administrative support (Kezar & Eckel, 2002b). Communicating and making visible the value of democratic engagement may be powerful tools to receive such support (American Association of State Colleges and Universities, 2002; Kezar & Eckel, 2002b). Another tool is working with respective university leadership and governing bodies to appraise their success in realizing higher education's civic mission (Gibson, 2006). In addition, the Kellogg Commission (1999) suggests that change agents work with administrators to develop a plan for engagement that encourages interdisciplinarity in research and teaching and incentivizes faculty involvement. It proposes that this plan include

> responsiveness; our willingness to collaborate respectfully with the communities we serve; our capacity for maintaining our role as neutral facilitators; access to our complex institutions; integrating scholarship with outreach, service, and engagement; coordination of the engagement agenda; and the adequacy of resources committed to the task. (p. 47)

This plan should further advance a culture that integrates engagement as a philosophy throughout the university and aligns with power structures in order to make engagement central to the institutional mission (American Association of State Colleges and Universities, 2002; Checkoway, 2001; Kellogg Commission, 1999; Plater, 2011).

CEPs who lead from the grassroots will have to know to work with rather than against the administration in order to limit resistance as they try to achieve holistic organizational change (Meyerson, 2003). They must be able to temper their approaches based on cultural expectations (Kezar et al., 2011). Thus, CEPs need to be able to serve in supportive roles when working with administrators to make visible engaged practices, appraise the institution's alignment with its civic mission, and develop a plan that advances community engagement throughout all aspects of the institution. Inferred personal attributes that CEPs need in this role include being collaborative, cooperative, innovative, patient, and articulate.

Enacting Change

Leaders enact change in a myriad of ways. In their 2011 study on change strategies used by faculty and staff in U. S. colleges and universities, Kezar and colleagues (2011) point out nine strategies that they found to be common across various change initiatives:

1. intellectual opportunities,
2. professional development,
3. leveraging curricula,
4. joining existing networks,
5. engaging students,
6. hiring like-minded people,
7. gathering data,
8. garnering resources, and
9. partnering with external stakeholders.

These nine strategies emerged from 165 interviews conducted with faculty and staff at five different institutions who held a variety of positions and ranks within their respective institutions. While Kezar and colleagues (2011) found that the strategies were consistent across a variety of professional positions and change initiatives (service-learning, diversity, etc.), they also found that the effectiveness of each strategy was dependent on institutional context. Thus, understanding institutional context is critical in enacting change.

CEPs use their knowledge and skills as democratic change agents when employing diverse strategies to effect change, including many of the strategies that Kezar and colleagues identified. Many strategies critical to institutional change and that reflect best practices in higher education community engagement, such as leading faculty development and building sustainable campus-community partnerships, are covered in other chapters in this volume (Chapters 5, 9, and 8, respectively). In the following section we focus on the broad and crosscutting strategy of bridging silos.

Leveraging Shared Institutional Context to Develop a Unified Voice
In 2005 Campus Compact and Tufts University convened 22 scholars from research universities considered to be leaders in civic and community engagement to share best practices. Recognizing the power of research universities as the producers of graduates who are likely to be future faculty, and as the recipients of a large amount of federal research dollars, the convened scholars decided to create a statement on the importance of engaged scholarship at research universities as well as a set of recommendations for supporting it. The statement addressed the barriers to engaged scholarship at research universities, many of which stemmed from the existence of silos or compartmentalization, such as the focus on individual disciplines and the disconnect between theory and practice (Gibson, 2006). The report's recommendations included, among other things, that community engagement leaders at research institutions aim to bridge these silos by integrating engaged scholarship with engaged pedagogies and creating multidisciplinary forums to discuss and promote engaged scholarship (Gibson, 2006). Kezar and Eckel (2002b) suggest that change leaders should organize opportunities to catalyze and support meaning-making related to the change agenda. Such opportunities should be for diverse audiences—individuals and groups campus-wide—and can be in the format of roundtables, workshops, interest groups, professional development, retreats, and town meetings.

Being an institutional citizen. Sturm and colleagues (2011) argue for the potential impact of bridging and integrating the change agendas of community engagement and diversity in higher education. Underlying their argument is the idea that these change agendas "grow out of a commitment to changing practices and settings that do not provide full participation for all the constituents" (p. 4). Similarly, in their study of grassroots change leaders, Kezar and colleagues (2011) found that such leaders share the common task of "act[ing] as the conscience of the organization— often bringing up ethical issues" and champion "ethical dilemmas found broadly in social and campus life" (p. 131). In addition to collaborating across common change agendas within institutions, Kezar (2014) argues for the importance of utilizing formal structures within institutions, such as governance committees, to forward change agendas by gaining seats at various influential tables.

Integrating curricular and cocurricular pathways of student learning. Several scholars discuss the importance of integrating community engagement into both curricular and cocurricular agendas and learning activities in order to create more powerful and sustained civic activities (Checkoway, 2001; Gibson, 2006; Hoy & Meisel, 2008; Kezar et al., 2011). A 1999 Kellogg Commission report argues that incorporating community engagement into the curriculum and cocurriculum helps to achieve comprehensive university engagement. Hoy and Meisel (2008) build on the work of colleges and universities that are part of the Bonner Network to present models for curricular and cocurricular programming that address Association of American Colleges & Universities' essential learning outcomes of personal and social responsibility and integrative learning. The report emphasizes the important role of community engagement as well as the importance of integrating the curriculum and cocurriculum in order to promote deep student learning as well as institutional change.

Centers as gathering places. Scholars recognize the important role that centers for community engagement have as gathering places to bring scholars and professionals together for campus-focused as well as local, regional, and national meetings. In a study that included a review of literature, an analysis of over 100 successful applications for the 2010 Carnegie Community Engagement Classification, and a survey of over 300 directors of community engagement centers, Welch and Saltmarsh (2013) identified the key infrastructure characteristics and program functions of community engagement centers. Among their findings were programming to advance student, faculty, and community partnership development; cross-campus collaboration; and communication practices that foster relationship building.

CEPs should position and use the centers, offices, and departments they lead to serve as gathering places for cross-role problem-based collaboration (American Association of State Colleges and Universities, 2002) and as "a powerful organizing center for total university engagement" (Kellogg Commission, 1999). Gathering should be designed to inspire and empower scholar-practitioners to discuss the advancement of the civic mission of universities and identify strategies to integrate their work with that of other leaders of the civic engagement movement (Gibson, 2006).

When envisioning change, CEPs need to recognize the broader campus context and to identify other initiatives with goals and values that align with the community engagement change agenda. In order to *enact* change, CEPs need to implement strategies that bring people together—across divisions, departments, and agendas—for dialogue, professional development, and strategic planning. In order to bridge silos to further the development of the engaged university, CEPs need to know how to identify other stakeholders as well as change agendas that complement the community engagement movement. CEPs need to possess the skills to articulate goals and objectives that can be shared across normally disconnected initiatives, plan gatherings that meet set goals, facilitate productive discussions, and follow up on meeting outcomes to sustain relationships and momentum in order to fulfill the change agenda. CEPs need to value collaboration, solidarity, and persistence.

Conclusion

CEPs are critical to the institutional change process and contribute to it in a myriad of ways, from convening stakeholders for professional development and strategic planning to demonstrating and articulating the importance of community engagement to the mission of higher education. In this chapter, we identified the critical knowledge, skills, and values that CEPs need to lead change, particularly the second-order change that scholars are calling for as part of the next-generation phases of the community engagement movement (Saltmarsh et al., 2009; Saltmarsh & Hartley, 2011; Welch & Saltmarsh, 2013).

Table 5.1 summarizes the competencies outlined within this chapter. Noticeable key characteristics that cross the categories of envisioning, leading, and enacting change are collaboration, importance of relationship building, and integration. Future research on institutional change in relation to community engagement could test the impact of collaborative efforts, such as advancing compatible change initiatives—that is, community engagement and diversity—to better understand the potential for building capacity for change.

The importance of institutional context to the type and success of change processes also stood out in this literature review. Further research could focus on the types of change strategies most appropriate for particular campus contexts. Finally, this literature review uncovered a wide range of knowledge and skills important in enabling CEPs to lead change. Although we acknowledged early on that one should not come to the conclusion that a single CEP needs to possess or employ all of the knowledge and skills at one time, future research could study how centers for community engagement can build among their collective staff the range of knowledge and skills identified in this review. For example, What are the critical professional positions and titles that map to these knowledge and skills? What areas of study can best prepare individuals to hold these positions? What ongoing professional development is needed to support CEPs in leading change in the next phases of the community engagement movement?

TABLE 5.1
CEP Competencies for Leading Institutional Change to Support Higher Education Community Engagement

	Knowledge	*Skills and Abilities*	*Attributes*
Envisioning change	• Personal agency • Available resources • Context of institution • Other initiatives that align with community engagement • Currents of community engagement movement • Relevance of community engagement to campus and departmental goals	• Relationship building • Conflict management • Work in fluid environment • Integrate goals and strategies of common initiatives • Address accountability • Resourceful • Articulate vision and goals • Strategic planning: identification of goals, objectives, and outcomes • Collaboration • Interpret and communicate connection between university mission and community engagement • Reflect on self	• Proactive • Collaborative • Analytical • Innovative • Adaptable • Resourceful • Articulate • Self-reflective • Strategic
Leading change	• Democratic principles and practices: debate, dialogue, facilitation, consensus building, conflict resolution • Cultural versus structural change • How to work with authority	• Develop and practice relational habits of democracy • Tolerate ambiguity • Work across roles and disciplinary silos • Foster inclusivity • Work against the grain • Move beyond distinct programs to integrated work • Make connections across initiatives • Be familiar with organizing methods • Connect community engagement to self-interests of others • Work authority	• Collaborative • Inclusive • Persevering • Flexible • Patient • Courageous/risk-taking • Cooperative
Enacting change	• Complementary initiatives and change agents	• Articulate goals and objectives and shared vision • Plan and implement meetings • Facilitate discussions • Follow up on ideas	• Collaborative • Show solidarity • Persistent

References

American Association of State Colleges and Universities. (2002). *Stepping forward as stewards of place: A guide for leading engagement at state colleges and universities*. Washington, DC: Author. Retrieved from www.aascu.org/WorkArea/DownloadAsset.aspx?id=5458

Bartha, M., Carney, M., Gale, S., Goodhue, E., & Howard, A. (2014). This bridge called my job: Translating, revaluing, and leveraging intermediary administrative work. *Public: A Journal of Imagining America: Hybrid, Evolving, and Integrative Career Paths, 2*(2), Part 1: A Manifesto From the Middle Ground of Campus-Community Partnerships.

Boyer, E. L. (1990). *Scholarship reconsidered: Priorities of the professoriate*. Princeton, NJ: Carnegie Foundation for the Advancement of Teaching.

Boyer, E. L. (1996). The scholarship of engagement. *Bulletin of the American Academy of Arts and Sciences, 49*(7), 18–33.

Boyte, H. C. (2000). The struggle against positivism. *Academe, 86*(4), 46–51.

Boyte, H. (2004). *Everyday politics: Reconnecting citizens and public life*. Philadelphia: University of Pennsylvania Press.

Boyte, H. C. (2008). Public work: Civic populism versus technocracy in higher education. In D. W. Brown & D. Witte (Eds.), *Agents of democracy: Higher education and the HEX journey* (pp. 79–102). Dayton, OH: Kettering Foundation.

Boyte, H. C. (2009). *Civic agency and the cult of the expert*. Dayton, OH: Kettering Foundation.

Boyte, H. C. (2011). Constructive politics as public work organizing the literature. *Political Theory, 39*(5), 630–660.

Boyte, C., & Fretz, E. (2011). Civic professionalism. In J. Saltmarsh & M. Hartley (Eds.), *"To serve a larger purpose": Engagement for democracy and the transformation of higher education* (pp. 82–101). Philadelphia, PA: Temple University Press.

Boyte, H. C., & Mehaffy, G. (2008). *The civic agency initiative*. Washington, DC and Minneapolis, MN: American Association of State Colleges and Universities & Center for Democracy and Citizenship, University of Minnesota. Retrieved from www.changemag.org/Photos/Civic%20Agency.pdf

Checkoway, B. (2001). Renewing the civic mission of the American research university. *The Journal of Higher Education, 72*(2), 125–147.

Cuban, L. (1988). A fundamental puzzle of school reform. *Phi Delta Kappan, 69*(5), 341–344.

Eatman, T. K. (2012). The arc of the academic career bends toward publicly engaged scholarship. In A. Gilvin, G. M. Roberts, & C. Martin (Eds.), *Collaborative futures: Critical reflections on publicly active graduate education* (pp. 25–48). Syracuse, NY: Graduate School Press.

Eckel, P. D., & Kezar, A. J. (2003). *Taking the reins: Institutional transformation in higher education*. Westport, CT: Greenwood.

Eckel, P., Hill, B., & Green, M. (1998). *On change: En route to transformation*. Washington, DC: American Council on Education.

Finley, A. (2011). *Civic learning and democratic engagement: A review of the literature on civic engagement in post-secondary education*. Washington, DC: U.S. Department of Education.

Fisher, R., Fabricant, M., & Simmons, L. (2004). Understanding contemporary university-community connections: Context, practice, and challenges. *Journal of Community Practice, 12*(3-4), 13-34.

Gibson, C. M. (2006). *New times demand new scholarship: Research universities and civic engagement—a leadership agenda*. Boston, MA: Tufts University and Campus Compact. Retrieved from kdpol43vw6z2dlw631ififc5.wpengine.netdna-cdn.com/wp-content/uploads/initiatives/research_universities/conference_report.pdf

Goettel, R., & Haft, J. (2010). *Imagining America: Engaged scholarship for the arts, humanities, and design*. Imagining America. Paper 12. Retrieved from surface.syr.edu/cgi/viewcontent.cgi?article=1006&context=ia

Hartley, M. (2011). Idealism and compromise and the civic engagement movement. In J. A. Saltmarsh & M. Hartley (Eds.), *"To serve a larger purpose": Engagement for democracy and the transformation of higher education* (pp. 27-48). Philadelphia, PA: Temple University Press.

Hoy, A., & Meisel, W. (2008). *Civic engagement at the center: Building democracy through integrated cocurricular and curricular experiences*. Washington, DC: Association of American Colleges & Universities.

Kellogg Commission. (1999). *Returning to our roots: The engaged institution* (3rd report). New York, NY: National Association of State Universities and Land-Grant Colleges.

Kezar, A. J. (2014). *How colleges change: Understanding, leading, and enacting change*. New York, NY: Routledge.

Kezar, A., & Eckel, P. D. (2002a). The effect of institutional culture on change strategies in higher education: Universal principles or culturally responsive concepts? *The Journal of Higher Education, 73*(4), 435-460.

Kezar, A., & Eckel, P. (2002b). Examining the institutional transformation process: The importance of sensemaking, interrelated strategies, and balance. *Research in Higher Education, 43*(3), 295-328.

Kezar, A., Gallant, T., & Lester, J. (2011). Everyday people making a difference on college campuses: The tempered grassroots leadership tactics of faculty and staff. *Studies in Higher Education, 36*(2), 129-151.

Mathews, D. (2011). Preface. In J. A. Saltmarsh & M. Hartley (Eds.), *"To serve a larger purpose": Engagement for democracy and the transformation of higher education* (pp. vii-xi). Philadelphia, PA: Temple University Press.

Meyerson, D. E. (2003). *Tempered radicals: How everyday leaders inspire change at work*. Boston, MA: Harvard Business School Press.

Meyerson, D. E., & Scully, M. (1995). Tempered radicalism and the politics of ambivalence and change. *Organization Science, 6*(5), 585-600.

Plater, W. M. (2011). Collective leadership for engagement: Reclaiming the public purpose of higher education. In J. A. Saltmarsh & M. Hartley (Eds.), *"To serve a larger purpose": Engagement for democracy and the transformation of higher education* (pp. 102–129). Philadelphia, PA: Temple University Press.

Ramaley, J. A. (2006). Governance in a time of transition. In W. G. Tierney (Ed.), *Governance and the public good* (pp. 157–177). Albany, NY: SUNY Press.

Ramaley, J. A. (2014). The changing role of higher education: Learning to deal with wicked problems. *Journal of Higher Education Outreach and Engagement, 18*(3), 7–22.

Rice, E. R. (2003). Rethinking scholarship and engagement: The struggle for new meanings. *Campus Compact Reader, 3,* 1–9.

Saltmarsh, J., & Hartley, M. (2011). Conclusion: Creating the democratically engaged university—possibilities for constructive action. In J. A. Saltmarsh & M. Hartley (Eds.), *"To serve a larger purpose": Engagement for democracy and the transformation of higher education* (pp. 289–299). Philadelphia, PA: Temple University Press.

Saltmarsh, J., Hartley, M., & Clayton, P. H. (2009). *Democratic engagement white paper.* Boston, MA: New England Resource Center for Higher Education.

Snyder, C. R. (2008). Should higher education have a civic mission? Historical reflections. In D. W. Brown & D. Witte (Eds.), *Agent of democracy: Higher education and the HEX journey* (pp. 53–75). Dayton, OH: Kettering Foundation.

Sturm, S., Eatman, T., Saltmarsh, J., & Bush, A. (2011). *Full participation: Building the architecture for diversity and public engagement in higher education.* Columbia University Law School, Center for Institutional and Social Change, White Paper. Retrieved from imaginingamerica.org/wp-content/uploads/2011/10/Catalyst-Paper.pdf

Welch, M., & Saltmarsh, J. (2013). Current practices and infrastructures for campus centers of community engagement. *Journal of Higher Education Outreach and Engagement, 17*(4), 25–56.

Whitchurch, C. (2013). *Reconstructing identities in higher education: The rise of "third space" professionals.* New York, NY: Routledge.

Chapter Six

ATTRIBUTES OF COMMUNITY ENGAGEMENT PROFESSIONALS SEEKING TO INSTITUTIONALIZE COMMUNITY-CAMPUS ENGAGEMENT

Laura Weaver and B. Tait Kellogg

Traditional conceptions of the role of the university as an authoritarian revealer and disseminator of knowledge have been challenged in recent decades as more collaborative notions of knowledge creation have become more legitimized. Most institutional missions have long included language around public service, referring to the role of knowledge in solving problems locally and globally as well as preparing students as democratic citizens (Ward, 1996). Yet traditional scholarship has long been revered over community knowledge, while lecture-style classroom environments are often valued over experiential education (Boyer, 1994). Because of this deep-seated organizational culture in higher education, community engagement initiatives were initially considered anti-institutional and a challenge to the traditional roles of the university (Lounsbury & Pollack, 2001). However, support for higher education has been challenged, causing many institutions to participate in a national conversation surrounding the university's responsibility to the public (Checkoway, 2001; Holland, 1997) and reexamine their core assumptions and priorities (Zlotkowski, 1995). In his groundbreaking work, Ernest Boyer (1994) calls for the "New American College," an institution where "faculty members would build partnerships with practitioners who would, in turn, come to campus as lecturer and student advisers" (p. A48). As a result of this national conversation, many colleges and universities have incorporated practices such as service-learning, community-based research, and reciprocal community-campus partnerships into the fabric of their institutional structure, bringing these once marginalized practices to the mainstream.

What does it take to establish the goals and values of community engagement as norms within the well-established organizational culture of a university campus? This chapter seeks to ask that question from the perspective of community engagement professionals (CEPs) aiming to institutionalize community engagement programs and practices. Many tasks, such as encouraging faculty development and cultivating community-campus partnerships, are necessary for the institutionalization of community engagement to occur and are addressed in greater depth in other chapters of this book. This chapter specifically provides an overview of the competencies necessary for the process of embedding community engagement within the university as a whole. For scholars and practitioners seeking to understand the professional orientation of CEPs, this review of the literature at the institutional level is essential. After all, the skills, abilities, knowledge, and personal attributes of capable CEPs navigating the complex organizational structure of universities have been vital to the institutional success of engagement practices on campuses nationwide.

To compile this literature review we limited our search to peer-reviewed research published between 1990 and 2015. This search was based on the foundational terms *community engagement* and *institutionalization* and *higher education*, but many other terms were substituted in combinations, including *service-learning*, *civic engagement*, and *public good*. Once we pushed deeper into the literature, other terms central to institutionalization emerged. In another round of searching we included the terms *assessment, rubric, centers for community engagement, Carnegie Community Engagement Classification, project planning, institutional mission, policy,* and *strategic planning.* Databases used include JSTOR, SocINDEX, Academic Search Complete, Education Resources Information Center, ProQuest, and Google Scholar. Once relevant literature was identified, we reviewed the works with an eye for which competencies were central to the process of institutionalizing community engagement initiatives within an individual institution of higher education.

Community Engagement Across Higher Education

The movement to institutionalize community engagement on the national level of higher education shaped and simultaneously was informed by a move toward engagement at individual institutions. Community engagement practices have been a campus priority since the mid-1980s with the formation of the Campus Outreach Opportunity League (COOL) and the founding of Campus Compact by college and university presidents (Hollander, Saltmarsh, & Zlotkowski, 2002). In 1999, the Kellogg Commission on the Future of State and Land-grant Universities released a report calling for publicly engaged institutions, or universities that are "fully committed to direct, two-way interaction with communities and other external constituencies through the development, exchange, and application of knowledge, information, and expertise for mutual benefit" (American Association of State Colleges and Universities, 2002, p. 9; Holland, 2000). Boyer (1990, 1994, 1996) further echoed this two-way partnership, signaling a shift in the culture of higher education toward greater institutionalization of community engagement. In 2001, the International Association for Research on Service-Learning & Community Engagement was established, which further promoted greater scholarship within community engagement. Participation in and assessment of community engagement practices has also been incorporated into the criteria for several major accreditation boards, including the North Central Association (NCA) and Western Association of Schools and Colleges (WASC; Butin, 2010).

In 2006 the Carnegie Foundation for the Advancement of Teaching established the elective Community Engagement Classification to recognize institutions for their commitment to community engagement. The application and reporting process created a common measure for postsecondary institutions to internally assess community engagement practices (Driscoll, 2008; Welch & Saltmarsh, 2013b). Within the academic literature, data from recognized institutions have allowed for more robust comparisons of how colleges and universities institutionalize community engagement (Sandmann, Thornton, & Jaeger, 2009). In her article on the introduction of Carnegie, Driscoll (2009) notes that the Carnegie Classification was designed to include institutions from a variety of backgrounds. Her characterization highlights the many ways institutions with dissimilar missions, structures, and practices are incorporating community engagement.

Although many CEPs are contributing to the institutionalization of community engagement on the national stage and across institutions of higher education—such as within the civic associations, accreditation entities, and standard-bearing organizations discussed here—we intentionally did not include competencies necessary for work outside the context of an individual university and its local community. Parallel to the institutionalization of engagement across the field of higher education has been the embedding of an engagement culture within many individual institutions. While national organizations such as the Carnegie Foundation, Campus Compact, and the Kellogg Commission were examining community engagement on the macro level, some campuses across the country were early adopters of community engagement, working to forge a path toward institutionalization. Indiana University–Purdue University Indianapolis (IUPUI), Portland State University (PSU), and University of Pennsylvania (Penn) are three examples of such institutions. In the early 1990s each of these institutions made intentional efforts to embed community engagement practices into the curriculum while building community-campus partnerships that linked intellectual, human, and fiscal resources (Bringle & Hatcher, 2004; Hartley, Harkavy, & Benson, 2005; Holland, 2001b; Wiewel, Kecskes, & Martin, 2011).

Institutionalization of Community Engagement

As community-engaged practices have expanded at colleges and universities across the country, researchers have sought to identify contributing factors to their institutionalization (e.g., Bringle & Hatcher, 2000; Furco & Holland, 2004; Holland, 1997; Sandmann et al., 2009; Welch & Saltmarsh, 2013a). Furco and Holland (2009) point out that the overall goal of institutionalizing community engagement is to capitalize on its unifying nature "as an integral strategy for advancing broader institutional goals" (p. 52). Community engagement as an integrative educational strategy is found across various academic disciplines and campus units. While it links multiple institutional goals and fosters reciprocal community-university partnerships, it also develops strong student leaders through the creation of new knowledge and abilities (Furco, 2002; Furco & Holland, 2004).

Greater understanding of the organizational structure of academic institutions and a common model for institutionalization provides a clearer context for further examination of the institutionalization of community engagement practices. Organizational theorist Weick (1976), as well as others (Goodman & Dean, 1982; Harkavay & Hartley, 2012; Hartley et al., 2005; Ward, 1996), describes academic organizations as *loosely coupled*, wherein each unit within the institution is somehow attached to the others, yet still retains its own identity and separateness. For example, Ward (1996) describes how, within a university, the guidelines and policies governing the faculty reward system of promotion and tenure are set by the highest administrative level, but are then interpreted and carried out by each department and unit individually, creating inconsistency across the institution. Goodman and Dean (1982) take these coupling behaviors into consideration in their framework for institutionalization of a new idea or practice. This model moves individuals through a process from initially becoming aware of a new behavior or activity, to greater experimentation with the behavior, to establishment of an institutional norm, and finally institutionalization—when the behavior or activity is viewed as a core value and purpose of the organization. This area of community engagement is ever expanding. Furco and Holland (2013) have highlighted organizational culture, organizational change theory, and change purpose, explained as "the rational or ultimate goal(s) for the change" (p. 448), as core to the institutionalization research agenda.

Competencies Across Themes, and a Caveat

In order for a CEP to successfully support institutionalization efforts, a set of competencies is essential in the form of skills, abilities, knowledge, and personal attributes. Throughout much of the literature on institutionalizing community engagement, the studies do not directly address the work of CEPs or required competencies. Thus, we often inferred what competencies would be necessary based on the qualities and characteristics of successful institutionalization presented within the literature. A few studies did include the CEP as an essential ingredient for institutionalizing community engagement (e.g., Ostrander, 2004; Vogel, Seifer, & Gelmon, 2010).

During this examination of the relevant literature four themes central to the work of CEPs emerged:

1. alignment with institutional philosophy, mission, and values;
2. organizational infrastructure and strong leadership;
3. essential institutional support and resources; and
4. collaborating with and supporting stakeholders.

Common within each of these themes, four key competencies surfaced (see also Figure 6.1):

1. possessing political capital,
2. cultivating and managing relationships across stakeholders,
3. capturing data and assessing outcomes for sustainability, and
4. honing communication and marketing skills.

Figure 6.1. Themes and Key Competencies for CEPs Institutionalizing Community Engagement.

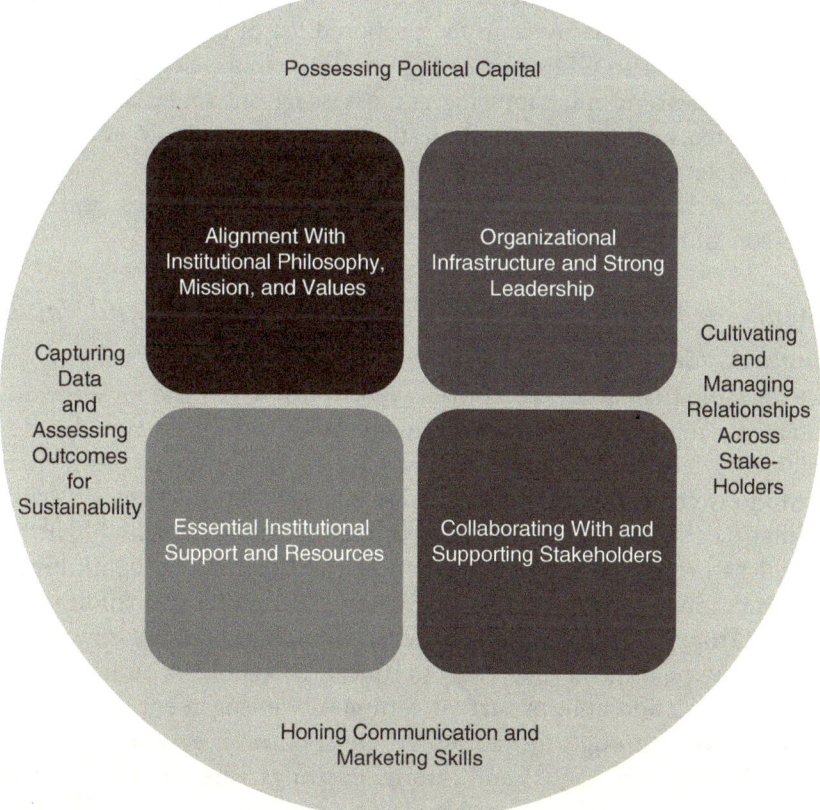

First, the ability to navigate the university's political environment in order to generate institutional change arises in each step of the institutionalization process. For example, political capital serves a professional when seeking buy-in from high-level administrators, and it is equally vital in the work of aligning institutional mission with university practice. Second, the social skills necessary for cultivating relationships may aid a professional as she or he effectively assesses community partnerships and also comes into play in interactions with faculty representatives. Third, comprehensive and effective assessment and evaluation skills aid a CEP in ensuring that community-campus partnerships are meeting the goals and needs of all stakeholders and serve to provide the necessary data needed to sustain these initiatives. Finally, communication and marketing skills emerge as central for a professional seeking to represent a campus's community engagement initiatives to both internal and external audiences.

Because no two institutions are the same, no one-size-fits-all framework applies to community engagement institutionalization (Furco & Holland, 2013), the lack of which points to the critical role of context when considering any of these themes or core competencies. Contextual variation is an important caveat in the proposed list of competencies found here. In addition to CEPs possessing political capital, being relationally oriented and proficient, capturing and assessing outcomes, and exercising sharp marketing and communication skills, the ability to adapt these competencies depending on one's context is critical.

In this chapter, we discuss the knowledge, skills, abilities, and attributes constituent to each theme.

Alignment With Institutional Philosophy, Mission, and Values

Institutions of higher education have been grounded in the tenet of service for more than 400 years (Boyer, 1996; Ward, 1996) and have mission statements that reflect this commitment. Within the past two decades, statements dedicated to public service have evolved to focus more on an institution's commitment to community engagement practices (Welch & Saltmarsh, 2013b). Holland (1997) was among the first to highlight the critical nature of the relationship between an institution's commitment to community engagement and its mission statement. Later studies (e.g., Pigza & Troppe, 2003; Thornton & Jaeger, 2006) highlight the importance of CEPs having the skills necessary to educate stakeholders on the institution's civic mission and its current community engagement efforts. This could be done through formal, university-sponsored events or publications (Hartley et al., 2005) and informal settings where the focus is on building or nurturing a relationship (Jacoby, 2015). It is essential that CEPs have the ability to clearly articulate how community-campus engagement activities are an integral part of the mission and philosophy of the institution.

In their empirical study of engagement centers among Carnegie-classified institutions, Welch and Saltmarsh (2013a, 2013b) validated findings from earlier studies (e.g., Bringle & Hatcher, 2000; Furco, 2002; Furco & Holland, 2004, 2013; Pigza & Troppe, 2003; Vogel et al., 2010) that call for CEPs who possess political capital. These professionals should be able to work with institutional leaders to set campus-wide strategic goals and the development of a common language germane to its community engagement practices. This requires a CEP who is a big-picture thinker—one who understands the historical context of community engagement at the institution (Furco & Holland, 2004; Ostrander, 2004), understands how community engagement is connected to other institution-wide educational goals (Furco, 2002; Furco & Holland, 2004; Jacoby, 2015), and is *committed* to regular information sharing among university leaders (Pigza & Troppe, 2003). We infer from the literature that CEPs must be able to articulate these strategic goals and their impact to internal and external stakeholders, as well as be skilled in communicating with, listening to, and collaborating with other administrative units to ensure the strategic positioning of community engagement.

Organizational Infrastructure and Strong Leadership

Much of the small but rich body of empirical work focused on the institutionalization of community engagement has concluded that a critical factor to sustainability and success is establishing an organizing unit or center to "provide leadership and assistance" (Holland, 1997, p. 36). The national study on Learn and Service America, Higher Education (LSAHE) by Gray and colleagues (1998; Gray, Ondaatje, Fricker, & Geschwind, 2000) showed that institutions with a coordinating center were able to advance engagement initiatives with greater sustainability over a three-year period than those without such a center. Furco and Holland (2004) noted that positioning these centers within the academic affairs area is "most effective in garnering academic legitimacy, faculty participation, and sustained institutional support" (p. 36). This positioning was later reflected by Welch and Saltmarsh (2013a, 2013b) in their examination of those institutions earning the Carnegie Community Engagement Classification. Once established and positioned within the institution, it is critical that the coordinating center be staffed with CEPs who understand higher education organization structure and theory (Furco & Holland, 2013; Hartley et al., 2005;) and are able to effectively work with other administrative units across campus (Bringle & Hatcher, 2000; Furco, 2002; Hollander et al., 2002).

Much of the literature examining the organizational structures of campus-wide centers noted that CEPs must be able to cultivate a "critical mass" of supporters for community engagement among all members of the institution (Furco, 2002; Hartley et al., 2005; Pigza & Troppe, 2003; Vogel et al., 2010; Welch & Saltmarsh, 2013a, 2013b). This is directly linked back to the common thread of CEPs possessing the political capital necessary to garner support for community engagement not only among top university administrators but also across the faculty and student body. Welch and Saltmarsh (2013a) note,

> Finally, while the results . . . reflect and support these findings, they also reveal the important role of informal faculty leadership to promote this work. This is related yet separate from the topic of faculty development, but the cultural and political implications suggest the importance of a critical mass of influential faculty. . . . Similarly, . . . responses revealed the important role of institutional administrators in publicly advocating centers and their mission to establish legitimacy across campus. (pp. 191–192)

CEPs need to apply their knowledge of organizational theory and institutionalization as they synthesize and translate information between stakeholders (Bringle & Hatcher, 1996, 2000; Pigza & Troppe, 2003; Walshok, 1999).

Vogel and colleagues (2010) conducted a retrospective, qualitative examination of how institutions that had participated in a national program to implement curricular community engagement into professional health education programs during the 1990s sustained their practices across 10 years. They found that appointing CEPs who act as strong leaders and advocates for community engagement at the institution is one of the critical factors for sustainability (Vogel et al., 2010, p. 64). Additionally, these individuals must be knowledgeable of formalized institutional and program assessment methods and learning outcomes and then use this knowledge to capture and assess community engagement initiatives. Finally, they must be able to report these data in order to further strengthen institutional support (Furco, 2002; Jacoby, 2015; Vogel et al., 2010; Welch & Saltmarsh, 2013a, 2013b).

An essential responsibility of community engagement centers is to serve as the campus unit charged with organizing and disseminating a wide range of operational, logistical, and programmatic policies connected to community engagement activities (Jacoby, 2015). CEPs need to have a working knowledge of higher education risk management as it relates to community engagement and the skills to work with the university's risk management department to develop appropriate policies and procedures necessary to protect the interest, health, and safety of all stakeholders (Furco, 2002; Jacoby, 2015). These tools can involve the development of standardized partnership agreements, applications and liability waivers, learning contracts and agreements, progress reports, and assessment instruments. Additionally, once partnerships have been established, CEPs use their ability to communicate across boundaries to continually correspond with community partners to ensure that any health and safety requirements are met. Many of the competencies related to these responsibilities involve CEPs' knowledge, skills, and abilities as they relate to faculty development and students' civic learning and development, which are discussed in greater detail in Chapters 9 and 7, respectively.

Essential Institutional Support and Resources

The literature on institutional support relies heavily on skill-based competencies. These skills, often garnered through professional training, fall into the categories of funding, marketing, human resources, and assessment. Central to this aspect of the institutionalization process is the core competency of the CEP possessing political capital.

Essential to the successful institutionalization of community engagement is funding. To ensure that institutionalization is not vulnerable, CEPs must have the skills necessary to balance several funding streams, internal and external (Holland, 2009), and possess the political capital necessary to advocate for community engagement as a continual budget priority (Bringle & Hatcher, 1996, 2000; Furco, 2002; Walshok, 1999; Weerts & Hudson, 2009). The success of that balance requires grant-writing skills, or at minimum the skills to link community engagement work with potential funding sources (Weerts & Hudson, 2009). Connecting community engagement and institutional advancement requires the skill to include alumni and other stakeholders as a part of community engagement efforts (Weerts, 2007). These efforts might also include creating faculty incentives to participate in institutional advancement projects as they relate to community engagement. State-supported funding streams have dwindled in recent years, but a study by Weerts and Ronca (2006) notes a link between successful community engagement marketing and an increase in state financial support. The authors call for "sturdy, recognizable structures set up to coordinate and communicate these outreach and engagement initiatives" (p. 954). Thus, CEPs who offer honed promotion skills geared toward outside parties, including the public in the institution's home state, may reap financial benefits for community engagement programs.

For CEPs, marketing skills hinge on the clear articulation of the institution's community engagement vision and needs (Weerts, 2007). Marketing skills must be carefully crafted so that the message portrayed is not too top down or focused on one leader, but instead weaves in the institution's most appropriate stories and reports (Furco, 2002; Holland, 1997, 2009; Vogel et al., 2010). A number of researchers (Furco, 2002; Holland, 1997; Thornton & Zuiches, 2009; Vogel et al., 2010; Weerts & Hudson, 2009) have noted the importance of being able to market to internal audiences as a method for garnering institutional support for community engagement. Correspondingly, they must have internal communication skills to clearly articulate institutional choices made regarding structural changes (Holland, 2009).

Equally important is the application of marketing skills to external audiences in communicating an institution's "brand of engagement" (Thornton & Zuiches, 2009). Partnering with institutional advancement offices to incorporate community engagement programs into institution-wide marketing has the potential to assist with funding projects that benefit both the university and the community as well as to further centralize community engagement in the institution's mission (Holland, 2009; Weerts & Hudson, 2009). In his article on using engagement as a brand position, Blanton (2007) recommends that CEPs create a clear message via a centralized staff. But professionals must remain careful that marketing does not outpace the reality of community engagement efforts, in that if marketing efforts portray an engagement program more cohesive or expansive than the one that currently exists, these efforts may damage the program's credibility and the institution's reputation.

Another set of skills needed for CEPs institutionalizing a structure of support is rooted in human resources, or empowering people in the institution to serve. Thornton and Zuiches (2009) recommend honing hiring skills that ensure that staff will be committed to supporting community engagement efforts. This includes the human resource skills necessary to support the hiring of faculty and staff supportive of community engagement practices (Jacoby, 2015; Ostrander, 2004) and the political savvy needed to encourage policy changes such as those surrounding a promotion and tenure system that allows faculty to become more enmeshed in community-engaged scholarship (Bringle & Hatcher, 2000; Furco, 2002; Hollander et al., 2002; Welch & Saltmarsh, 2013a, 2013b).

In addition to hiring practices, professional development skills aid CEPs in educating faculty and staff on what is included in community engagement and how to participate (Holland, 2009). These skills in professional preparation also abet the CEP who seeks to link leadership training with fund-raising efforts (Weerts & Hudson, 2009). Sharp social skills in "mapping the political terrain" will help CEPs to build networks, bargain and negotiate, and navigate the hyperpolitical environment of the university (Weerts & Hudson, 2009, p. 78). Lastly, community-engaged professionals must be able to track and assess engagement efforts, as well as evaluate the outcomes of engagement programs (Bringle & Hatcher, 2000; Thornton & Zuiches, 2009). Using these assessment data is an important skill that can help strengthen the institution's overall community engagement marketing, communication, and funding efforts.

Social abilities, such as collaboration, are important, including internally cooperating with institutional advancement offices to communicate community engagement efforts to the public (Weerts & Hudson, 2009). Holland (2009) notes that this collaboration might also help bring other stakeholders, such as board members, into the conversations surrounding mission alignment. For a professional at a state university, external collaboration might include working with state relations departments to develop a unified image of the university and its public commitment (Blanton, 2007). The successful collaboration with community partners should include a capable CEP introducing these outside perspectives into the campus political arena (Thornton & Zuiches, 2009).

CEPs seeking to institutionalize campus support must maintain many different bodies of knowledge in order to successfully utilize the skills outlined by the literature. To apply fund-raising skills, professionals must understand donation trends, particularly the trend toward donors seeking tangible community outcomes that might align with community engagement work (Weerts & Hudson, 2009). CEPs must understand the symbols that contribute to a community engagement–oriented campus environment and know more generally how symbolism plays a role in institutional culture (Thornton & Zuiches, 2009). CEPs must cultivate knowledge on human resources, including how to allocate work and how to coordinate roles once responsibilities have been assigned (Thornton & Zuiches, 2009). In building a faculty culture of engagement, CEPs must understand traditional barriers, including who controls expertise and reward in the faculty review system (Thornton & Zuiches, 2009). Finally, for CEPs designing institutional structure, understanding the impacts of these structural choices is essential. This structural knowledge might include whether engagement efforts will be centralized or decentralized or how a coordinating center might fit within the university structure (Holland, 2009).

Collaborating With and Supporting Stakeholders

CEPs interact with and support a number of internal and external stakeholders. Within the university, CEPs collaborate with their counterparts in other administrative units to plan and implement programming for faculty and students. They work to cultivate two-way, reciprocal community-campus partnerships, which are at the center of community engagement work and an essential component of its institutionalization.

Considerable scholarship has been devoted to the challenges of institutionalizing community engagement when it comes to ensuring faculty involvement. Some scholars point to the foundation of the community engagement movement as having been built by civic-minded faculty (Stanton, 1999) or the future of service-learning lying with faculty leadership (Zlotkowski, 1995). Though many individual faculty members may continue to be personally devoted to the values of engagement, the conventional pathways to tenure and promotion place value on traditional scholarship over engaged scholarship, particularly at research institutions (Bringle, Hatcher, & Clayton, 2006; Ellison & Eatman, 2008; Ferman & Hill, 2004; Weerts & Sandmann, 2008). In her analysis of the Carnegie Engaged Campus applications, Driscoll (2009) highlights the major challenges surrounding faculty promotion and tenure for the future of institutionalizing community engagement. Nevertheless, institutions across higher education are seeking new structures of support for faculty. The competencies employed by CEPs play a significant role in successfully institutionalizing systems that not only encourage and reward faculty (O'Meara, 2003) but also support faculty as they engage in this work.

CEPs seeking to institutionalize systems of faculty support must possess the skills for building institutional structures as well as assessment. To build strong structures of support, CEPs must begin with clear and consistent language surrounding the faculty role in community engagement, including the parameters of community-engaged scholarship (Saltmarsh, Giles, Ward, & Buglione, 2009). A strong structure of support must include institutional methods of rewarding engaged faculty (Bringle & Hatcher, 2000; Holland, 2009). CEPs not only need the knowledge of these reward systems and the pressures that traditional scholarship expectations place on faculty but also must possess the political capital necessary to advocate for their change. Ideally, institutional reward systems provide a kind of "cultural armor" for faculty who might encounter pushback from the emphasis on more traditional forms of scholarships (O'Meara, 2002, p. 174). Building these systems, including changes to the requirements for promotion and tenure, requires skills in policy-making and political discernment (O'Meara, 2003). These structures also demand the administrative, logistical, and training skills to aid faculty in implementing community engagement (Furco, 2002; Hartley et al., 2005; Holland, 1997; Welch & Saltmarsh, 2013b). In terms of personal attributes, these professionals should prioritize the knowledge of community members in order to challenge traditional notions in the peer review process of who is a peer (Saltmarsh et al., 2009).

Assessment skills allow CEPs to help faculty assess the impact of community engagement projects on students, the community, and themselves (O'Meara, 2003). Particularly important for faculty is the assessment of student learning through surveys or instruments for measuring student development, which requires particular skills on the part of CEPs (Bringle & Hatcher, 2009). CEPs aiming to institutionalize must analyze service-learning curriculum as a whole rather than just quantifying isolated courses (Bringle & Hatcher, 2009).

The scholarship on institutionalizing community engagement highlights a set of abilities that CEPs must possess, primarily social abilities that assist in bridging the potential divide among community needs, institutional constraints, and traditional demands on faculty. CEPs must have the ability to cultivate relationships with faculty in order to incorporate their voices in major institutional changes (Saltmarsh et al., 2009). These professionals should be able to intentionally create an open environment for faculty to interact and share their community engagement experiences (Bringle & Hatcher, 1996, 2000; O'Meara, 2003). CEPs need to be able to translate the value of incorporating community-engaged pedagogies and work with faculty to become advocates for this work.

A central tenet of community engagement is that the partnership between the university and community organization be reciprocally beneficial. The mutual nature of engagement stands in opposition to traditional notions of one-sided "outreach" (Boyer, 1996). In order for community engagement work to take root at an institution, strong community-campus partnerships must be a central priority. The literature on successful institutionalization alludes to an assemblage of skills, abilities, knowledge, and personal attributes that CEPs might cultivate in their pursuit of quality community partnerships. The competencies listed here are geared toward a CEP who seeks to institutionalize engagement on his or her campus and, thus, seeks to assess and maintain partnerships throughout the institution. Note that a separate set of competencies is needed for the CEP whose work entails creating and maintaining one individual community partnership at a time. The competencies for creating and sustaining reciprocal community-campus partnerships are discussed at length in Chapter 8.

For a community-engaged professional seeking to forge and maintain strong partnerships throughout his or her institution, a set of interpersonal, program management, and assessment skills is required. Interpersonal skills are central to strong community-campus partnerships, including those needed to bridge boundaries that exist between an institution and its community partners (Ferman & Hill, 2004; Furco, 2002; Hollander et al., 2002; Weerts & Sandmann, 2010). A CEP must have the social ability to cultivate two-way dialogue with community partners (Weerts & Sandmann, 2010), and for that he needs the communication skills to articulate internally the goals and mission for partnerships from the institution's perspective (Holland, 2001a). The professional then must use these communication skills to clearly express the mutual needs and commitment of the community and institution (Beere, 2009). Program design competencies required include the skill to outline an institutional vision for partnerships, which might include focusing on one geographic location or type of partnership (Beere, 2009; Hollander et al., 2002).

In order to maintain partnerships, CEPs must possess the skills necessary for securing funding, the internal social dexterity for managing resources, and the knowledge to meet any regulations that may be in place (Weerts & Sandmann, 2010). Also required is the skill to manage faculty requirements and expectations as they relate to partnerships (Vogel et al., 2010; Walshok, 1999; Weerts & Sandmann, 2010). Finally, assessment is a key aspect of institutionalizing quality partnerships, which necessitates nurturing skills for translating partnership goals into measurable indicators, conducting data tracking and analysis on those indicators, and successfully reporting results from assessment (Holland, 2001a; Weerts & Sandmann, 2010).

CEPs need critical thinking skills that allow them to question if the institution has the capacity to establish or support high-quality partnerships (Beere, 2009; Ferman & Hill, 2004). Critical thinking abilities contribute to successfully clarifying an institution's partnership-related mission (Weerts & Sandmann, 2010), while social abilities allow professionals to build on existing positive relationships for future growth (Beere, 2009).

CEPs must comprehend the significance of social problems (Weerts & Sandmann, 2010) as compared to the resources and commitment required for the institution to address them (Beere, 2009). They must have a working knowledge of the language and behavioral expectations of both the institution and the community—enough to know what potential conflicts might arise due to differences in goals, language, or time commitments (Weerts & Sandmann, 2010). CEPs must possess knowledge of the goals of partnerships for the university (Holland, 2009) and from the perspective of the community partner (McNall, Reed, Brown, & Allen, 2009). Finally, Ferman and Hill (2004) note the importance of cultivating a deep knowledge of the tensions and boundaries between the institution and wider community.

In addition to knowledge of the community, a body of knowledge is required for successfully assessing community partnerships. CEPs must understand the assessment instruments available, including how to use and interpret them, in order to appreciate the health of partnerships (Holland, 2001a). In order to conduct assessment successfully, CEPs must also have an extensive knowledge of the community engagement activities across the campus as well as a deep understanding of the institution's mission (Furco, 1999).

Finally, a set of personal attributes is required of CEPs seeking to institutionalize community partnerships. These attributes revolve around a commitment to the principles of community engagement and include an orientation toward community integration (Weerts & Sandmann, 2010), respect for the community and the assets that partners bring (Beere, 2009; Ferman & Hill, 2004), and a commitment to the goals of the partnership (Beere, 2009). In seeking to value the perspectives of community partners, Ferman and Hill (2004) call for a willingness to listen, sensitivity toward the organization's objectives, and a willingness to share the institution's resources.

Avenues for Further Exploration

CEPs seeking a lasting commitment to partnerships with the community must strategically consider how to most effectively institutionalize engagement practices on their campus. Though literature directly focusing on these professionals is only now emerging (Dostilio, forthcoming; Dostilio & McReynolds, 2015; McReynolds, 2015; McReynolds & Shields, 2015), the existing body of research on the institutionalization of engagement at individual colleges and universities points to the competencies needed by these professionals. However, further exploration is warranted. Welch and Saltmarsh (2013b) note the varied "background and professional pathways" (p. 195) that CEPs take. Further research of how and why individuals enter the field may lead to clearer and more established pathways for future professionals and a greater understanding of how competencies are developed and honed. It is currently unclear how a CEP's previous work experience supports the development of key social competencies, such as relationship building and garnering political support. Future research on CEPs in this field should explore how these professionals came to learn about and understand their roles within the process of institutionalization.

Though the many scholars outlined in this review point to the benefits of institutionalizing engagement, future research may focus on the trade-offs CEPs have to make in order to embed engagement programs on campus. Weerts and Sandmann (2010) introduce differentiated roles that community-engaged professionals might play, including individuals who focus more on community or institutional needs. Though this relatively short review of the literature did not delve into the significant variation in institutional roles those CEPs seeking to institutionalize likely hold, future research on these professionals should explore these nuances within different CEP positions. Finally, assessment emerges as a core competency in each of the themes outlined, including assessing the impacts of engagement on students, faculty, and community members. Future research may also consider methods for evaluating impacts of engagement on the CEPs who work to institutionalize these practices.

References

American Association of State Colleges and Universities. (2002). *Stepping forward as stewards of place*. Washington, DC: Author.

Beere, C. (2009). Understanding and enhancing the opportunities of community-campus partnerships. *New Directions for Higher Education, 2009*(147), 55–63.

Blanton, J. (2007). Engagement as a brand position in the higher education marketplace. *International Journal of Educational Advancement, 7*(2), 143–154.

Boyer, E. L. (1990). *Scholarship reconsidered: Priorities of the professoriate*. Princeton, NJ: Princeton University Press.

Boyer, E. L. (1994). Creating the new American college. *The Chronicle of Higher Education, 40*(27), A48.

Boyer, E. L. (1996). The scholarship of engagement. *Journal of Public Service and Outreach, 1*(1), 11–20.

Bringle, R. G., & Hatcher, J. A. (1996). Implementing service learning in higher education. *The Journal of Higher Education, 67*(2), 221–239.

Bringle, R. G., & Hatcher, J. A. (2000). Institutionalization of service learning in higher education. *The Journal of Higher Education, 71*(3), 273–290.

Bringle, R. G., & Hatcher, J. A. (2004). Indiana University–Purdue University Indianapolis: Advancing civic engagement through service-learning. In M. Langseth & W. M. Plater (Eds.), *Public work and the academy: An academic* administrator's guide to civic engagement and service-learning (pp. 23–39). Bolton, MA: Anker.

Bringle, R. G., & Hatcher, J. A. (2009). Innovative practices in service-learning and curricular engagement. *New Directions for Higher Education, 2009*(147), 37–46.

Bringle, R. G., Hatcher, J. A., & Clayton, P. H. (2006). The scholarship of civic engagement: Defining, documenting, and evaluating faculty work. *To Improve the Academy, 25*, 257–279.

Butin, D. W. (2010). *Service-learning in theory and practice: The future of community engagement in higher education*. New York, NY: Palgrave Macmillan.

Checkoway, B. (2001). Renewing the civic mission of the American research university. *The Journal of Higher Education, 72*(2), 125–147.

Dostilio, L. D. (forthcoming). The professionalization of community engagement: Associations and professional staff. In C. Dolgan, T. Eatman, & T. D. Mitchell (Eds.), *The Cambridge handbook of service-learning and community engagement*. Cambridge, MA: Cambridge University Press.

Dostilio, L. D., & McReynolds, M. (2015). Community engagement professionals in the circle of service-learning and the greater civic enterprise. *Michigan Journal of Community Service Learning, 21*(2), 113–116.

Driscoll, A. (2008). Carnegie's community-engagement classification: Intentions and insights. *Change: The Magazine of Higher Learning, 40*(1), 38–41.

Driscoll, A. (2009). Carnegie's new community engagement classification: Affirming higher education's role in community. *New Directions for Higher Education, 2009*(147), 5–12.

Ellison, J., & Eatman, T. K. (2008). *Scholarship in public: Knowledge creation and tenure policy in the engaged university*. Syracuse, NY: Imagining America.

Ferman, B., & Hill, T. L. (2004). The challenges of agenda conflict in higher-education-community research partnerships: Views from the community side. *Journal of Urban Affairs, 26*(2), 241–257.

Furco, A. (1999). *Self-assessment rubric for the institutionalization of service-learning in higher education*. Berkeley: University of California Press.

Furco, A. (2002). Institutionalizing service-learning in higher education. *Journal of Public Affairs, 6*, 39–67.

Furco, A., & Holland, B. (2004). Institutionalizing service-learning in higher education: Issues and strategies for chief academic officers. In M. Langseth & W. M. Plater (Eds.), *Public work and the academy: An academic administrator's guide to civic engagement and service-learning* (pp. 23–39). Bolton, MA: Anker.

Furco, A., & Holland, B. (2009). Securing administrator support for service-learning institutionalization. In J. R. Strait & M. Lima (Eds.), *The future of service-learning: New solutions for sustaining and improving practice* (pp. 52–64). Sterling, VA: Stylus.

Furco, A., & Holland, B. (2013). Improving research on service learning institutionalization through attention to theories of organizational change. In P. H. Clayton, R. G. Bringle, & J. A. Hatcher (Eds.), *Research on service learning:*

Conceptual frameworks and assessment. Volume 2B: Communities, institutions, and partnerships (pp. 441–469). Sterling, VA: Stylus.

Goodman, P. S., & Dean, J. W. (1982). Creating long-term organization change. In P. S. Goodman (Ed.), *Change in organizations* (pp. 226–279). San Francisco, CA: Jossey-Bass.

Gray, M. J., Ondaatje, E. H., Fricker, R. D., & Geschwind, S. A. (2000). Assessing service-learning: Results from a survey of "Learn and Service America, Higher Education." *Change: The Magazine of Higher Learning, 32*(2), 30–39.

Gray, M. J., Ondaatje, E. H., Fricker, R. D., Geschwind, S. A., Goldman, C. A., Kaganoff, T., . . . Klein, S. P. (1998). *Coupling service and learning in higher education: The final report of the evaluation of the Learn and Serve America, Higher Education Program.* Santa Monica, CA: RAND.

Harkavy, I., & Hartley, M. (2012). Integrating a commitment to the public good into the institutional fabric: Further lessons from the field. *Journal of Higher Education Outreach and Engagement, 16*(4), 17–36.

Hartley, M. J., Harkavy, I., & Benson, L. (2005). Putting down roots in the groves of academe: The challenges of institutionalizing service-learning. In D. W. Butin (Ed.), *Service-learning in higher education: Critical issues and directions* (pp. 205–222). New York, NY: Palgrave Macmillan.

Holland, B. (1997). Analyzing institutional commitment to service: A model of key organizational factors. *Michigan Journal of Community Service Learning, 4*(1), 30–41.

Holland, B. A. (2000). Institutional impacts and organizational issues related to service-learning [Special issue]. *Michigan Journal of Community Service Learning, 1,* 52–60.

Holland, B. A. (2001a). A comprehensive model for assessing service-learning and community-university partnerships. *New Directions for Higher Education, 2001*(114), 51–60.

Holland, B. A. (2001b). Toward a definition and characterization of the engaged campus: Six cases. *Metropolitan Universities, 12*(3), 20–29.

Holland, B. A. (2009). Will it last? Evidence of institutionalization at Carnegie classified community engagement institutions. *New Directions for Higher Education, 2009*(147), 85–98.

Hollander, E. L., Saltmarsh, J., & Zlotkowski, E. (2002). Indicators of engagement. In M. E. Kenny, L. A. K. Simon, K. Kiley-Brabeck, & R. M. Lerner (Eds.), *Learning to serve: Promoting civil society through service learning* (pp. 31–49). Boston, MA: Kluwer Academic.

Jacoby, B. (2015). *Service-learning essentials: Questions, answers, and lessons learned.* San Francisco, CA: Jossey-Bass.

Lounsbury, M., & Pollack, S. (2001). Institutionalizing civic engagement: Shifting logics and the cultural repackaging of service-learning in US higher education. *Organization, 8*(2), 319–339.

McNall, M., Reed, C., Brown, R., & Allen, A. (2009). Brokering community-university engagement. *Innovative Higher Education, 33*(5), 317–331.

McReynolds, M. (2015). The practice of engagement: Developing as a practitioner-scholar. In O. Delano-Oriaran, M. W. Penick-Parks, & S. Fondrie (Eds.), *Service-learning and civic engagement: A sourcebook* (pp. 3–9). Thousand Oaks, CA: SAGE.

McReynolds, M., & Shields, E. (2015). *Diving deep in community engagement: A model for professional development*. Des Moines, IA: Iowa Campus Compact.

O'Meara, K. (2002). *Scholarship unbound: Assessing service as scholarship for promotion and tenure*. New York, NY: Routledge Falmer.

O'Meara, K. (2003). Reframing incentives and rewards for community service-learning and academic outreach. *Journal of Higher Education Outreach and Engagement, 8*(2), 201–220.

Ostrander, S. A. (2004). Democracy, civic participation, and the university: A comparative study of civic engagement on five campuses. *Nonprofit and Voluntary Sector Quarterly, 33*(1), 74–93.

Pigza, J. M., & Troppe, M. L. (2003). Developing an infrastructure for service-learning and community engagement. In B. Jacoby & Associates (Eds.), *Building partnerships for service-learning* (pp. 106–130). San Francisco, CA: Jossey-Bass.

Saltmarsh, J., Giles, D. E., Ward, E., & Buglione, S. M. (2009). Rewarding community-engaged scholarship. *New Directions for Higher Education, 2009*(147), 25–35.

Sandmann, L. R., Thornton, C. H., & Jaeger, A. J. (2009). The first wave of community-engaged institutions. *New Directions for Higher Education, 2009*(147), 99–104.

Stanton, T. (1999). *Service-learning: A movement's pioneers reflect on its origins, practice, and future*. San Francisco, CA: Jossey-Bass.

Thornton, C. H., & Jaeger, A. J. (2006). Institutional culture and civic responsibility: An ethnographic study. *Journal of College Student Development, 47*(1), 52–68.

Thornton, C. H., & Zuiches, J. J. (2009). After the engagement classification: Using organization theory to maximize institutional understandings. *New Directions for Higher Education, 2009*(147), 75–83.

Vogel, A. L., Seifer, S. D., & Gelmon, S. B. (2010). What influences the long-term sustainability of service-learning? Lessons from early adopters. *Michigan Journal of Community Service Learning, 17*(1), 59–76.

Walshok, M. (1999). Strategies for building the infrastructure that supports the engaged campus. In R. G. Bringle, R. Games, & E. A. Malloy (Eds.), *Colleges and universities as citizens* (pp. 74–95). Needham Heights, MA: Allyn & Bacon.

Ward, K. (1996). Service-learning and student volunteerism: Reflections on institutional commitment. *Michigan Journal of Community Service Learning, 3*(1), 55–65.

Weerts, D. J. (2007). Toward an engagement model of institutional advancement at public colleges and universities. *International Journal of Educational Advancement, 7*(2), 79–103.

Weerts, D., & Hudson, E. (2009). Engagement and institutional advancement. *New Directions for Higher Education, 2009*(147), 65–74.

Weerts, D. J., & Ronca, J. M. (2006). Examining differences in state support for higher education: A comparative study of state appropriations for research I universities. *The Journal of Higher Education, 77*(6), 935–967.

Weerts, D. J., & Sandmann, L. R. (2008). Building a two-way street: Challenges and opportunities for community engagement at research universities. *The Review of Higher Education, 32*(1), 73–106.

Weerts, D. J., & Sandmann, L. R. (2010). Community engagement and boundary-spanning roles at research universities. *The Journal of Higher Education, 81*(6), 702–727.

Weick, K. E. (1976). Educational organizations as loosely coupled systems. *Administrative Science Quarterly, 21*(1), 1–19.

Welch, M., & Saltmarsh, J. (2013a). Best practices and infrastructures for campus centers of community engagement. In A. Hoy & M. Johnson (Eds.), *Deepening community engagement in higher education: Forging new pathways* (pp. 183–198). New York, NY: Palgrave Macmillan.

Welch, M., & Saltmarsh, J. (2013b). Current practices and infrastructures for campus centers of community engagement. *Journal of Education Outreach and Engagement, 17*(4), 25–56.

Wiewel, W., Kecskes, K., & Martin, S. (2011). Portland State University's second (r)evolution: Partnering to anchor the institution in sustainable communities. *Metropolitan Universities, 22*(2), 8–20.

Zlotkowski, E. (1995). Does service-learning have a future? *Michigan Journal of Community Service Learning, 2*, 123–133.

Chapter Seven

SUPPORTING STUDENT CIVIC LEARNING AND DEVELOPMENT

Jodi Benenson, Kevin M. Hemer, and Kara Trebil

The college years serve as a prime time for young people to develop their civic identities (Colby & Damon, 1992). Higher education institutions can serve as a key venue for college students to develop a sense of civic responsibility through curricular, cocurricular, and community-engaged experiences that deliberatively engage students in accordance with their own developmental readiness. Community engagement professionals (CEPs) play a role in students' civic learning and development. Collaborating with students, faculty, community organizations, and other institutional leaders, CEPs serve as critical access points to civic learning opportunities in higher education.

The extant community engagement literature reflects decades of research on civic learning and development. Indeed, the literature offers evidence that civic learning can enhance other forms of learning during college and influence other indicators of student success. Topics that focus on civic attitudes and behaviors of students in higher education can inform our understanding of the competencies CEPs need to understand and influence student civic learning and development. Moreover, demographic shifts in higher education necessitate a discussion to identify the competencies required of CEPs to equitably promote student civic learning and development.

This chapter is organized into three sections. We begin by providing background on civic learning and development in higher education, finding that while much is known about the competencies students need to be active citizens, the literature has not yet distilled corollary competencies for CEPs. We then consider the competencies required of CEPs to engage students in effective civic learning and development. Table 7.1 provides an overview of the competencies this literature review explores. We conclude by offering insights for future research on competencies required of CEPs to effectively support student civic learning and development.

This chapter was developed through the use of multiple online databases, including Google Scholar, EBSCO, and ProQuest, and focused on literature published in peer-review journals and scholarly research reports from 1990 to the present. The literature review began by searching the terms *higher education* and *student civic learning* and *civic development*. Based on the articles found and keywords identified, the search was expanded to include *civic identity, civic knowledge, civic values, civic outcomes, service-learning,* and *political learning*. Studies that did not pertain

TABLE 7.1
Overview of Competencies

Knowledge	*Abilities*	*Personal Attributes*
Knowledge of students' developmental trajectories and expression of civic learning and development	Establishing authentic relationships	An asset-based mind-set that guides work with students
Knowledge of the ways in which students' identities inform and frame their community engagement experience, particularly those students from historically marginalized groups	Facilitating peer-to-peer discussion that positively impacts student learning	Visible embodiment of the value of contributing to the larger community as a role model for students
Knowledge of civic learning pedagogies	Creating partnerships and collaborating with other campus professionals who share desired student learning outcomes	

to college students or college environments were largely excluded from the review.

This literature review is based on the assumption that there is already a level of civic learning and engagement taking place in higher education institutions and focuses on competencies that are necessary for effective, high-impact student learning, particularly for underserved students. Moreover, because CEPs are situated differently at various types of institutions, we recognize competencies may take different shapes and forms within different institutions in which CEPs reside. Context affects where CEPs need to spend their time and attention. However, we want to emphasize that context is not the same as institutional characteristics or classifications. There are multiple studies that suggest institution type is not as important as the kinds of engagement and learning experiences a student has on campus (Pascarella & Terenzini, 2005). Context is represented by the cultures and policies that affect students. For example, an institution-wide commitment to service or global learning might change how or where CEPs need to spend their time to support student learning and development.

Background on Civic Learning and Development in Higher Education

Civic learning and development have long been at the core of higher education's mission to cultivate and prepare students for principled citizenship in a democratic society (Braskamp, 2011). Leaders in higher education have committed to learning that is related to developing the civic capabilities of students, implementing and assessing a variety of pedagogical approaches, programs, and content (Ehrlich, 1997; Saltmarsh, 2005; Torney-Purta, Cabrera, Roohr, Liu, & Rios, 2015). Today, more than 70% of all college students report participating in some form of volunteering, community service, or service-learning during their time in college (Astin, Vogelgesang, Ikeda, & Yee, 2000; National Task Force on Civic Learning and Democratic Engagement, 2012). Moreover, about 50% of college students report participating in credit-bearing service-learning activities in college (National Survey of Student Engagement, 2010). Research suggests that service-learning is associated with a variety of other learning outcomes (Finley, 2011) and has taken off as a leading form of civic engagement in higher education.

As a national framework for student civic learning in higher education has unfolded, various definitions around *civic learning* have developed. Over the years, frameworks and initiatives such as the Political

Engagement Project (PEP), Saltmarsh's (2005) framework around democracy and higher education, the Association of American Colleges & Universities' *A Crucible Moment: College Learning and Democracy's Future* report (National Task Force on Civic Learning and Democratic Engagement, 2012), and other work have shaped the role of civic learning in higher education. In January 2012, based on the National Task Force on Civic Learning and Democratic Engagement report and other efforts in higher education, the Obama administration and the U.S. Department of Education (2012) issued *Advancing Civic Learning and Engagement in Democracy*, a "call to action" to make civic learning and engagement in democracy core for all levels of education.

Upon reviewing these definitions and frameworks, we sought to identify common features of civic learning. This includes the learning and development of knowledge (e.g., historical, political, contemporary, civic), skills (e.g., civic imagination, critical thinking), values (e.g., inclusion, participation), and collective action (e.g., community organizing) through academic and community experiences (Ehrlich, 2000; Musil, 2009; National Task Force on Civic Learning and Democratic Engagement, 2012; Saltmarsh, 2005). Students' civic learning can occur through civic engagement, curricular and cocurricular activities, and off-campus programming and can be used to inform and shape students' civic development. Civic development, then, refers to the development of one's identity where one makes sense of one's relationship to the larger society through voluntary participation and collaboration (McIntosh & Youniss, 2010).

Centering Competencies Around Student Civic Learning and Development

For the purposes of this literature review, we consider the competencies CEPs need to facilitate civic learning and to support the civic development of students during college. Furthermore, CEPs should consider and reflect on their own development over the course of their lives and careers alongside the development of students. Given what we know about the increased focus on civic learning, particularly in the context of service-learning and other curricular and cocurricular approaches over the past 20 years, the question becomes, What are the competencies required by CEPs to promote and support effective student civic learning and engagement in higher education? Following, we outline competencies categorized as knowledge, abilities, and personal attributes required of CEPs to foster high-impact and effective student civic learning and development.

Knowledge

This section describes the different forms of knowledge required of CEPs: knowledge of (a) students' developmental trajectories and expression of civic learning and development, (b) the ways these civic learning contexts can impact learning for marginalized groups, and (c) students' civic learning pedagogies.

Knowledge of Students' Developmental Trajectories and Expression of Civic Learning and Development

Research demonstrates that civic identity, particularly during college, is not fixed or uniform. In fact, Youniss, McLellan, and Yates (1997), taking a developmental perspective, support the idea that civic identity begins to develop during adolescence by linking social participation in adolescence to civic engagement in later adulthood. Because students' civic identity is constructed over time, higher education has the potential to serve as a support structure in further developing students' sense of agency and social responsibility.

The "civic-minded" graduate (CMG) model (Steinberg, Hatcher, & Bringle, 2011), one conceptualization of civic identity, integrates educational and civic domains with the student's identity. According to Steinberg and colleagues (2011), civic-minded students are knowledgeable of and involved in the community after leaving a course of study and have a commitment and sense of responsibility to act as a member of that community. The authors suggest that the CMG model provides a clear end goal, and for this reason, program staff and organizations, including CEPs, can "design stronger programs, use resources wisely, and collaborate with colleagues to support and advance the agreed upon mission" (Steinberg et al., 2011, p. 29). Bringle, Clayton, and Bringle (2015) take this a step further and consider the development of a democratic civic identity in students. The authors contend that citizens with identities as democratic agents are what are needed for democracy to flourish; they propose four components of developing such identities: democratic thinking, action, critical reflection, and partnership.

CEPs must be aware of how students are developing their civic identities and consider the following factors when building competencies. Utilizing previous findings (Weerts, Cabrera, & Pérez Mejías, 2014) around civic behaviors, Weerts and Cabrera (2015) examined the characteristics of students and how they vary in their civic identity expression. Researching super-engagers, students who engaged in all eight of the measured civic behaviors, as their reference category, Weerts and Cabrera used a variety of demographic and psychological factors to examine differential preferences for civic identity expression. Students who engaged in none of the eight measured civic behaviors were less likely than super-engagers to intend to participate in religious activities and less likely to have participated in high school leadership activities. Apolitical engagers are more likely to be female and less likely to study social majors (e.g., liberal arts and social sciences). This knowledge allows CEPs to guide their thinking about which students they should reach out to on campus. For example, working to identify and reach out to first-year students who are less involved in high school leadership activities would allow CEPs to identify a group that is much less likely to engage in civic-related behaviors of their own volition. Information such as this allows targeted marketing to students who may not otherwise engage in civic-related behaviors while in college. Such a strategic approach allows CEPs to engage students whose civic learning and development may be lower than their peers'—a status that has effects on individuals across the life span.

In addition to behavioral differences there are developmental differences that relate to students' civic-learning skills. *Pluralistic orientation* is a construct that utilizes cognitive, intrapersonal, and interpersonal dimensions (Engberg & Hurtado, 2011). It assesses students' ability to work effectively with others of diverse backgrounds and their openness to new ideas and perspectives, including being empathetic to others' perspectives (Hurtado, Engberg, Ponjuan, & Landrewman, 2002). Pluralistic orientation is necessary for students to engage in a diverse democracy and should be a disposition CEPs support. It is a desirable student outcome that both manifests as an attitude and can be utilized as a skill that can be enacted.

There are unique typologies of students. Examining first-year students, Denson and Ing (2014) identified four latent groups of students based on their pluralistic orientation. The two most straightforward groups were those with high (14% of the sample) and low (56%) pluralistic orientation. There were also groups that classify as either low disposition, high skill (10%) or high disposition, low skill (20%) on the pluralistic orientation scale. Identifying which group students belong to, or even just knowing over half of students enter college with a low pluralistic orientation, allows CEPs to develop programs to support specific students in developing this important construct.

The previous paragraphs demonstrate what many CEPs already know: College students are not a homogeneous group. Therefore, it makes sense that students are unique in their behavior and engagement. Bowman (2014) found that a student's openness to experience directly relates to how students engage in their campus community (e.g., students with higher openness to experience are more likely to interact with faculty outside of class). Knowing that a student's engagement with college varies based on mental dispositions leads to the question, What are different ways students engage in civic-related behaviors to express their civic identity? Weerts and colleagues (2014) examined college graduates' engagement in eight different civic-related categories. Through a latent class analysis, four groups of students emerged: super-engagers (30% of the sample, highly engaged), social-cultural engagers (6% of the sample, engaged in only social and cultural activities), apolitical engagers (39% of the sample, engaged in professional, service, social, and community-oriented activities), and non-engagers (25% of the sample, unlikely to engage in any civic-related activities). While 75% of the students engaged in some or all of the eight civic-related behaviors measured, their preferences were not uniform. Thirty-nine percent of all students, more than half of those who were civically engaged, had a preference for apolitical engagement. If CEPs are on a campus where political engagement is valued as part of the educational experience, it is important to recognize that just because a student appears civically engaged, it does not mean that the student is engaged in political behavior. Therefore, CEPs could use this knowledge to develop more programs that support politically oriented civic engagement behaviors.

Knowledge of the Ways in Which Students' Identities Inform and Frame Their Community Engagement Experience, Particularly Those Students From Historically Marginalized Groups
We know that students' intersecting identities and lived experiences inform how they engage with and respond to their community engagement experiences (Green, 2003; Henry, 2005). However, much of the research addressing college student learning and civic development rarely considers these as factors. The scholars who have given attention to students' identities have found that those from a lower socioeconomic status have the highest civic returns upon graduating from college (Brand, 2010) and that non-traditional-age students are more likely than traditional-age students to participate in community service during their time in college (Cruce & Moore, 2007). During and after college, women are more likely than men to participate in their community through volunteerism (Cruce & Moore, 2007; Lopez & Elrod, 2006), while men are more likely to engage politically (Vogelgesang & Astin, 2005).

There remains a significant lack of empirical information regarding the lived experiences of college students of color participating in community engagement, particularly at predominantly White institutions. Scholars have attended to racial and class differences between students and those being served (Chesler & Scalera, 2000; Green, 2001, 2003; T. D. Mitchell, Donahue, & Young-Law, 2012), and to community engagement experiences embedded within ethnic studies programs and minority-serving institutions (V. Garcia, 2007; Yep, 2011; Zlotkowski et al., 2005). Others disaggregate student outcome data by race and ethnicity but fail to ask questions that allow students to frame their responses through their lived experiences (Astin & Sax, 1998; Eyler & Giles, 1999).

This lack of attention to an important group within the college student population is in direct opposition to the espoused values of community engagement and a result of the historical traditions and unspoken norms of higher education. Community engagement continues to be framed by the notion that the students who are doing service work are coming to the experience from a position of privilege—White and middle to upper class—and that those who are being served are low-income people of color (Butin, 2006; Green, 2003; Gilbride-Brown, 2011; T. D. Mitchell & Donahue, 2009). As such, the experiences of students of color and those coming from a low-income background are ignored, even when they are most salient to the service experience (Lee, 2005). As professionals working directly with students, CEPs can disrupt this norm by making an intentional effort to better understand who their students are and the lenses through which they view their community engagement experience and forming learning opportunities that validate and honor those lenses.

Fortunately, a small number of scholars have taken steps to fill this gap in the literature, providing us with some preliminary findings on which we can build future research. T. D. Mitchell and Donahue (2009) in particular have called for instructors of service-learning courses to pay close attention to the experiences of students of color in their classroom. In interviews with 10 students of color who participated in a service-learning course at a small public university, the authors uncovered a variety of responses that students of color might have to a service-learning experience, including

- feelings of empowerment to serve a community with which they are familiar,
- resistance to serving in a community from which they are trying to distance themselves or that triggers memories from negative past experiences,
- frustration with classmates who lack understanding and verbalize deficit perspectives of their home communities rooted in stereotypes,

- a desire to disengage with the class or a responsibility to defend their community when such comments are made, and
- the burden of being in the position to "teach" their White peers and instructors about the realities of the communities in which they are serving.

This is especially challenging when White students, faculty, and staff have been conditioned to avoid the topic of race and are unwilling to engage in the discussion in constructive ways (Green, 2003; T. D. Mitchell, Donahue, & Young-Law, 2012; Vaccarro, 2009).

Further, students of color and those coming from low-income backgrounds participating in community engagement often find themselves balancing their intersecting and sometimes conflicting identities (Henry, 2005; T. D. Mitchell & Donahue, 2009). Their service site may simultaneously bring to the surface their personal experiences with oppression, but also the privilege they carry as a result of their college student status. This can lead to feelings of isolation at both their service site and on their college campus, as neither place feels completely comfortable. These findings indicate a need for CEPs to not only acknowledge the dynamics of power and privilege that are present in the relationship between students and the communities in which they are serving but also apply these same principles to the experiences of the students themselves to ensure all students' lived experiences are centered and affirmed.

Knowledge of Civic Learning Pedagogies

In their direct work with students, and via support for faculty who are implementing community engagement in their courses, CEPs should understand the pedagogical approaches that have been used in higher education to foster student civic learning. Specifically, CEPs must ensure that students are engaged in active community-based activities that directly relate to, and are core components of, learning objectives and outcomes. CEPs must consider the ways civic learning pedagogies contribute to the current and future development of students as contributors to the community.

Kuh (2008) outlines a variety of high-impact practices that educational research suggests increase rates of college student retention and engagement. According to Kuh, high-impact practices encourage mindful interactions with diverse groups, should provide spaces for frequent and meaningful feedback, facilitate learning through cocurricular opportunities, and demand time and effort. Service-learning emerged as high-impact pedagogy (Kuh, 2008) and a vehicle for cultivating citizenship and change agency because it involves participants in community-engaged activities that promote civic learning (e.g., civic knowledge, civic skills, civic dispositions) and also enriches academic learning. Much of this work also suggests that students learn through hands-on, active learning, which, when done with explicit attention to civic learning and development, can foster civic responsibility and future civic engagement. Research demonstrates that students benefit more from civic learning pedagogies that provide opportunities for direct service and provide opportunities to interact with diverse individuals than when they do not provide direct service (Eyler & Giles, 1999). Additionally, Astin and colleagues (2000) found the greatest indicator of a positive service-learning experience was whether the student had an interest in the subject at hand.

While service-learning has become a core pedagogical approach for student civic learning and development alongside cocurricular opportunities such as volunteerism and community service, scholars in the field of civic learning have questioned whether service-learning provides students with the knowledge and capacities needed to influence systemic, structural social and political problems (Densmore, 2000). If not done well, service-learning can reinforce, rather than disrupt, the dominant narrative that results in students' ill-informed preconceived notions of communities and the social issues affecting them. Finley (2011), in an extensive literature review on civic learning and democratic environments, suggests that while service-learning and community service offer opportunities to volunteer as a means to help others, these forms of engagement do not always provide opportunities for students to work with others through differences to solve public problems. Furthermore, the National Task Force on Civic Learning and Democratic Engagement (2012) in its *A Crucible Moment* report emphasized that although community service can serve as a pathway toward civic learning, community service is not always "the same as democratic engagement with others across differences to collectively solve public problems" (p. 5). Thus, civic learning cannot be developed among students if the form of learning is not civic.

In response to this criticism, some instructors and scholars have adopted a critical approach to service-learning. Unlike traditional service-learning, *critical service-learning* takes a social change orientation, emphasizes the redistribution of power, and requires authentic relationships to be developed among faculty/staff, students, and community partners (T. Mitchell, 2008). Using a critical framework, Clark and Nugent (2011) conducted a comprehensive analysis of the *Michigan Journal of Community Service Learning* from 1994 to 2007 and triangulated their findings with interview data from both pioneers and emerging leaders within the field of community engagement who claim a social justice orientation to their work. From the data, six best practices of critical service-learning emerged:

1. identify and build relationships with all stakeholders in the service learning process,
2. develop the personal power of all involved in the service learning experience,
3. create authentic learning environments,
4. create long-term partnerships with all involved,
5. explicitly name and discuss power relationships in the service experience, and
6. produce meaningful action toward change. (Clark & Nugent, 2011, p. 15).

For these reasons, CEPs must know the difference between apolitical and political forms of civic learning. If CEPs are not expressly knowledgeable about what is and is not civically oriented, they will not be civically mindful when working with students.

Abilities

This section describes three abilities required of CEPs: establishing authentic relationships, facilitating peer-to-peer discussions, and creating democratic partnerships in collaboration with other campus professionals.

Ability to Establish Authentic Relationships

The emphasis on authenticity and relationships that is found in the critical service-learning literature is echoed in other bodies of literature as well. Relationships are also a core tenet of transformative learning (Cranton, 2006), college student engagement (Kuh, 2009), and culturally engaging campus environments (Museus, 2014). Just as CEPs must develop relationships with their colleagues and community partners, building authentic relationships with students is key to their learning and development.

In order to understand others, one must first understand oneself. To effectively create authentic relationships, CEPs must first develop their own self-awareness, which includes identifying and acknowledging their own positionality in their community engagement work. Maher and Tetreault (2001) describe the idea of positionality, "in which people are defined not in terms of fixed identities, but by their location within shifting networks of relationships, which can be analyzed and changed" (p. 164). While navigating their work as educators, CEPs must constantly reflect on how their own identities and lived experiences inform and affect their interactions with students.

Furthermore, authentic relationships between CEPs and students are facilitated and strengthened by an environment in which students are seen as equal partners in the learning process. Rather than CEPs playing the role of expert with knowledge and skills to pass along to students, this approach assumes students have unique and valuable perspectives that provide new insights and contribute to the learning of those around them. One way in which CEPs can facilitate such an educational process is through critical reflection and meaningful dialogue.

Ability to Facilitate Peer-to-Peer Discussion That Positively Impacts Student Learning
Engagement in curricular and cocurricular community-based programs has many beneficial outcomes (Jacoby, 2009; Pascarella & Terenzini, 2005). However, these experiences are not all the same quality and do not lead to the same levels of student learning. The shape and style of these programs are important.

J. J. Mitchell, Gillon, Reason, and Ryder (in press) found that participating in community-based programs (both curricular and cocurricular) increased how much students valued the importance of contributing to the larger community as well as students' personal and social responsibility. More importantly, Mitchell and colleagues (in press) found that meaningful discussion with peers mediated both outcomes. Moreover, Barnhardt, Sheets, and Pasquesi (2015) examined students' civic commitments and capacities for community action. After controlling for students' precollege dispositions, the strongest predictors for students' developing the commitment and skill to contribute to the larger community are participation in curricular service-learning and peer-to-peer conversations around community-based experiences. Pascarella and Terenzini (2005) have identified the importance of peer culture in student learning, development, and socialization. This research builds on that, showing that while participating in community engagement—specifically curricular service-learning—is a good start, peer-to-peer dialogue has an added benefit beyond just participating. Effectively facilitating peer-to-peer dialogue as a form of reflection allows CEPs to maximize student learning and development beyond what mere participation can achieve.

Ability to Create Partnerships and Collaborate With Other Campus Professionals Who Share Desired Student Learning Outcomes
The modern state of higher education rarely involves a surplus of human or financial resources. Understanding this, CEPs must be able to utilize their resources for maximum student learning and development. One

strategy is collaboration with other campus partners. In order to best approach campus partners, CEPs must understand and articulate what kinds of experiences result in mutually shared outcomes in the eyes of other campus professionals. Utilizing 27 studies representing over 175,000 undergraduate students, Bowman (2011) conducted a meta-analysis testing the assertion that meaningful engagement with diversity is important in order to prepare college students for participation in a globalized and demographically diverse society—a commonly espoused goal within the community engagement field. Bowman found that college diversity experiences are related to increased civic engagement, which is true for student development related to attitudes, skills, behaviors, and motivations across several types of diversity experiences. This will improve student learning and has the potential to lead to organizational change that will better support students (Sturm, Eatman, Saltmarsh, & Bush, 2011). Utilizing this information, CEPs should connect with professionals on campus who specialize in work around diversity or multiculturalism.

CEPs don't just hope to engage students during their time in college; they hope the civic learning and development that occurs during college persists beyond graduation. Examining postcollegiate civic outcomes six years after graduation, Bowman, Park, and Denson (2015) examined the effects of participating in racial/ethnic student organizations on 11 different civic engagement outcomes. They found that participation in racial/ethnic student organizations was positively associated with all 11 desirable civic outcomes 6 years after graduation, and 8 of the 11 outcomes when utilizing propensity score matching, a quasiexperimental technique that allows for even stronger claims of causation. This is true regardless of race/ethnicity, gender, or institution attended. CEPs who want to support underrepresented and minoritized students should recognize the value and importance of racial/ethnic student organizations and make it a priority to support the groups themselves as well as participation in these groups. Reaching out to campus professionals to support or advise student organizations, specifically racial/ethnic organizations, might be one way to stretch the limited resources already on campus.

A body of scholarship is developing around faculty supporting civic learning through their curriculum and pedagogy. However, we found limited research that examines the relationship among CEPs, faculty, and student learning. We know that CEPs and faculty both work with students to support student learning and development, but the relationship between these two groups is underexamined.

Personal Attributes

This final section describes two particular personal attributes that are required of CEPs: possessing an asset-based mind-set that guides work with students, and visibly embodying the value of civic learning as a role model for students.

Possess an Asset-Based Mind-Set That Guides Work With Students
Kretzmann and McKnight (1993) developed a framework for community development that focuses on *asset mapping*, or identifying and building on the strengths and resources of a community rather than centering on its needs and deficiencies. The model assumes that every person has gifts, and a strong community is one that empowers its members to use and share those gifts.

This framework was developed with the community in mind and, appropriately so, is commonly applied as a tool to teach students to challenge the dominant and damaging deficit narrative of communities, and the importance of working in solidarity. This means serving alongside, rather than for, community members and recognizing the people who live and work there are most knowledgeable about the community and best suited to identify and implement solutions to social problems. That said, students are also community members; to engage them effectively, CEPs must acknowledge and leverage the knowledge, skills, and assets they bring.

In a qualitative study using community-based research techniques, Sandy and Holland (2006) conducted focus groups with 99 established community partners of eight communities in California. The community partners were asked to provide insight into the community-campus relationships, and for their perspective on building effective partnerships. They reported that college students who engaged in their organization through community-campus partnerships had a positive direct impact on their clientele as they were able to build quality relationships, helped to build capacity within the organization with their volunteer time and efforts, provided new insight and encouraged professional staff to reflect more critically about their work, and enabled community partners to bridge the gap between theory and practice. Perhaps even more important, community partners benefit from the energy and enthusiasm that young, idealistic college students bring to their organizations (C. Garcia, Nehrling, Martin, & SeBlonka, 2009; Jones, 2003; Pickeral, 2003).

Similar to the deficit perspective Kretzmann and McKnight (1993) oppose, higher education literature often frames a diverse student body and the engagement of historically underrepresented students as a challenge to overcome, largely ignoring their assets and pointing out all the ways in which they lack the support and preparation to be successful in college (Bensimon, 2005). However, it is critical to the goals of community engagement and to the community partners that students from diverse backgrounds be participating, particularly when they identify with the communities in which they are doing service, or have themselves been objects of such service.

For example, students of color and those from low-income backgrounds have skills to be effective in their service that White, upper-class students often lack. Reflecting on eight years of instructing service-learning courses at a predominantly White institution, Vaccaro (2009) compared and contrasted the quotes from, and observations of, White and Black students to explore the ways their racial identity impacted their engagement in communities of color. Community site leaders reported that, while well intentioned, White students were uncomfortable, and therefore less natural, when interacting with people of color at the service site; often failed to recognize the structural inequities faced by communities of color; and demonstrated a lack of awareness of the aversive racism to which they were subscribing in some of their comments and responses to people of color. In contrast, Black students were able to name how institutionalized cultures and systems of oppression contributed to the experiences of people in the community, had "instant credibility" with community members, and were better equipped to build positive and more effective relationships as mentors to youth of color.

Furthermore, students of color typically have a more nuanced view, and deeper understanding of, the social issues at play within their community site (Green, 2001; T. D. Mitchell & Donahue, 2009; Vaccaro, 2009). Racially minoritized students, first-generation students, and those coming from a low-income background are more likely to self-identify with the community in which they are serving, and as a result engage more deeply in the learning environment (Lee, 2005; Wilsey, Friedrichs, Gabrich, & Chung, 2014). These attributes positively contribute to students' abilities to be effective at their community sites. Henry (2005) asks CEPs to "disrupt the server/served dichotomy" as it is too simplistic to take into account the multiple identities and positions of the various stakeholders and participants in a community engagement experience. In doing so, all participants are valued as contributing members, aligning with the principles of asset-based community development.

Visibly Embody the Value of Contributing to the Larger Community as a Role Model for Students

Students learn and develop from their experiences both inside and outside the classroom, and students' peers are strong socializing agents for supporting civic learning. Student outcomes from college do not solely rely on individual experiences and peer culture; organizational context matters. One way to think of organizational context is campus climate. CEPs likely value campus climates that deliver the message that contributing to the larger community is an important part of college.

One aspect of this climate is how students perceive professionals on their campus (faculty, student affairs staff, and upper-level administrators) as advocates for their own values. Barnhardt, Sheets, and Pasquesi (2015), utilizing mixed methods, found that students' perceptions of campus administrators, faculty, and student affairs staff influenced students' capacities and skills for contributing to the larger community. Less than half of all students (9,710 students at 23 institutions) perceived campus professionals as frequently advocating for students to become active and involved citizens—a worrying sign if contributing to the larger community is a shared desire of higher education. Students most commonly reported advocacy for contributing to the larger community by their peers (43.4% of students) and least commonly by senior campus administrators (35%), with faculty (38.9%) and student affairs staff (41.1%) falling somewhere in the middle.

The degree to which professionals advocate for contributing to the larger community was the strongest predictor of students developing the commitment and skills to contribute to the larger community. This advocacy factor can be interpreted as an expression of values. CEPs would be wise to acknowledge that students recognize how campus professionals express their values. Striving to be a civic-minded professional is one way to embody this ideal. A *civic-minded professional* is "defined as one who is (a) skillfully trained through formal education, (b) with the ethical disposition as a social trustee of knowledge, and (c) the capacity to work with others in a democratic way, (d) to achieve public goods" (Hatcher, 2008, p. 21). CEPs should openly express values that support the commonly cited goal of student civic learning and strive to be civic-minded professionals.

This introspective work is necessary, because it demonstrates to students that CEPs and other campus professionals personally embody the value of contributing to the larger community through public advocacy.

Conclusion

This chapter demonstrates the ways CEPs must be equipped with the knowledge, abilities, and personal characteristics to effectively engage students in civic learning. This includes competencies related to their own work with students, as well as competencies that enable CEPs to support faculty and staff who engage students and contribute to their civic learning and development. In doing so, CEPs must critically reflect on their roles as practitioners in the same space as students. Brookfield (1998) developed a model of critically reflective practice that asks educators to examine their own work through the following lenses: (a) their autobiography as a learner of practice, (b) their learners' eyes, (c) their colleagues' experiences, and (d) the theoretical literature.

The first lens, our autobiography as learners of practice, asks CEPs to analyze and learn from their own experiences. When professionals utilize their own experiences rather than learning from conceptual or textbook situations, it is more likely to stick with them in the long term. Additionally, understanding our own autobiography helps to explain our motivation, the particular ways we approach our work, why we prioritize one responsibility over another, and how we respond to different situations. It can also enable CEPs to consider how experiences that might feel individual may actually be reflective of a collective experience within the profession.

Reflecting on our work through the second lens of our learners' eyes is of particular importance to the practice of CEPs. Seeking to understand how our students are processing their learning means understanding their interpretation of our teaching, advising, guidance, and support. It can be surprising to learn the various ways in which diverse students will interpret and respond to one action or comment by an educator. In order to generate authentic responses and perspectives, CEPs must strive to ensure that their students feel safe to learn and express themselves in educational spaces.

CEPs have the benefit and challenge of working with colleagues across their institution and within the community. Understanding the third lens in which they see our work is critical to the success of a relationship and partnership. Our colleagues serve as sounding boards, challenge our assumptions, and provide alternative perspectives to our own realities and the conclusions we have drawn. In this way, they are a significant source of support that should not be disregarded. While we have evidence that demonstrates the value of strong community-campus partnerships, we know little about the CEP's role in that relationship. An area on which future research should focus is the relationship between CEPs and the community, and the ways in which their familiarity with and knowledge of the community impacts students' learning.

Finally, the fourth lens is theoretical literature on community engagement that can offer an even broader perspective and serves to name and normalize phenomena that CEPs might assume are unique to their individual circumstances. This knowledge enables CEPs to put their experiences into context and recognize that not all interpretations of and responses to their work by students and colleagues are a reflection of themselves as professionals. Rather, many other factors can and do come into play.

References

Astin, A. W., & Sax, L. J. (1998). How undergraduates are affected by service participation. *Journal of College Student Development, 39*(3), 251–263.

Astin, A. W., Vogelgesang, L. J., Ikeda, E. K., & Yee, J. A. (2000). *How service learning affects students*. Los Angeles, CA: Higher Education Research Institute, University of California Los Angeles. Retrieved from heri.ucla.edu/pdfs/hslas/hslas.pdf

Barnhardt, C. L., Sheets, J. E., & Pasquesi, K. (2015). You expect what? Students' perceptions as resources in acquiring commitments and capacities for civic engagement. *Research in Higher Education, 56*(6), 622–644. doi://10.1007/s11162-014-9361-8

Bensimon, E. M. (2005). Closing the achievement gap in higher education: An organizational learning perspective. *New Directions for Higher Education, 131,* 99–111.

Bowman, N. A. (2011). Promoting participation in a diverse democracy: A meta-analysis of college diversity experiences and civic engagement. *Review of Educational Research, 81*(1), 29–68.

Bowman, N. A. (2014). Conceptualizing openness to diversity and challenge: Its relation to college experiences, achievement, and retention. *Innovative Higher Education, 39*(4), 277–291.

Bowman, N. A., Park, J. J., & Denson, N. (2015). Student involvement in ethnic student organizations: Examining civic outcomes six years after graduation. *Research in Higher Education, 56*(2), 127–145.

Brand, J. E. (2010). Civic returns to higher education: A note on heterogeneous effects. *Social Forces, 89*(2), 417–433.

Braskamp, L. A. (2011). Higher education for civic learning and democratic engagement: Reinvesting in longstanding commitments. *Diversity & Democracy, 14*(3), 1–3.

Bringle, R. G., Clayton, P. H., & Bringle, K. E. (2015). From teaching democratic thinking to developing democratic civic identity. *Partnerships: A Journal of Service-Learning and Civic Engagement, 6*(1), 1–26.

Brookfield, S. (1998). Critically reflective practice. *Journal of Continuing Education in the Health Professions, 18*(4), 197–205.

Butin, D. W. (2006). The limits of service-learning in higher education. *The Review of Higher Education, 29*(4), 473–498.

Chesler, M., & Scalera, C. V. (2000). Race and gender issues related to service-learning research. [Special issue]. *Michigan Journal of Community Service Learning, 7,* 18–27.

Clark, A. Y., & Nugent, M. (2011). Power and service-learning: Salience, place and practice. In B. Porfilio & H. Hickman (Eds.), *Critical service-learning as revolutionary pedagogy: A project of student agency in action* (pp. 3–27). Charlotte, NC: Information Age Publishing.

Colby, A., & Damon, W. (1992). *Some do care: Contemporary lives of moral commitment.* New York, NY: Free Press.

Cranton, P. (2006). Fostering authentic relationships in the transformative classroom. *New Directions for Adult and Continuing Education, 109,* 5–13.

Cruce, T. M., & Moore, J. V. (2007). First-year students' plan to volunteer: An examination of the predictors of community service presentation. *Journal of College Student Development, 48*(6), 655–673. doi://10.1353/csd.2007.0063

Densmore, K. (2000). Service learning and multicultural education: Suspect or transformative? In C. R. O'Grady (Ed.), *Integrating service learning and multicultural education in colleges and universities* (pp. 45–58). Mahwah, NJ: Lawrence Erlbaum Associates.

Denson, N., & Ing, M. (2014). Latent class analysis in higher education: An illustrative example of pluralistic orientation. *Research in Higher Education, 55*(1), 101–122.

Ehrlich, T. (1997). Civic learning: Democracy and education revisited. *Educational Record, 8*(3/4), 56–65.

Ehrlich, T. (2000). *Civic responsibility and higher education.* Westport, CT: American Council on Education and Oryx Press.

Engberg, M. E., & Hurtado, S. (2011). Developing pluralistic skills and dispositions in college: Examining racial/ethnic group differences. *The Journal of Higher Education, 82*(4), 416–443.

Eyler, J., & Giles, D. E., Jr. (1999). *Where's the learning in service-learning?* San Francisco, CA: Jossey-Bass.

Finley, A. (2011). *Civic learning and democratic engagements: A review of the literature on civic engagement in post-secondary education.* Association of American Colleges & Universities. Retrieved from www.aacu.org/sites/default/files/files/crucible/LiteratureReview.pdf

Garcia, C., Nehrling, S., Martin, A., & SeBlonka, K. (2009). Finding the best fit: How organizations select service learners. In R. Stoecker & E. Tyron (Eds.), *The unheard voices: Community organizations and service learning* (pp. 38–56). Philadelphia, PA: Temple University Press.

Garcia, V. (2007). Social justice and community service learning in Chicano/Latino/Raza studies. In J. Calderon (Ed.), *Race, poverty, and social justice: Multidisciplinary perspectives through service learning* (pp. 207–224). Sterling, VA: Stylus.

Gilbride-Brown, J. (2011). Moving beyond the dominant: Service-learning as a culturally relevant pedagogy. In T. Stewart & N. Webster (Eds.), *Exploring cultural dynamics & tensions within service-learning* (pp. 27–44). Charlotte, NC: Information Age Publishing.

Green, A. E. (2001). "But you aren't White": Racial perceptions and service-learning. *Michigan Journal of Community Service Learning, 8*(1), 18–26.

Green, A. E. (2003). Difficult stories: Service-learning, race, class, and whiteness. *College Composition and Communication, 55*(2), 276–301.

Hatcher, J. A. (2008). *The public role of professionals: Developing and evaluating the civic-minded professional scale*. (Doctoral dissertation). Retrieved from ProQuest Dissertations & Theses (AAT 3331248).

Henry, S. E. (2005). "I can never turn my back on that": Liminality and the impact of class on service-learning experience. In D. W. Butin (Ed.), *Service-learning in higher education* (pp. 45–66). New York, NY: Palgrave Macmillan.

Hurtado, S., Engberg, M. E., Ponjuan, L., & Landrewman, L. (2002). Students' precollege preparation for participation in a diverse democracy. *Research in Higher Education, 42*(2), 163–186.

Jacoby, B. (2009). *Civic engagement in higher education: Concepts and practices*. San Francisco, CA: Jossey-Bass.

Jones, S. R. (2003). Principles and profiles of exemplary partnerships with community agencies. In B. Jacoby (Ed.), *Building partnerships for service-learning* (pp. 151–173). San Francisco, CA: Jossey-Bass.

Kretzmann, J. P., & McKnight, J. L. (1993). *Building communities from the inside out: A path toward finding and mobilizing a community's assets*. Evanston, IL: Center for Urban Affairs and Policy Research, Northwestern University.

Kuh, G. D. (2008). *High-impact educational practices: What they are, who has access to them, and why they matter*. Washington, DC: Association of American Colleges & Universities.

Kuh, G. D. (2009). What student affairs professionals need to know about student engagement. *Journal of College Student Development, 50*(6), 683–706.

Lee, J. J. (2005). Home away from home or foreign territory? How social class mediates service-learning experiences. *Journal of Student Affairs Research and Practice, 42*(3), 572–587.

Lopez, M. H., & Elrod, B. (2006). *College attendance and civic engagement among 18- to 25-year-olds*. Retrieved from www.civicyouth.org/PopUps/FactSheets/FS06_coll_att.pdf

Maher, F. A., & Tetreault, M. K. T. (2001). *The feminist classroom: Dynamics of gender, race, and privilege*. Oxford, UK: Rowman & Littlefield.

McIntosh, H., & Youniss, J. (2010) Toward a political theory of political socialization of youth. In L. R. Sherrod, J. Torney-Purta, & C. A. Flanagan (Eds.), *Handbook of research on civic engagement in youth* (pp. 23–41). Hoboken, NJ: John Wiley & Sons.

Mitchell, J. J., Gillon, K. E., Reason, R. D., & Ryder, A. J. (in press). Improving student outcomes of community-based programs through peer-to-peer conversation. *Journal of College Student Development*.

Mitchell, T. (2008). Traditional vs. critical service-learning: Engaging the literature to differentiate two models. *Michigan Journal of Community Service Learning, 14*(2), 50–65.

Mitchell, T. D., & Donahue, D. M. (2009). "I do more service in this class than I ever do at my site": Paying attention to the reflections of students of color in service-learning. In J. Straight & M. Lima (Eds.), *The future of service-learning: New solutions for sustaining and improving practice* (pp. 172–190). Sterling, VA: Stylus.

Mitchell, T. D., Donahue, D. M., & Young-Law, C. (2012). Service learning as a pedagogy of Whiteness. *Equity & Excellence in Education, 45*(4), 612–629.

Museus, S. D. (2014). The culturally engaging campus environments (CECE) model: A new theory of success among racially diverse college student populations. In M. B. Paulsen (Ed.), *Higher education: Handbook for theory and research: Volume 29* (pp. 189–227). Dordrecht, Netherlands: Springer.

Musil, C. T. (2009). Educating students for personal and social responsibility. In B. Jacoby (Ed.), *Civic engagement in higher education* (pp. 49–68). San Francisco, CA: Jossey-Bass.

National Survey of Student Engagement. (2010). *NSSE 2010 grand frequencies by major, first-year students and seniors*. Bloomington, IN: Indiana University Center for Postsecondary Research; data from the Higher Education Research Institute cited in N. O'Neill, *Practices that matter: Educating students for personal and social responsibility*. Washington, DC: Association of American Colleges & Universities.

National Task Force on Civic Learning and Democratic Engagement. (2012). *A crucible moment: College learning and democracy's future*. Washington, DC: Association of American Colleges & Universities.

Pascarella, E. T., & Terenzini, P. T. (2005). *How college affects students*. San Francisco, CA: Jossey-Bass.

Pickeral, T. (2003). Partnerships with elementary and secondary education. In B. Jacoby (Eds.), *Building partnerships for service-learning* (pp. 174–191). San Francisco, CA: Jossey-Bass.

Saltmarsh, J. (2005). The civic promise of service learning. *Liberal Education, 91*(2), 50–55.

Sandy, M., & Holland, B. A. (2006). Different worlds and common ground: Community partner perspectives on campus-community partnerships. *Michigan Journal of Community Service Learning, 13*(1), 30–43.

Steinberg, K. S., Hatcher, J. A., & Bringle, R. G. (2011). Civic-minded graduate: A north star. *Michigan Journal of Community Service Learning, 18*, 19–33.

Sturm, S., Eatman, T., Saltmarsh, J., & Bush, A. (2011). *Full participation: Building the architecture for diversity and public engagement in higher education*. White paper. New York, NY: Columbia University Law School Center for Institutional and Social Change.

Torney-Purta, J., Cabrera, J. C., Roohr, K. C., Liu, O. L., & Rios, J. A. (2015). *Assessing civic competency and engagement in higher education: Research background, frameworks, and directions for next-generation assessment* (Research Report No. RR-15-34). Princeton, NJ: Educational Testing Service. http://dx.doi.org/10.1002/ets2.12081

U.S. Department of Education. (2012). *Advancing civic learning and engagement in democracy: A road map and call to action*. Retrieved from http://www.ed.gov/sites/default/files/road-map-call-to-action.pdf

Vaccaro, A. (2009). Racial identity and the ethics of service-learning as pedagogy. In S. Y. Evans, C. M. Taylor, M. R. Dunlap, & D. S. Miller (Eds.), *African Americans and community engagement in higher education: Community service, service-learning, and community-based research* (pp. 119–133). Albany, NY: State University of New York Press.

Vogelgesang, L. J., & Astin, A. W. (2005). *Post-college civic engagement among graduates.* Research Report No. 2. Retrieved from www.heri.ucla.edu/PDFs/Atlantic%20-%20Report%202.pdf

Weerts, D. J., & Cabrera, A. F. (2015). Understanding civic identity in college: Profiles of civically engaged. *Journal of College and Character, 16*(1), 22–36.

Weerts, D. J., Cabrera, A. F., & Pérez Mejías, P. P. (2014). Uncovering categories of civically engaged college students: A latent class analysis. *The Review of Higher Education, 37*(2), 141–168.

Wilsey, S. A., Friedrichs, J., Gabrich, C., & Chung, T. T. (2014). A privileged pedagogy for privileged students? A preliminary mixed-methods analysis comparing first-generation and non-first-generation college students on post-evaluations of service-learning courses. *PRISM: A Journal of Regional Engagement, 3*(2), 79–97.

Yep, K. (2011). To reform or to empower: Asian American studies and social justice service learning. In C. Cress & D. Donahue (Eds.), *Democratic dilemmas of service-learning: Curricular strategies for success* (pp. 157–166). Sterling, VA: Stylus.

Youniss, J., McLellan, J. A., & Yates, M. (1997). What we know about engendering civic identity. *American Behavioral Scientist, 40*(5), 620–631.

Zlotkowski, E., Jones, R., Lenk, M., Meeropol, J., Gelmon, S., & Norvell, K. (2005). *One with the community: Indicators of engagement at minority-serving institutions.* Boston, MA: Campus Compact.

Chapter Eight

HIGH-QUALITY COMMUNITY-CAMPUS PARTNERSHIPS

Approaches and Competencies

Laura Martin and Sean Crossland

If you have come here to help me, then you are wasting your time. But if you have come because your liberation is bound up in mine, then let us work together.

—Aboriginal elder Lila Watson (as cited in Hidayat, Pratsch, & Stoecker, 2009, p. 160)

If institutions of higher education are to fulfill their mission to the public good by applying their scholarship and resources to address societal needs, then community partnerships are critical to the success of those endeavors. Community-campus partnerships guide institutions of higher education to understand how they can most effectively collaborate to address pressing social and environmental challenges by contributing their expertise and resources. This joint process of knowledge and resource exchange is referred to as community engagement.

The Carnegie Foundation defines *community engagement* as a reciprocal, mutually beneficial partnership between higher education institutions and communities at the local, state, regional, national, and international levels (New England Resource Center for Higher Education, n.d., para. 9). Community-based organizations, frequently nonprofit or public-sector entities that partner with universities in this problem-solving work, are key stakeholders that help colleges and universities navigate the dynamics of working with communities.

This chapter explores the competencies exhibited by community engagement professionals (CEPs) involved in the cultivation, development, and maintenance of high-quality community-campus partnerships. These competencies and their component characteristics are inferred from peer-reviewed literature on community-campus partnerships in the context of community engagement.

The authors began the literature review process by creating guiding questions exploring the concept of CEP competencies relative to the cultivation of high-quality partnerships. From the guiding questions, a list of key search terms was established to identify scholarly, empirical, and peer-reviewed literature from 1990 to the present. Key search terms for online databases included *campus/university/community partnership* in conjunction with the following terms: *community/civic engagement, service-learning, mutually beneficial,* and *reciprocal*. The authors sought to include the community perspective on these partnerships, and to incorporate a balance of quantitative and qualitative approaches. Google Scholar and the University of Mississippi Libraries, which includes the Education Resources Information Center (ERIC) and the Professional Development Collection, were the primary avenues of search to access articles from journals including the *Journal of Higher Education Outreach and Engagement, Michigan Journal of Community Service Learning,* and *Partnerships: A Journal of Service Learning & Civic Engagement*. The authors also consulted the bibliographies of several works deemed critical to the subject matter.

The discussion begins by defining *community-campus partnerships*. Then the competencies—knowledge, personal attributes, skills, and abilities—are discussed in turn. Finally, the analysis reveals a disposition of CEPs to view community stakeholders as valued contributors to the partnership process, suggesting an overarching ethical competency for CEPs seeking to build high-quality partnerships.

Defining *Community-Campus Partnerships*

This chapter intentionally uses the term *community-campus partnerships* out of a desire to foreground the community dimension of these collaborative endeavors. This is a departure from community engagement literature that refers to *campus-community engagement, university-community engagement,* or *community-university engagement*. Yet the term *community* is imperfect, as it can "downplay the complex nature of community by treating it in the abstract" (Dempsey, 2010, p. 365). Nonetheless, the term *community* is used here in an effort to represent and elevate involvement beyond the campus. The term *campus*, in turn, is intended to encompass the broad spectrum of higher education institutions.

Bringle, Clayton, and Price (2009) highlight the heterogeneity of community and campus groups in the SOFAR model. SOFAR maps 10 dyadic relationships that reflect lines of communication and influence among stakeholder groups, including students, community organizations, faculty, administrators, and community residents. The SOFAR model is instructive for cultivating community-campus partnerships as it challenges CEPs to view neither the community nor the campus as monolithic.

Community partnerships can be understood as a type of formal relationship; namely, a relationship "in which the interactions possess three particular qualities: closeness, equity, and integrity" (Bringle et al., 2009, p. 3). The degree of closeness influences equity, when outcomes are commensurate with inputs and evenly distributed, and integrity, which is expressed as an alignment in values and worldview that shapes shared problem-solving approaches. In sum, *relationships* and *partnerships* are not interchangeable terms. This analysis focuses on partnership cultivation, development, and maintenance.

High-quality partnerships share several characteristics. Jacoby (2003) observed that principles of good community partnership include shared mission, open communication, and a balance of power. This spirit of open communication and collaboration among partners is echoed by Schulz, Israel, and Lantz (2003), who identify several items influencing group dynamics, including shared leadership, vision, decision-making, power, and resources, which signals the importance of integrating goals and processes in effective partnerships.

Enos and Morton (2003) challenge all parties engaged in community-campus collaboration to pursue the transformative potential of these partnerships by transcending self-interest to seek mutual benefit. Their work considers the depth, complexity, and time frame of partnerships ranging from transactional to transformational. The joint creation of work and knowledge in transformative partnerships creates greater meaning and triggers shifts in identity that embrace a "larger definition of *community*" (Enos & Morton, 2003, p. 25; emphasis added). By practicing the open communication and integration of goals discussed by Jacoby (2003) and Schulz and colleagues (2003), CEPs can nurture a long-term commitment to reciprocity and transformation, as outlined by Enos and Morton (2003). Additionally, Bringle and colleagues (2009) noted that, like relationships, partnerships are fluid and can shift along the transactional to transformational spectrum over time.

In examining roles that campus actors play in engaging community stakeholders, Sandmann, Jordan, Mull, and Valentine (2014) observed that scholarship has "focused less attention on how community engagement is nurtured and developed at the individual level among faculty, staff, students, and community partners" (p. 84). Their research pertains to boundary spanning, where CEPs play a key role in bridging the threshold that separates academia from the community setting. This process of partnership cultivation, development, and maintenance is an essential element of community-campus engagement, and CEPs are central to this work. CEPs can develop personal relationships as well as institutional partnerships, which are the focus of this analysis. Understanding the competencies and practices of CEPs who engage in high-quality partnership work will contribute directly to the gap in the literature identified by Sandmann and colleagues (2014).

This review of the literature on community-campus partnerships seeks to infer the competencies that allow CEPs to develop and sustain high-quality partnerships. We should note at the outset that we authors are engaged in this work as practitioner-scholars at centers of engagement at our respective institutions. Given our community orientation, this literature review seeks to give special consideration to the perspectives of community partners, particularly as community voices seem to be underrepresented in the literature (Littlepage, Gazley, & Bennett, 2012; Sandy & Holland, 2006).

The literature on community partnerships revealed an ethical orientation woven throughout the competencies: a propensity to consider community partners as legitimate stakeholders and meaningful contributors in the partnership process. This orientation informs how CEPs approach how they do the work of partnership, which includes how they

- apply theoretical understandings of partnership to the practice of partnership cultivation;
- build relationships;
- preference collaborative ways of building knowledge, valuing the synthesis of academic expertise and the lived experience; and
- foster open, two-way communication in all aspects of partnership development and maintenance.

With this ethical orientation underpinning an understanding of competencies, our analysis explores the component domains of knowledge,

TABLE 8.1
Community-Campus Partnership Competencies

Knowledge	*Personal Attributes*	*Skills*	*Abilities*
Context	**Relationship building**	**Democratic engagement**	Organizational
Practices informed by theory	Passion	Conflict resolution	**Two-way communication**
Resources	Self-awareness	Partnership management	**Developing closeness**

personal attributes, skills, and abilities that CEPs use to cultivate high-quality partnerships. Table 8.1 delineates specific competencies that are discussed in this chapter. Boldfaced items are qualities that elevate and validate the ethical commitment of valuing community stakeholders as full partners.

Knowledge

The specific knowledge sets necessary to develop high-quality partnerships can be classified into three groups: historical, institutional, and environmental context; theoretical frameworks; and knowledge of internal and external resources.

Historical, Institutional, and Environmental Context

Knowing the history and environment within which a partnership develops provides a strong foundation for high-quality partnerships. The partnership history between an organization and an institution provides knowledge that influences the community partner's perspective. If past partnerships involved conflicts, this may provide insight into potential obstacles to collaboration and how to address them. CEPs should also understand the history of the institution's relationship with a community and how a community has responded to the institution (Bringle & Hatcher, 2002; Leiderman, Furco, Zapf, & Goss, 2002; Schulz et al., 2003). This historical perspective also interacts with other contextual factors.

CEPs who wish to mobilize partnerships effectively will benefit from understanding how to navigate inside their respective institutions. Enos and Morton (2003) refer to this as being *organizationally literate*, where CEPs "understand how their institution works, how it makes decisions, how resources are allocated, what problems and issues are important to leaders, and what opportunities exist for innovation and change" (p. 33). CEPs who seek to validate partnership work will understand how a partnership will connect with their institutional mission and resonate with institutional leaders.

Environmental context requires a knowledge set ranging from detailed information about individual community partners to an overall understanding of a community's geography, cultural diversity, agendas, and resources. In order to work toward reciprocity, external expectations must be clearly articulated (Bringle & Hatcher, 2002; Schulz et al., 2003). CEPs must have an understanding of the work culture, needs, goals, and quality of student engagement as perceived by the community partner (Littlepage et al., 2012; Sandy & Holland, 2006). It is also important to understand the learning outcomes, demographics, volunteer standards, organizational capacity, and most urgent needs of the community (Bringle & Hatcher, 2002; Leiderman et al., 2002; Littlepage et al., 2012). Finally, the motivation for partnership must be taken into consideration in order to prevent the creation of dependency (Kindred & Petrescu, 2015).

Theoretical Frameworks

One can choose to develop partnerships ad hoc, but high-quality partnerships have been the subject of significant empirical and best practice literature. Therefore, CEPs should look to the models and theories already in existence and practice around the country rather than starting from scratch. CEPs should have a well-defined method, grounded in one or more theories that endorse democratic, transformative, or constructive learning approaches, or a combination of them, before initiating partnerships.

Knowledge of theoretical frameworks allows CEPs to operationalize historical and environmental context in partnership cultivation, development, and maintenance. Dostilio (2014) identifies the knowledge of democratic engagement processes, roles, and qualities as foundational in the ability to integrate the historical and environmental context in community-campus partnerships. A partnership built on the framework of democratic engagement will be much more likely to embody the transformational qualities identified by Enos and Morton (2003). Thus, knowledge of theories pertaining to democratic engagement undergirds a democratic approach to partnership development.

Leiderman and colleagues (2002) identify eight core elements of effective partnerships:

1. mutually determined processes and goals;
2. shared resources, rewards, investments, and risks;
3. capacity-dictated roles and responsibilities;
4. parity and recognition of value of all;
5. benefits derived from the partnership justifying the costs and/or risks involved;
6. shared vision based on shared passion;
7. clearly defined system of accountability; and
8. shared commitment to reciprocity and mutual benefit.

While this list may not be comprehensive, it can be considered a baseline framework to be used for partnership development (Leiderman et al., 2002).

An additional concept to be considered when developing a theoretical framework for partnership development is the notion of how knowledge and learning are perceived. Weerts and Sandmann (2008) contend that knowledge must be developmental, internally constructed, and socially and culturally mediated by partners. In order to prevent the development of the negative connotation of "town and gown" tension (Leiderman et al., 2002), one must recognize the knowledge process as local, complex, dynamic, and living outside the boundaries of the institution. Learning takes place within the context in which knowledge is applied (Weerts & Sandmann, 2008), which is precisely why community-campus partnerships contain transformative potential for all involved.

Knowledge of Internal and External Resources

Knowledge of internal and external resources is crucial to effectively maximize partnership potential. Internal resources exist within the context of the community-campus partnership, while external resources are outside of the partnership but can be leveraged to benefit the collaboration.

Internal resources are housed at the campus-based institution and community-based organization engaged in partnership. These can range from community partner capacity, education and expertise of senior staff, and connection to the knowledge, resources, and existing research at the institution (Bringle & Hatcher, 2002; Leiderman et al., 2002; McNall, Reed, Brown, & Allen, 2009; Sandy & Holland, 2006). When identifying internal resources, it is essential to include community partner perspective in the conversation, as many higher education professionals may take for granted on-campus resources that community organizations would consider very useful (Leiderman et al., 2002). Many prominent service and community engagement centers also offer meeting space for community partner programs and activities.

CEPs should be aware that while research can be an asset or a resource, research not conducted with a community-based approach has the potential to perpetuate the town-gown tension wherein a community is viewed as a research subject rather than a vested partner. Community engagement is rich with opportunities for community-based research from both the programmatic focus of the engagement work and the study of engagement itself (McNall et al., 2009). Existing and emerging research provides significant opportunities for CEPs to connect and contribute to the work of community partners. One of the main perceived benefits identified by community partners is "access to knowledge and research on campus" (Leiderman et al., 2002).

External resources exist outside of the partnership between institution and organization. These can take the form of grants, federal programming, and other funding sources (Bringle & Hatcher, 2002). Community assets and strengths existing outside the partnership can also be considered external resources (Leiderman et al., 2002). CEPs with knowledge of these resources and how to access them can significantly raise capacity on campus and at community partner organizations.

Personal Attributes

Personal attributes are another dimension of competencies that influence the ability of CEPs to cultivate high-quality partnerships. Key personal attributes include a capacity for relationship building, a high degree of passion and commitment to engagement work, and a keen sense of self-awareness.

Relationship Building

Community engagement work is fertile ground for collaboration, particularly for practitioners who value learning alongside other stakeholders (Dostilio, 2014). Openness to diverse opinions and sensitivity to community concerns (Bringle & Hatcher, 2002) will allow CEPs to become attuned to community dynamics. This receptivity can demonstrate authentic concern for the community and allow CEPs to establish credibility with internal and external stakeholders (Weerts & Sandmann, 2010).

Leiderman and colleagues (2002) found that a commitment to ensure mutual benefit leads to the development of trust and accountability in a community partnership. Trust is a critical component of community partnerships, and Schulz and colleagues (2003) consider the role of mutual trust in assessing the effectiveness of participatory research partnerships. The relationship-building attributes that influence the ability of CEPs to nurture partnerships are rooted in the unifying ethical competency that values community contributions to the partnership process and outcomes. These relationships are built on a two-way exchange that explicitly seeks mutual benefit and, ultimately, transformation.

Passion and Commitment

Community stakeholders report that effective partnerships take root when "the members of the partnership have a shared vision that is built on genuine excitement and passion for the issues at hand" (Leiderman et al., 2002, p. 7). Passion for the work can also draw CEPs deeper into the partnership itself; Dostilio (2014) found that democratically oriented partnerships were facilitated by "depth of social involvement in relation to partnership involvement" (p. 240). Partnerships, particularly those that are transformational in nature, require intensive, ongoing involvement. Passion for and commitment to the work can sustain the energy of CEPs in the long-term (and frequently nonlinear) effort to cultivate high-quality partnerships. Finally, passion and commitment can also serve as a litmus test for gauging a potential or current partnership. CEPs can assist other campus stakeholders to assess if an authentic commitment to engagement work exists, and if not, they can identify an opportunity to redirect a collaboration.

Self-Awareness

Work by Duck (1988, 1994) suggests the importance of self-awareness in relationship development (as cited in Bringle et al., 2009), which can guide CEPs in how to approach community partners in the partnership initiation process. Once the partnership is established, there are many ways in which CEPs can facilitate partnership development and maintenance.

Weerts and Sandmann (2010) developed a framework with task orientation (technical/practical/socioemotional/leadership on the x-axis) and social closeness (institutional focus to community focus on the y-axis) to illustrate four predominant roles taken by boundary spanners at public research universities. These roles are community-based problem solvers, technical experts, engagement advocates, and engagement champions. Weerts and Sandmann (2010) posit that understanding where an individual falls on these spectrums can mitigate role conflict in navigating community-campus partnerships.

Bringle and Hatcher (2002) cite work by Morton (1997) regarding the importance of qualities that facilitate positive relationships and seek to address unmet expectations (p. 512). Bringle and Hatcher (2002) use the term *integrity* to refer to this personal attribute that nurtures relationships while taking appropriate action to hold partnership members accountable.

An understanding of personal strengths and growth areas can guide CEPs as they seek to cocreate and develop partnerships alongside community stakeholders, ideally aligning themselves to seek compatibility (Bringle & Hatcher, 2002) with community partners. The sense of shared ownership that stems from codeveloping and implementing a joint vision reinforces the ethical competency of democratic orientation toward community partnerships. Bearing in mind the influence of personal attributes, the next section addresses skills that facilitate the development of high-quality partnerships.

Skills

Key skills for CEPs to nurture in the development of high-quality partnerships include democratic engagement, conflict resolution, and partnership management.

Democratic Engagement

In 2009 Saltmarsh, Hartley, and Clayton published *Democratic Engagement White Paper*. The paper posits that "civic engagement without an intentional and explicit democratic dimension keeps academics and universities disengaged from participating in the public culture of democracy" (p. 11). Table 8.2 compares civic engagement focused on activity and place to democratic civic engagement focused on purpose and process (Saltmarsh et al., 2009).

CEPs who develop high-quality partnerships possess an orientation toward democratic engagement. The concepts of cocreation of knowledge, coplanning, cotraining, shared design, shared control, and the ability to develop a mutually beneficial agenda are highlighted throughout the literature and stress the necessity for collaboration throughout the partnership process (Littlepage et al., 2012; McNall et al., 2009; Sandy & Holland, 2006). Stoecker and Tryon highlight the "critical nature of collaboration and communication between higher education and community partners to develop projects and timelines, agree on expectations, and determine appropriate student products and course outcomes" (as cited in Littlepage et al., 2012, p. 317). It should also be noted that partners need to reserve the

TABLE 8.2
Comparison of Civic and Democratic Civic Engagement

	Civic Engagement (Focus on Activity and Place)	Democratic Civic Engagement (Focus on Purpose and Process)
Community relationships	Partnerships and mutuality	Reciprocity
	Deficit-based understanding of community	Asset-based understanding of community
	Academic work done *for* the public	Academic work done *with* the public
Knowledge production/ research	Applied	Inclusive, collaborative, problem oriented
	Unidirectional flow of knowledge	Multidirectional flow of knowledge
Epistemology	Positivist, scientific, technocratic	Relational, localized, contextual
	Distinction between knowledge producers and knowledge consumers	Cocreation of knowledge
	Primacy of academic knowledge	Shared authority for knowledge creation
	University as the center of public problem-solving	University as a part of an ecosystem of knowledge production addressing public problem-solving
Political dimension	Apolitical engagement	Facilitating an inclusive, collaborative, and deliberative democracy
Outcome	Knowledge generation and dissemination through community involvement	Community change that results from the cocreation of knowledge

Source: Saltmarsh et al., 2009.

right to decline partnering in situations that may cause undue burden or mission skew for the organization (Sandy & Holland, 2006).

Conflict Resolution

Conflict resolution can be considered as the process of solving conflicts when they surface as well as the ability to anticipate misunderstandings and issues before they arise (Kindred & Petrescu, 2015). It should be noted that the skill of conflict resolution differs from the creation of processes and programming that address potential conflicts at the outset of a partnership. The latter is identified and discussed in the following section on partnership management

The skill of conflict resolution requires that individuals, institutions, and organizations have processes in place and are willing to encourage mediation; negotiate shared power, influence, and resources; and determine "agreed upon problem-solving processes" (Bringle & Hatcher, 2002; Sandmann et al., 2014; Schulz et al., 2003). Ring and Van de Ven (1994) highlight the need to reduce uncertainty, determine obligations and expectations, and clearly define roles early in the partnership (as cited in Kindred & Petrescu, 2015).

Partnership Management

Partnership management refers to the necessary skills for the initiation and maintenance of effective partnerships. For clarity, the skill of partnership management can be divided into two categories: infrastructure and implementation.

Partnership infrastructure is the system developed to initiate and sustain partnerships. The initiation of effective partnership may begin with a request for proposals (RFP) or memorandum of understanding (MOU). These documents allow for the clear definition of parameters and goals in partnership and minimize opportunity cost (Bushouse, 2005). It is essential that this process defines clear goals, creates accountability, and considers the opportunity for equitable leadership. Many of the frameworks discussed within this chapter should be considered in the creation of partnership infrastructure. Once the infrastructure is established, CEPs need to be able to implement it.

Partnership implementation requires, at a minimum, for CEPs to effectively organize and facilitate meetings and develop agendas (Schulz et al., 2003). It is essential that this be done with a democratic process. At the core, CEPs should have the skills necessary to liaise among various constituencies (Walshok, 1999, as cited in Bringle et al., 2009) at all stages of partnership: planning, design, analysis, and implementation (Weerts & Sandmann, 2008). Once adequate infrastructure is in place, there is a skill set required to implement the process.

Perhaps as important as the initiation of partnership is the integration of reflection and assessment. Assessment should include both the processes utilized in partnership and the outcome of said partnership (McNall et al., 2009) and should happen on a regular basis (Gass, 2010). Dostilio (2014) highlights the need to facilitate deliberation and reflection exercises as a means to foster inclusivity. Both Bringle and Hatcher (2002) and Leiderman and colleagues (2002) articulate the need for partnerships to advance the organization's mission. This is a process that evolves from partnership creation through facilitated, collaborative reflection and assessment (Schulz et al., 2003). Input and assessment from students, community partners, faculty, and any other relevant parties are necessary to ensure effectiveness of partnership and also provide the opportunity to publicly celebrate successful partnerships (Bringle & Hatcher, 2002).

Abilities

Abilities that shape partnership cultivation are the final domain of competencies. The literature contains three areas in which the abilities of CEPs facilitate the development of high-quality partnerships: organizational strength, two-way communication, and the ability to foster closeness in relationships. Both two-way communication and nurturing relationships reflect the ethical competency that affirms community involvement in partnership cultivation, development, and maintenance.

Organizational Strength

Organizational strength is best understood as the ability to act on the knowledge of internal and external resources by connecting partnership stakeholders and following up on partnership activities. Bringle and Hatcher (2002) note that a campus clearinghouse function can be an effective tool to broker connections among various campus and community representatives, though Sandy and Holland (2006) found that CEPs at service-learning offices can unwittingly function as gatekeepers for seasoned partners who desire direct contact with faculty.

The ability to connect stakeholders is a crucial function in partnership cultivation, as "practitioners play an important role in connecting the constituents in SOFAR, whose relationships, in turn, deeply influence the processes and outcomes of service-learning and civic engagement" (Clayton, Bringle, Senor, Huq, & Morrison, 2010, p. 17). Bringle and colleagues (2009) note the importance of developing personal relationships into broader partnership networks, remarking that this may entail "reaching up, out, and across existing institutional and social structure to engage members with greater or complementary influence, power, and resources" (p. 15).

At the operational level, Leiderman and colleagues (2002) echo the importance of the ability to connect campus and community assets by noting concrete actions such as granting access to university resources, an important benefit to community partners, as well as inviting partners to share their knowledge and expertise on campus. Explicitly placing community partners in the teaching role presents an opportunity to shift the traditional paradigm of academics as experts and also capitalizes on the desire of community partners to contribute to student learning outcomes (Sandy & Holland, 2006).

Leiderman and colleagues (2002) identified an additional organizational strength, which is "careful preparation, excellent implementation, and meticulous follow-through" (p. 6); that follow-through is an important dimension of bringing accountability to a partnership. Simply having the capacity to respond to community concerns (Bringle & Hatcher, 2002) is a necessary prerequisite to deliver this degree of detailed planning and implementation.

Enos and Morton (2003) recognize the decentralized nature of institutions of higher education, where there is traditionally a high degree of autonomy among campus units. Individuals pursuing engagement activities must understand how to navigate the landscape of their institutions to connect with would-be partners. CEPs will be most successful in brokering these partnerships if they possess the ability to visualize the landscape and connect the stakeholders, as well as a detail-oriented nature that ensures execution and follow-up.

Two-Way Communication

The ability to engage in two-way communication is characterized by a commitment to include community partner voices, communicate with clarity, and seek consensus. Tushman (1977) notes the critical nature of "effective lines of communication between internal and external agents" (as cited in Weerts & Sandmann, 2010, p. 709). Establishing two-way conversations is simply not possible without the inclusion of community partner voices.

The quality of community-campus interactions is vital to distinguishing high-quality partnerships. As communications ensue across campus and community lines, it is important to maintain a sense of equality between organizations and institutions (Weerts & Sandmann, 2008). Community partners should feel that they have an influence in the decision-making process, which is facilitated by open and honest communication (Gass, 2010).

When campus and community stakeholders are able to communicate openly, they have the freedom to mutually determine potential benefits, goals, roles, responsibilities, and expectations (Leiderman et al., 2002). While these items were addressed in the previous section on skills, the ability to communicate effectively informs the process through which these items are created.

The literature suggests that CEPs need to communicate clearly in both the affirmative and negative sense. This entails the ability to know when a partnership is mutually desirable, as well as the discernment to decline or postpone partnership development (Bringle & Hatcher, 2002).

Consensus building (Dostilio, 2014; Weerts & Sandmann, 2008) is the culminating element of two-way communication. Consensus is more likely to result from inclusive and clear communication, though it may not be necessary for every decision with which a partnership contends. In the framework developed by Schulz and colleagues (2003), consensus is recommended for important decisions that flow from a model of participatory decision-making.

The concept of parity reveals the transformative potential of inclusive, bidirectional communication, in that it delineates how effective communication processes can affect a community. Leiderman and colleagues (2002) refer to parity as when "campus and community partners are interested in creating long-term relationships to produce meaningful change in community outcomes" (p. 13). Thus, CEPs who practice two-way communication are positioned to transform partnerships and the communities in which they are rooted.

Ability to Foster Closeness

The ability to foster relationships enhances partnership work by developing a sense of closeness. The literature describes a continuum within this area, suggesting that relationships built on inclusiveness and trust will lead to a sense of closeness.

Inclusive relationship building takes on many dimensions. One feature of democratically engaged partnerships is that diverse collaborators are able to contribute to the shared agenda (Dostilio, 2014). This broad participation can be facilitated by effective communication with diverse audiences (Bringle et al., 2009). When these dialogues acknowledge and respect the expertise and experience of all individuals, each participant can share a unique perspective, which can lead to an ability to discuss racial, ethnic, and economic issues in a way that advances the work of the partnership (Leiderman et al., 2002).

Communication can both build connections (Fariar, 2010, as cited in Sandmann et al., 2014) and foster the development of interpersonal relationships, which are critical throughout the life cycle of a partnership (Bringle & Hatcher, 2002; Kindred & Petrescu, 2015). Kindred and Petrescu (2015) also note the importance of attending to the partnership process as much as the outcomes. Continually validating stakeholder feedback and participation creates trust, a critical component of a successful collaboration (Schulz et al., 2003).

A sense of closeness develops in partnerships that are characterized by interdependence, which involves frequent interaction and collaboration on activities such as shared governance, grant writing, and service on advisory groups (Bringle & Hatcher, 2002, p. 510). Clayton and colleagues (2010) found that closer relationships are also described as being more transformational. This finding suggests that building relationships is a crucial function not only for partnership maintenance but also for influencing the overall quality and outcomes of the collaboration.

Conclusion

This examination of knowledge, personal attributes, skills, and abilities provides a starting point for discussion of the competencies that CEPs can utilize to cultivate high-quality partnerships. If CEPs exhibit the ethical competency of holding community partners as legitimate stakeholders and meaningful contributors in the partnership process, then competencies related to collaboration, communication, and relationship building will be particularly useful in developing high-quality partnerships. Furthermore, if transformational relationships are considered to be the highest expression of a successful community-campus partnership, then CEPs should strongly consider developing these competencies in their work.

While the literature devotes significant effort to understanding and measuring collaboration, communication, and relationships, there has been comparatively little investigation into the leadership styles required to facilitate community-campus partnerships. Dostilio (2014) found that the role of leaders can facilitate a democratically engaged partnership that "promotes structures and facilitation techniques that create space for transparency, deliberation, and inclusion of diverse stakeholders" (p. 241). Additional research can help CEPs understand leadership styles that best convene, facilitate, and when necessary direct stakeholder involvement, as well as how and when to adapt those roles in order to cultivate high-quality community partnerships.

References

Bringle, R. G., Clayton, P. H., & Price, M. (2009). Partnerships in service learning and civic engagement. *Partnerships: A Journal of Service Learning & Civic Engagement, 1*(1), 1–20.

Bringle, R. G., & Hatcher, J. A. (2002). Campus–community partnerships: The terms of engagement. *Journal of Social Issues, 58*(3), 503–516.

Bushouse, B. K. (2005). Community nonprofit organizations and service-learning: Resource constraints to building partnerships with universities. *Michigan Journal of Community Service Learning, 12*(1), 32–40.

Clayton, P. H., Bringle, R. G., Senor, B., Huq, J., & Morrison, M. (2010). Differentiating and assessing relationships in service-learning and civic engagement: Exploitative, transactional, or transformational. *Michigan Journal of Community Service Learning, 16*(2), 5–21.

Dempsey, S. E. (2010). Critiquing community engagement. *Management Communication Quarterly, 24*(3), 359–390.

Dostilio, L. D. (2014). Democratically engaged community-campus partnerships: Reciprocal determinants of democratically oriented roles and processes. *Journal of Higher Education Outreach and Engagement, 18*(4), 235–244.

Duck, S. W. (1988). *Relating to others*. Chicago, IL: Dorsey.

Duck, S. W. (1994). *Meaningful relationships*. Thousand Oaks, CA: SAGE.

Enos, S., & Morton, K. (2003). Developing a theory and practice of community-campus partnerships. In B. Jacoby & Associates (Eds.), *Building partnerships for service-learning* (pp. 20–41). San Francisco, CA: Jossey-Bass.

Fariar, M. (2010). Social science resources for restoration outreach programs. *Ecological Restoration, 28*(2), 150–153.

Gass, E. (2010). New model of university-community partnerships. *Partnerships: A Journal of Service-Learning and Civic Engagement, 1*(2), 1–14.

Hidayat, D., Pratsch, S., & Stoecker, R. (2009). Principles for success in service learning: The three Cs. In R. Stoecker & E. Tryon (Eds.), *The unheard voices: Community organizations and service learning* (pp. 147–161). Philadelphia, PA: Temple University Press.

Jacoby, B. (2003). Fundamentals of service-learning partnerships. In B. Jacoby & Associates (Eds.), *Building partnerships for service-learning* (pp. 1–19). San Francisco, CA: Jossey-Bass.

Kindred, J., & Petrescu, C. (2015). Expectations versus reality in a university-community partnership: A case study. *VOLUNTAS: International Journal of Voluntary and Nonprofit Organizations, 26*(3), 823–845.

Leiderman, S., Furco, A., Zapf, J., & Goss, M. (2002). *Building partnerships with college campuses: Community perspectives*. Retrieved from files.eric.ed.gov/fulltext/ED481879.pdf

Littlepage, L., Gazley, B., & Bennett, T. A. (2012). Service learning from the supply side: Community capacity to engage students. *Nonprofit Management and Leadership, 22*(3), 305–320.

McNall, M., Reed, C. S., Brown, R., & Allen, A. (2009). Brokering community-university engagement. *Innovative Higher Education, 33*, 317–331. doi:10.1007/s10755-008-9086-8

Morton, K. (1997). Campus and community at Providence College. In *Expanding boundaries: Building civic education within higher education* (Vol. 2, pp. 8–11). Washington, DC: Corporation for National Service.

New England Resource Center for Higher Education. (n.d.). *Carnegie Community Engagement Classification*. Retrieved from nerche.org/index.php?option=com_content&view=article&id=341&Itemid=92

Ring, P., & Van de Ven, A. (1994). Developmental processes of cooperative interorganizational relationships. *Academy of Management Review, 19*(1), 90–118.

Saltmarsh, J., Hartley, M., & Clayton, P. H. (2009). *Democratic engagement white paper*. Boston, MA: New England Resource Center for Higher Education.

Sandmann, L. R., Jordan, J. W., Mull, C. D., & Valentine, T. (2014). Measuring boundary-spanning behaviors in community engagement. *Journal of Higher Education Outreach and Engagement, 18*(3), 83–96.

Sandy, M., & Holland, B. A. (2006). Different worlds and common ground: Community partner perspectives on community-campus partnerships. *Michigan Journal of Community Service Learning, 13*(1), 30–43.

Schulz, A. J., Israel, B. A., & Lantz, P. (2003). Instrument for evaluating dimensions of group dynamics within community-based participatory research partnerships. *Evaluation and Program Planning, 26*(3), 249–262.

Tushman, M. L. (1977). Special boundary roles in the innovation process. *Administrative Science Quarterly, 22*(4), 587–605.

Walshok, M. L. (1999). Strategies for building the infrastructure that supports the engaged campus. In R. G. Bringle, R. Games, & E. A. Malloy (Eds.), *Colleges and universities as citizens* (pp. 74–95). Needham Heights, MA: Allyn & Bacon.

Weerts, D. J., & Sandmann, L. R. (2008). Building a two-way street: Challenges and opportunities for community engagement at research universities. *The Review of Higher Education, 32*(1), 73–106.

Weerts, D. J., & Sandmann, L. R. (2010). Community engagement and boundary-spanning roles at research universities. *The Journal of Higher Education, 81*(6), 702–727.

Chapter Nine

COMPETENCIES COMMUNITY ENGAGEMENT PROFESSIONALS NEED FOR FACULTY DEVELOPMENT

J. Shannon Chamberlin and Johanna Phelps-Hillen

Recruiting faculty to incorporate community engagement into their research and teaching and helping faculty develop as practitioners are essential to the success, expansion, and institutionalization of community engagement (Butin, 2007). Faculty champions are necessary for any educational program to be fully embraced within higher education (Wood, 1990), and institutionalization literature suggests building a critical mass of faculty who understand and promote engagement practices, such as service-learning (Furco, 1999; Welch & Saltmarsh, 2013). Community engagement professionals (CEPs) are those individuals with administrative duties who contribute to the overall institutionalization of community engagement within an institution of higher education and who often support and guide faculty as they adopt and champion community-engaged work. Therefore, faculty development is an important aspect of the CEP's role. Faculty development is a form of professional development offering unique learning and growth experiences for university and college faculty (Camblin & Steger, 2000). This chapter focuses on the competencies (knowledge, skills, abilities, and attributes) that CEPs need in order to encourage faculty to take advantage of the potential for personal growth and professional development possible through community engagement activities.

To identify literature relevant to this review, we restricted our search to empirical and peer-reviewed literature published in the past 20 years. We searched online databases, journal archives, and reference lists of scholarly sources that were pertinent to the topic of faculty development. The databases we used included Academic Search Complete, Education Research Information Center (ERIC), SocINDEX with Full Text, Education Research Complete, Google Scholar, JSTOR, and ProQuest. Although the key search terms *community engagement* and *faculty development* yielded the most relevant results, we also searched other terms in various combinations.

We included literature that defined *faculty* as individuals with positions primarily in teaching or research at institutions of higher education. The literature suggests that individuals with a variety of faculty designations (these are not exclusive)—pretenure/junior, tenured, full, non-tenure-track, instructors, and graduate students—often undertake duties traditionally considered to be occupied by "faculty," such as teaching, research, and service.

Model of Contextualized Practice

This literature review is dependent on an assumption that community-engaged work, and specifically faculty development specific to that work, is highly contextual and dependent on one's environment of practice and the people found within. As a whole, the literature included in this review indicates that the development of faculty capacity for community engagement takes place in the context of an institution situated within any number of geographic or thought communities; it is further contextualized by the current thought and practice advocated across the community engagement field via professional associations and scholarly publications. A CEP at a given institution may be responsible for inviting faculty interest, engaging them in community engagement activities, and providing development and support to build faculty capacity for engagement as needed. Faculty may already be interested but may not be engaged, and so they need assistance in developing specific skills and drawing on support as they form community partnerships, adopt engaged pedagogies, or develop and design engaged research. Faculty who have already adopted community engagement may welcome ongoing support as they continue to integrate and balance their commitments to teaching, research, the institution, and the community. To support faculty capacity for community engagement, the CEP may facilitate relationship development between faculty and community partners and may advocate for engagement-friendly policies and programs within the institution.

The literature promoted the following areas of activity related to CEPs' role in faculty development: (a) recruiting and preparing faculty to do community engagement; (b) customizing ongoing training and support for engaged faculty; (c) building faculty capacity for developing high-quality community partnerships; and (d) facilitating faculty reflection on workload, tenure and promotion, and community engagement integration. Figure 9.1 illustrates the variety of activities that impact the competencies necessary for CEPs to facilitate faculty development in community engagement.

Figure 9.1. Model of Contextualized Practice.

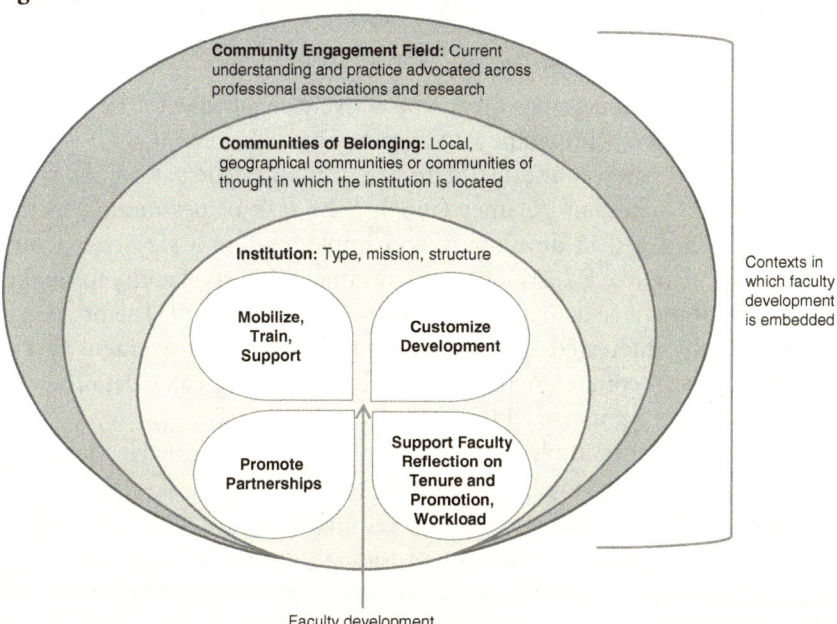

Our categorization of these activity groups illustrates the diversity of foci CEPs have when implementing faculty development; it is not meant to imply that the activities are discrete. Individual competencies (skills, knowledge, and dispositions) may be found within each activity group and also across more than one activity group. In many cases, desirable competencies for CEPs were not directly identified by the authors of the reviewed literature, but rather were inferred based on our experience in the field and understanding of CEP practices that were being promoted in the literature. Each of the four activity areas is described in a separate section of this chapter. Individual competencies embedded within each activity area are then discussed within each section and summarized in a table in each section.

A note about language: Although elsewhere in the field the term *development* may be replacing the term *training*, in the context of this chapter, *training* refers to disseminating information and enhancing specific skills as part of overall faculty development. Our purpose in differentiating the terms in this way is to remain consistent with the usage in the literature reviewed as well as to prevent possible confusion resulting from using *development* to represent both the development of specific skills and overall faculty development.

Attracting Faculty and Involving Them in Community Engagement

Some faculty members may already be actively engaged with the community, but for others who are new to community engagement, a CEP needs to attract their interest and facilitate their initial participation. As noted by Bringle, Hatcher, and Games (1997), "The task of persuading faculty to become engaged in developing and implementing a service learning course [for instance] is distinct from working with those faculty to further their development as instructors and professionals" (p. 46). The process of getting faculty interested and facilitating their initial involvement carries with it hallmark competencies that are discussed in greater detail within this section and summarized in Table 9.1.

In their model for implementing and institutionalizing service-learning, Bringle and Hatcher (1996) suggest that the first step in development for unengaged faculty is generating interest and helping faculty to see how community engagement can be incorporated into the courses they teach, aligned with their personal values, and integrated with their research and other scholarly endeavors. Bringle and Hatcher suggest these goals can be

TABLE 9.1
CEP Competencies for Attracting Faculty and Involving Them in Community Engagement

Actions	Knowledge	Ability/Skill	Personal Attribute
• Recruiting faculty to community engagement	• Understands how to approach differently motivated faculty using different strategies	• Helps faculty brainstorm how to incorporate community engagement into teaching and research	• Is flexible, can use a variety of approaches in faculty recruitment and development • Persuasive
• Supporting initial involvement	• Is familiar with the logistic support needed to implement engaged teaching and research • Is aware of institutional constraints and possibilities that prevent or support faculty engagement	• Organizes and disseminates resources and provides faculty with information • Facilitates faculty learning from one another	• Relationally oriented • Innovative: Good at designing and implementing new programs

accomplished by providing opportunities for newly interested faculty to meet with faculty experienced in community engagement and by facilitating course development through providing sample syllabi and relevant literature and through workshops. Abes, Jackson, and Jones (2002) and Jacoby (2015) similarly suggest that CEPs offer general topic workshops (e.g., an introduction to experiential learning) to attract interest in community engagement, publicize on campus its benefits so that faculty can see how service-learning and other forms of community engagement impact student learning, advocate for community engagement in conversations with faculty, and help faculty brainstorm how to incorporate service-learning or other forms of community engagement into their courses.

Within their programming, CEPs need to account for differences in what motivates faculty to become community engaged. In her document review of personal narrative essays by 68 community engagement exemplars, O'Meara (2008b) identified both extrinsic and intrinsic types of motivation for community engagement, which included institutional, disciplinary, professional, scholarly, and personal values and goals as well as desirable outcomes for students. Her findings suggest that "motivation for community engagement likely varies by type of engagement and depth of involvement" (p. 7). Because individual faculty members are inclined to try community engagement as the result of a variety of motivations, CEPs need to understand how to approach differently motivated faculty using different strategies.

Faculty may need support in their initial attempts to engage with communities. Logistical concerns related to the implementation of service-learning, or the construction of an effective community engagement initiative, may discourage some faculty (Gelmon & Agre-Kippenhan, 2002). Jacoby (2015) noted that supporting faculty with administrative issues "such as transportation, liability and risk management" (p. 116) is helpful for recruiting and retaining community-engaged faculty. This and similar forms of institutional commitment to community engagement specifically can help mitigate time commitments and enhance partner relationships. Partnership development support (Gelmon & Agre-Kippenhan, 2002), as well as support in the form of supplemental instructors and teaching assistants, grading rubrics for engaged deliverables (Shapiro, 2012), and release time for course preparation or syllabi construction (Abes et al., 2002), are all support mechanisms that both entice and enhance the faculty experience of community engagement. CEPs need to be prepared to locate resources; provide faculty with information related to time, logistics, and funding sources; and provide faculty training in how to use service-learning effectively (Abes et al., 2002; Bringle & Hatcher, 1996).

One frequent exemplar of infrastructural support for faculty is the development of faculty fellows programs (Bringle, Games, Foos, Osborne, & Osborne, 2000; Clayton & O'Steen, 2010; Hamel-Lambert, Millesen, Slovak, and Harter, 2012):

> It is assumed that faculty fellows not only focus on their own professional development but they will also be leaders in advancing institutional change. . . . The Faculty Fellows program attracts committed faculty and expands their involvement in service learning, community activities, and the scholarship of engagement. (Bringle et al., 2000, pp. 889–890)

Fellows programs are one place where faculty can interact with peers while "norming" their practice and assessments, yet these spaces also are generative in that they provide opportunities for conversations that generate a shared learning moment (Shapiro, 2012). Spaces for faculty to engage with each other can help "[build] a community . . . , [promote] curricular coherence, [identify] best practices, [and improve] courses and student learning" (Shapiro, 2012, p. 54). Such programs require committed resources—fiscal and otherwise—that are extensions of an institution's commitment to community engagement. Therefore, in addition to planning faculty fellow programs, CEPs may need to be able to secure funds for the development of these faculty learning communities.

To summarize, CEPs need competencies related to arousing interest in community engagement and persuading faculty to try community engagement, using a variety of approaches. CEPs need to demonstrate to faculty how community engagement can be incorporated into courses and research. They need to help faculty make initial connections with community partners and help faculty work out initial challenges and logistics. In addition, CEPs may set the stage for ongoing relationships between faculty and community partners and for supportive collegial relationships among faculty peers.

Customizing Ongoing Training and Support for Engaged Faculty

In addition to attracting faculty new to community engagement, faculty may also be encouraged to engage in research related to community engagement, participate in community engagement leadership, act as role models for other faculty, and advocate for community engagement on campus. In order to adequately support faculty beyond the initial attraction phase, CEPs need to be adept at customization. The same developmental approaches will not equally fit all institutional contexts and all needs of faculty. CEPs need to be prepared to customize faculty development to suit individuals within their institution (Clayton & O'Steen, 2010) and to consider individual faculty members' needs related to their individual attributes and circumstances as a function of where they are developmentally. The kind of development a faculty member needs depends upon several factors, including the type of institution, the type of community engagement in which faculty want to engage, and where individual faculty members are on their developmental journeys (their readiness for community engagement generally, and specifically for particular forms of community-engaged scholarship [CES]). These factors are discussed here, and their associated competencies are summarized in Table 9.2.

Faculty development strategies are highly dependent on the type of community engagement a faculty member is interested in performing. Community engagement is not a monolith but rather a collage of various types, ranging from direct faculty service in the community, research in the community (with, for, or about the community), social change work (Jordan et al., 2012), and course-related service-learning that may take the

TABLE 9.2
CEP Competencies for Customizing Ongoing Support for Engaged Faculty

Factors to Consider	Knowledge	Ability/Skill	Personal Attribute
Type of community engagement	Is familiar with various forms of community engagement in which faculty are interested or engaged	Provides a variety of training and support for faculty engaged in different types of community engagement	Interested in a broad range of community engagement activities and enthusiastic enough to advocate for them
Readiness/developmental journey	Knows various faculty career stages and ranks	Meets faculty where they are and helps them take the next step in development	Perceptive about where faculty are on their developmental journey and sensitive to what they may need at their current stage of development
			Flexible enough to customize developmental training and support to fit each faculty member's needs and interests
Possibility of pursuing CES	Knows about CES, including history, literature, and current community challenges that might be appropriately addressed through CES	Offers faculty "ever-more intense opportunities for involvement" (Clayton & O'Steen, 2010, p. 102)	Accepting of where faculty are in their journey and yet inspiring and challenging to help move them forward
	Is aware of the needs, research interests, and expertises of faculty engaging in CES		
Degree of integration among community engagement, teaching, and research	Knows how community engagement, teaching, and research can be symbiotic	Helps faculty synergize their teaching, research, and community engagement	Empathetic and understanding of possibly conflicting demands on faculty time
	Is aware of how various disciplines place value on categories of faculty work: teaching, research, and service	Helps faculty reflect on how they allot time to teaching, research, and community engagement	

form of onetime service experiences, multiple-visit service, and project-based service-learning (Chamberlin, 2015). CEPs need to be able to provide appropriate training and support for faculty who are engaged with the community in a variety of ways. From their quantitative analysis of 173 tenure and promotion documents, Glass, Doberneck, and Schweitzer (2011) concluded,

> The different types of publicly engaged scholarship suggest the need for a multitrack approach to building faculty capacity for engagement. Instead of the typical "one size fits all" approach, faculty development staff may tailor their activities to reach faculty members who are involved in different types of publicly engaged scholarship. (p. 22)

Customization is also made necessary by variations in faculty members' stages of career and levels of readiness for community engagement work. CEPs need to be prepared to recruit and support faculty in all stages of their careers, from graduate students through established scholars (O'Meara & Jaeger, 2006). This attention extends beyond recruitment of tenured or tenure-track faculty. Garrison and Jaeger (2014) noted that recruiting and enhancing graduate students' use of service-learning pedagogies, while contingent on a variety of factors related to self-motivation, is strongly influenced by existing institutional support, particularly professional assistance and workshops. O'Meara's (2008a) work also suggests that graduate students are a unique population. Therefore, a CEP at a graduate-degree-granting institution needs to attend to the diversity in education and experience level when recruiting and training graduate students.

Clayton and O'Steen (2010) also noted distinctions among faculty based on their readiness for community engagement: "We often think in terms of supporting *a developmental journey* among our faculty members—meeting them where they are and offering them ever-more intense opportunities for involvement" (p. 102). A faculty member's developmental journey may include progression from the singular use of engaged pedagogy to a more inclusive idea of CES. Clayton and O'Steen suggested that as faculty progress on their developmental journey beyond direct service and service-learning, CEPs need to be able to help faculty learn more about CES and then help them find ways to disseminate their work through publication and presentation. Other studies point to additional capacities that CEPs may help faculty develop if they choose to engage in CES, which include knowing CES history and literature, concepts of community engagement and CES, institutional policies that impact faculty inclination toward community engagement, and current community challenges that might be appropriate foci for CES (Axtell, n.d.; Jordan et al., 2012; Nyden, 2003).

Professional development opportunities, such as workshops, need to be customized not only in regard to type of community engagement, faculty career stage, and level of readiness but also in terms of when faculty have time to participate. In order to ensure faculty can take advantage of a range of developmental options, sessions need to be offered in a variety of formats and durations of commitment and at a variety of times in order to fit individual faculty members' schedules (Chamberlin, 2015).

To summarize, CEPs need to be flexible and willing to provide each faculty member with appropriate development opportunities as they continue past the initial attraction phase into sustained involvement. One size does not fit all. A number of factors influence the kinds of development necessary. CEPs need to help faculty plan their community engagement involvement in line with institutional priorities regarding faculty time allotment. Different variations of community engagement call for different sorts of preparation, so CEPs need to be knowledgeable about many forms of community engagement. Faculty members are at different levels of readiness and their availability varies. To be most effective, training and support for faculty need to be customized to fit their interests, needs, and availability.

Building Faculty Capacity for High-Quality Community-Campus Partnerships

One particularly salient aspect of the way CEPs support faculty through ongoing, targeted faculty development relates to brokering high-quality community-campus partnerships. CEPs often serve as moderators of partnerships (Bringle & Hatcher, 2002; Gelmon & Agre-Kippenhan, 2002) between campus representatives and community organizations, or are portrayed as intermediaries (Weerts & Sandmann, 2010, p. 643). In such capacities, they act as a model for faculty members to emulate when engaging with community partners. The ability of faculty to successfully implement community-engaged work depends in part on the skills, knowledge, and abilities that CEPs employ in pursuing successful community partnerships on behalf of and with faculty. Without models, faculty can unintentionally reinforce the town-and-gown divide (Mayfield, 2001), reifying a number of problematic practices seen in early community engagement initiatives (Stewart & Webster, 2011; Ward & Wolf-Wendel, 2000), rather than engaging in healthy reciprocal practices, such as those parsed by Dostilio and colleagues (2012) in their concept review of reciprocity. Within this chapter, we discuss the need for CEPs to competently attend to aspects of partnership facilitation *between faculty and community partners*. (General competencies for partnership development were discussed in Chapter 8.)

CEPs need to be knowledgeable about potential community partners and to provide opportunities for faculty to meet and build ongoing relationships with them (Abes et al., 2002; Chamberlin, 2015). Literature in the area of faculty involvement in community partnerships provides a window into the potential roles CEPs play when supporting faculty in their community-campus partnership development, which include acting as a model and guide for faculty, ameliorating faculty apprehension of working outside the bounds of their disciplinary expertise, and enhancing faculty appreciation of the diverse perspectives and experiences that community partners bring to engaged teaching and research.

In a seminal essay, Bringle and Hatcher (2002) outlined the phases and dynamics of community-campus relationships. They offered direct implications for CEPs: monitoring and soliciting feedback from partners, developing community advisory groups, developing multifaceted partnerships, assessing outcomes and being able to modify these assessments, and affirming healthy relationships.

In addition to enhancing partnerships, CEPs need to influence faculty perspectives of community that make engagement appealing (or intimidating). CEPs sometimes encounter a particular sort of apprehension among faculty interested in community engagement work. Butin (2007) wrote of this apprehension as an existential concern, wherein faculty fear that they are no longer the only subject-matter experts, and that by moving their courses and research to a different space, two varieties of expertise are offered to students. When recruiting and training faculty, CEPs need to be able to articulate this existential unease without alienating or discouraging faculty. In supporting the construction of healthy, reciprocal partnerships, CEPs can help faculty come to the realization that they

> may have to watch the theories in the textbook contradicted by the reality on the ground. They may have to face the fact their lectures do not speak to the situation that students encounter in their community. Or they may realize that their expertise, built up over many years of graduate school and teaching, may be next to useless in situations requiring different skills or more interdisciplinary knowledge than they have developed. (Butin, 2007, p. 35)

In their qualitative survey of 99 community partners, Sandy and Holland (2006) suggested that efforts to moderate this anxiety can be enhanced by shedding light on student learning that occurs because of exposing students to multiple expertises (not in spite of doing so). Axtell (n.d.) conducted a process for the University of Minnesota in which they mapped their existing community engagement faculty development resources and identified gaps among them. In doing so, Axtell identified the need for faculty to engage in critical reflection as a means to recognize the limits of their own expertise, respect community partners' knowledge and experience, and envision their respective roles in community-campus partnership.

The last area of capacity in which CEPs help faculty is recognizing the centrality of diverse perspectives and experiences to the bedrock of successful, democratic community-campus partnerships. In her exploratory case study of democratically engaged partnerships, Dostilio (2014) found that those partnerships that demonstrated high degrees of democratic practices valued inclusivity and full participation by all members (among other qualities). The partnership of primary interest to the study built the capacity of its members to behave democratically by promoting interorganizational collaboration and facilitating learning interactions among partnership members wherein inclusivity and full participation were expressly discussed. Before Dostilio's study, Stoecker, Tryon, and Hilgendorf (2009) offered what was at the time (and perhaps still remains) the broadest representation of community partners and their perceptions of community engagement. CEPs can support faculty in reorienting their work to be representative of both community and campus and help moderate the often dominant role of the university in community-campus partnerships.

Therefore, CEPs facilitate educational opportunities for faculty related to communication and community sensitivities (Weerts & Sandmann, 2010, p. 643), while also allowing faculty space to develop this understanding on their own. At the same time, CEPs' construction of wider institutional commitment to high-quality partnerships is a vital competency alongside successfully moderating community-faculty relationships. CEPs can serve as the first representatives of the community for faculty, balancing the diverse and equally rich knowledge sets in each space, while allaying faculty concerns. As community engagement initiatives expand, it is useful for CEPs to both understand and model the theoretical underpinnings of reciprocal, democratic relationships between communities and campuses. Table 9.3 provides an overview of CEP competencies for engaging faculty in the building of high-quality community-campus partnerships.

TABLE 9.3
CEP Competencies for Building Faculty Capacity for High-Quality Community-Campus Partnerships

Actions	Knowledge	Ability/Skill	Personal Attribute
• Act as model and guide for faculty	• Is aware of effective communication practices within community-campus partnerships • Knows community needs, priorities, and abilities and faculty needs, priorities, and abilities	• Models effective communication to enhance collaborative enterprises between community partners and faculty • Aligns community partners' needs, missions, priorities, and abilities with representative faculty on campus	• Flexible
• Ameliorate faculty apprehension about working outside of the bounds of disciplinary expertise	• Knows that some faculty experience an existential unease about community engagement	• Articulates existential unease without alienating or discouraging faculty • Facilitates critical reflection wherein faculty encounter the limits of their own experience and value of leveraging community expertise	• Patient • Perceptive
• Enhance faculty's appreciation of the diverse perspectives and experiences community partners bring	• Knows that inclusion and full participation are hallmarks of a democratic orientation	• When appropriate, serves as the first representative of the community for faculty, balancing the diverse and equally rich knowledge sets in each space	• Humble

Facilitating Faculty Reflection on Workload, Tenure, and Community Engagement Integration

In addition to helping faculty navigate community partnerships, CEPs influence the institutional conditions that affect faculty. (CEPs' role in institutionalization was discussed in great depth in Chapter 5.) This section outlines the competencies necessary for CEPs to raise faculty awareness of institutional conditions such as workload and tenure that influence the ability to pursue community engagement.

Faculty concerns are often related to the practical implications of their community engagement work in relation to their institutional position. Literature reviewed for this section suggested that effective faculty development projects take into consideration an institution's tenure and promotion structure; alignment of an institution's preferred balance among community engagement, teaching, and research with the way faculty allocate their time; and alignment between faculty identity and institutional identity. CEPs can help faculty navigate this institutional context.

The ability to discuss the implications of engagement activities in relation to a faculty member's rank, tenure, and promotion is vital for CEPs. In building their developmental framework for community engagement faculty, Gelmon and Agre-Kippenhan (2002) noted, "Many faculty are reluctant to venture too far into community-based activities when the traditional institutional mechanisms for promotion and tenure do not encourage community-based teaching or partnerships" (p. 161). Weerts and Sandmann (2010) also suggested that the possible outcomes of investing in community engagement may not seem to be in a faculty member's best interest (p. 646). Recognizing the tension at play allows CEPs to ascertain how faculty participation in community engagement can enrich their teaching, service, and research, thereby responding appropriately to faculty members' developmental needs. At the same time, the construction of new disciplinary-specific journals built upon the principles of civic engagement and community engagement (Jacoby & Associates, 2009), represented by journals like *Reflections* and *Perspectives on Politics*, indicates that CEPs need to stay attuned to new publications and initiatives in specific disciplines as well as maintain adequate research abilities. These abilities help allay concerns about requirements with representation of disciplinary-specific scholarship to help support tenure cases.

Advocating for incentives related to community engagement in rank, tenure, and promotion determinations at an institutional level, as well as articulating how community engagement work can support faculty's mobility within the university, are two abilities effective CEPs may have related to faculty development within the institutional infrastructure. As the Carnegie Community Engagement Classification increasingly supports models of tenure and promotion guidelines that embrace Boyer's concept of "scholarship of application" (Driscoll, 2008, p. 41), CEPs can leverage community engagement as a value-added opportunity for faculty focused on portfolio development. Driscoll, in her examination of the early applications for Carnegie Community Engagement Classification, found that successful institutional applications often represented institutions where service and engagement were embedded in missions, with trickle-down effects dispersed across campus.

CEPs' ability to construct these unique professionalization opportunities within their institutional framework helps faculty in finding the best balance among various aspects of their roles (Jordan et al., 2012). Another ability CEPs need is designing and conducting professional development sessions related to helping faculty maintain balance in their teaching, research, and service responsibilities while integrating community engagement (Chamberlin, 2015). Therefore, CEPs can encourage administrators to clarify their expectations regarding the relative priority of various faculty responsibilities. For that task, a desirable personal attribute for CEPs would be diplomacy.

CEPs need to be able to help faculty envision how community engagement can be integrated into the core of teaching and research, thereby encouraging faculty to enhance their scholarship with community engagement (Bloomgarden & O'Meara, 2007; Bringle et al., 2000; Bringle & Hatcher, 1996; Clayton & O'Steen, 2010; Colbeck & Wharton-Michael, 2006; Gelmon & Agre-Kippenhan, 2002). The relationship among teaching, research, and community engagement is symbiotic; they benefit one another when CES is integrated with faculty work rather than supplementary to core activities of teaching and research (Colbeck & Wharton-Michael, 2006). "Tying service-learning to what faculty members at research institutions already value—peer-reviewed scholarly publication and professional disciplinary conferences—helps raise its academic legitimacy" (Furco, 2001, p. 76). Not all faculty know how to integrate community engagement into their day-to-day practice and work, and they may not know quite how to strike a good balance in allotting their time among teaching, service, and research. In their focused study, Jordan and colleagues (2012) examined the effectiveness of a one-year pilot program for faculty development in community engagement, finding that faculty often conduct community engagement work but do not identify with the institution's broader community engagement initiatives, thereby losing opportunities to network and collaborate with peers and align their efforts with institutional expectations related to their work.

Furthermore, helping faculty find ways to overlap their time commitments may help overcome one of the major reservations faculty have about community engagement: finding the time for it (Bloomgarden & O'Meara, 2007). Additionally, to incentivize adoption of community engagement by faculty, CEPs need to be familiar with internal and external funding sources in order to attract faculty interest. Some institutions offer funding opportunities for faculty to develop, convert, and modify their courses to include community engagement. If afforded financial resources, CEPs then need to manage distribution of calls for proposals, proposal review, fund distribution, and project management. The success of these initiatives and funding to develop and maintain them are built within a context of institutional support; therefore, CEPs need to be able to garner institutional support for key programs and initiatives. In a number of circumstances, this entails knowing whom to contact and when. CEPs need to be adept at advocating with administration for institutional support of community engagement and its various manifestations.

Beyond offering funding opportunities for such projects as jump-starting research or enhancing curricula with service-learning, CEPs can help faculty link community engagement with research, thereby providing faculty with a way to document their community work (Bringle et al., 2000). Within institutional rewards systems, this often helps faculty use community engagement work toward tenure and promotion. "Faculty will be motivated to participate in faculty development activities when they are confident that their interests are aligned with . . . institutional reward structures" (Bringle, Hatcher, Jones, & Plater, 2006, p. 67). In fact, Gelmon and Agre-Kippenhan (2002) noted in their abstract that the impetus for developing models like the one they proposed is for universities to provide the initial framework. Like many evolutions in higher education, this notion hinges on the concept that institutions drive faculty to shape their work toward the infrastructure, yet faculty are also drivers of institutional change (Kezar, Gallant, & Lester, 2011). Here, the relationship between faculty identity and institutional identity is noteworthy.

In recruiting faculty, junior faculty can be selected based on affinity for, or fit with, the institution's and department's mission. In this way, faculty are seen as enactors of an institution's self-proclaimed vision, or as Driscoll (2008) noted, a self-selected classification such as Carnegie Community Engagement. New faculty are positioned so that institutional values and identities bear down on them for specific effect, and, once tenured, faculty are afforded a degree of freedom to engage with goals outside this scope and can harness grassroots tools to respect existing norms while challenging and reshaping them. Kezar and colleagues (2011) examined these tactics, suggesting that staff and faculty are important actors in leveraging classrooms and student mentoring as modes of driving institutional change. CEPs can interject their expertise anywhere along this spectrum.

CEPs can reflect an institution's tenure and promotion structure in their work with faculty, helping faculty align integration of community engagement into teaching and research with institutional incentives and identity. CEPs can be critical in helping faculty reflect and identify means of connecting community engagement with tenure and workload concerns. Table 9.4 provides an overview of the important ways in which CEPs can help faculty simultaneously integrate community engagement while reflecting on workload, tenure, and promotion processes.

Conclusion

The competencies that are desirable for CEPs to effectively support faculty development can be classified into the following activity sets: (a) attracting, preparing, and involving faculty in community engagement initially; (b) customizing ongoing training and support for faculty engaged in community engagement; (c) building faculty capacity for developing high-quality community partnerships; and (d) facilitating faculty reflection on workload, tenure and promotion, and community engagement integration. Depending on the context of practice for a given CEP, some competencies may be useful in multiple aspects of a CEP's faculty development endeavors. Others may be uniquely specialized and contingent on a CEP's institutional context.

Initially, CEPs may brainstorm with faculty who are new to community engagement on how community engagement can be incorporated into their courses, research, and other scholarly endeavors. CEPs may also help faculty realize how community engagement aligns with their personal values and with institutional mission. In addition, CEPs can be assets for community partners and faculty as new community engagement–related projects evolve. CEPs may facilitate peer interactions like learning communities, peer support groups, and mentoring to ease faculty into community engagement. Once faculty are engaged, CEPs can customize support to accommodate differences in faculty readiness, the type of community engagement they are engaged in, their career stages, and where they are in their developmental journeys in relation to community engagement. All along the way, CEPs may model communication and co-construction practices to help faculty develop high-quality community partnerships. CEPs can ameliorate uneasiness faculty may be feeling in this context and enhance faculty appreciation for community partners' expertise. In relation to the institution, CEPs can address pressure or impediments faculty may be experiencing and advocate with administrators to improve clarity of institutional expectations regarding appropriate balance among teaching, research, and community engagement in faculty workload. CEPs may need to manage calls for proposals, proposal review, and fund distribution as part of faculty development and support.

TABLE 9.4

CEP Competencies for Facilitating Faculty Reflection on Workload, Tenure, and Community Engagement Integration

Concerns	Knowledge	Ability/Skill	Personal Attribute
• Tenure and promotion concerns and institutional pressures for job maintenance or promotion	• Knows how to engage faculty based on the benefits of community engagement for their research, teaching, and service	• Stays attuned to new publications and initiatives in specific disciplines; maintains adequate research abilities • Ascertains how faculty participation in community engagement can enrich their teaching, service, and research, thereby responding appropriately to faculty's developmental needs • Advocates on behalf of faculty with administration for institutional support of community engagement and its various manifestations	• Perceptive • Enthusiastic
• Balance in faculty commitments		• Encourages administrators to clarify their expectations regarding the relative priority of various faculty responsibilities	• Informative • Encouraging
• Institutional constraints and possibilities that prevent or support faculty engagement	• Knows specific, tangible areas for programmatic influence and improvement within infrastructure	• Designs and conducts professional development sessions related to helping faculty determine and maintain balance in their teaching, research, and service responsibilities while integrating community engagement • Constructs unique professionalization opportunities reflective of the institution's framework • Grounds programs in institutional infrastructure	• Problem solver • Critical thinker
• Funding	• Manages funds, budgets, and grants related to faculty development	• Discusses the merit of and solicits funds for the development of faculty learning communities • Manages distribution of calls for proposals, proposal review, and fund distribution	• Persuasive

At every stage of faculty development, CEPs need to meet faculty where they are and help them move forward in community engagement by customizing professional development opportunities and support for each individual. By its nature, the role of the CEP is relational—getting to know faculty members as individuals and facilitating relationship-building among faculty members and between faculty and community partners. Faculty development is a respectful process, one undertaken *with* faculty, not done *to* faculty. CEPs can be more effective by engaging in interactive customization of training and support with faculty, rather than offering ready-made one-size-fits-all workshops, for instance. By working with faculty as they progress along their development journeys, CEPs can encourage faculty to tackle increasingly intense forms of community engagement. In this way, CEPs can contribute not only to an increased number of community engagement activities at their institutions but also to improved quality of community-campus engagements and useful research in the field as well.

The full diversity of competencies examined in this chapter, and throughout this project, may not be manifested by one individual. Those responsible for hiring CEPs may choose to prioritize those competencies most needed in their circumstances and aim at putting together over time a team with complementary competencies. To bolster their efforts, CEPs may also choose to encourage faculty to be institutional change-makers (Wood, 1990), enhancing the work of community engagement both in the community and on campus. The more faculty who are involved in community engagement and who are advocating for community engagement, the more likely that community engagement will be a sustainable presence on campus, and potentially a lasting and enriching aspect of campus culture.

References

Abes, E. S., Jackson, G., & Jones, S. R. (2002). Factors that motivate and deter faculty use of service-learning. *Michigan Journal of Community Service Learning, 9*(1), 5–17. Retrieved from hdl.handle.net/2027/spo.3239521.0009.101

Axtell, S. (n.d.). *Creating a community-engaged scholarship (CES) faculty development program.* Minneapolis, MN: University of Minnesota. Retrieved from Citeseerx.ist.psu.edu/index

Bloomgarden, A. H., & O'Meara, K. (2007). Faculty role integration and community engagement: Harmony or cacophony? *Michigan Journal of Community Service Learning, 13*(2), 5–18. Retrieved from hdl.handle.net/2027/spo.3239521.0013.201

Bringle, R. G., Games, R., Foos, C. L., Osgood, R., & Osborne, R. (2000). Faculty Fellows program. *American Behavioral Scientist, 43*(5), 882–894. Retrieved from ProQuest.

Bringle, R. G., & Hatcher, J. A. (1996). Implementing service learning in higher education. *Journal of Higher Education, 67*(2), 221–239. Retrieved from www.jstor.org/stable/2943981

Bringle, R. G., & Hatcher, J. A. (2002). Campus-community partnerships: The terms of engagement. *Journal of Social Issues, 58*(3), 503–516. doi:10.1111/1540-4560.00273

Bringle, R. G., Hatcher, J. A., & Games, R. (1997). Engaging and supporting faculty in service learning. *Journal of Public Service and Outreach, 2*(1), 43–51. Retrieved from openjournals.libs.uga.edu/index.php/jheoe/article/view/287/266

Bringle, R. G., Hatcher, J. A., Jones, S., & Plater, W. M. (2006). Sustaining civic engagement: Faculty development, roles, and rewards. *Metropolitan Universities, 17*(1), 62–74.

Butin, D. (2007). Focusing our aim: Strengthening faculty commitment to community engagement. *Change, 39*(6), 34–39. doi:10.3200/CHNG.39.6.34-39

Camblin, L., & Steger, J. (2000). Rethinking faculty development. *Higher Education, 39*(1), 1–18. doi:10.1023/A:1003827925543

Chamberlin, J. S. (2015). *College faculty experiences assigning service-learning and their inclination to continue* (Doctoral dissertation). Retrieved from scholarworks.waldenu.edu

Clayton, P. H., & O'Steen, W. L. (2010). Working with faculty: Designing customized developmental strategies. In B. Jacoby & P. Mutascio (Eds.), *Looking in, reaching out: A reflective guide for community service-learning professionals* (pp. 95–113). Boston, MA: Campus Compact.

Colbeck, C. L., & Wharton-Michael, P. (2006). Individual and organizational influences on faculty members' engagement in public scholarship. *New Directions for Teaching and Learning, 105*, 17–26. doi:10.1002/tl.221

Dostilio, L. D. (2014). Democratically engaged community-university partnerships: Reciprocal determinants of democratically oriented roles and processes. *Journal of Higher Education Outreach and Engagement, 18*(4), 235–244.

Dostilio, L. D., Brackmann, S. M., Edwards, K. E., Harrison, B., Kliewer, B. W., & Clayton, P. H. (2012). Reciprocity: Saying what we mean and meaning what we say. *Michigan Journal of Community Service Learning, 19*(1), 17–32. Retrieved from hdl.handle.net/2027/spo.3239521.0019.102

Driscoll, A. (2008). Carnegie's community-engagement classification: Intentions and insights. *Change: The Magazine of Higher Learning, 40*(1), 38–41. doi:10.3200/CHNG.40.1.38-41

Furco, A. (1999). *Self-assessment rubric for the institutionalization of service-learning in higher education.* Berkeley: University of California.

Furco, A. (2001). Advancing service-learning at research universities. *New Directions for Higher Education, 114*, 67–78. doi:10.1002/he.15

Garrison, J. D., & Jaeger, A. J. (2014). From serendipity to resolve: Graduate student motivations to teach using service-learning. *Michigan Journal of Com-

munity Service Learning, 20(2), 41–52. Retrieved from hdl.handle.net/2027/spo.3239521.0020.203

Gelmon, S. B., & Agre-Kippenhan, S. (2002). A developmental framework for supporting evolving faculty roles for community engagement. *Journal of Public Affairs,* 6(1), 161–182. Retrieved from Academic Search Complete database.

Glass, C. R., Doberneck, D. M., & Schweitzer, J. H. (2011). Unpacking faculty engagement: The types of activities faculty members report as publicly engaged scholarship during promotion and tenure. *Journal of Higher Education Outreach and Engagement,* 15(1), 7–30. Retrieved from openjournals.libs.uga.edu/index.php/jheoe/article/viewFile/504/435

Hamel-Lambert, J. M., Millesen, J. L., Slovak, K., & Harter, L. M. (2012). Reflections on community-engaged scholarship faculty development and institutional identity at Ohio University. *Journal of Higher Education Outreach and Engagement,* 16(1), 129–148. Retrieved from ERIC database.

Jacoby, B. (2015). *Service-learning essentials: Questions, answers, and lessons learned.* San Francisco, CA: Jossey-Bass.

Jacoby, B., & Associates. (2009). *Civic engagement in higher education: Concepts and practices.* San Francisco, CA: Jossey-Bass.

Jordan, C., Doherty, W. J., Jones-Webb, R., Cook, N., Dubrow, G., & Mendenhall, T. J. (2012). Competency-based faculty development in community-engaged scholarship: A diffusion of innovation approach. *Journal of Higher Education Outreach and Engagement,* 16(1), 65–95. Retrieved from openjournals.libs.uga.edu/index.php/jheoe/article/view/750

Kezar, A., Gallant, T. B., & Lester, J. (2011). Everyday people making a difference on college campuses: The tempered grassroots leadership tactics of faculty and staff. *Studies in Higher Education,* 36(2), 129–151. doi:10.1080/03075070903532304

Mayfield, L. (2001). Town and gown in America: Some historical and institutional issues of the engaged university. *Education for Health,* 14(2), 231–240. doi: 10.1080/13576280110056609

Nyden, P. (2003). Academic incentives for faculty participation in community-based participatory research. *Journal of General Internal Medicine,* 18(7), 576–585. doi:10.1046/j.1525-1497.2003.20350.x

O'Meara, K. (2008a). Graduate education and community engagement. *New Directions for Teaching and Learning,* 113, 27–42. doi: 10.1002/tl.306

O'Meara, K. (2008b). Motivation for faculty community engagement: Learning from exemplars. *Journal of Higher Education Outreach and Engagement,* 12(1), 7–29. Retrieved from www.google.com/url?q=http://openjournals.libs.uga.edu/index.php/jheoe/article/viewFile/123/111&sa=D&ust=1443375773989000&usg=AFQjCNHX0EpYH6yQz8SpGgqn7lUnWW7xGg

O'Meara, K., & Jaeger, A. J. (2006). Preparing future faculty for community engagement: Barriers, facilitators, models, and recommendations. *Journal of Higher Education Outreach and Engagement,* 11(4), 3–26. Retrieved from works.bepress.com/kerryann_omeara/15/

Sandy, M., & Holland, B. (2006). Different worlds and common ground: Community partner perspectives on campus-community partnerships.

Michigan Journal of Community Service Learning, 13(1), 30–44. Retrieved from hdl.handle.net/2027/spo.3239521.0013.103

Shapiro, D. (2012). Collaborative faculty assessment of service-learning student work to improve student and faculty learning and course design. *Michigan Journal of Community Service Learning, 19*(1), 44–57. Retrieved from hdl.handle.net/2027/spo.3239521.0019.104

Stoecker, R., Tryon, E. A., & Hilgendorf, A. (2009). *The unheard voices: Community organizations and service learning.* Philadelphia, PA: Temple University Press.

Stewart, T., & Webster, N. (Eds.). (2011). *Exploring cultural dynamics and tensions within service-learning.* Charlotte, NC: Information Age Publishing.

Ward, K., & Wolf-Wendel, L. (2000). Community-centered service learning: Moving from doing for to doing with. *American Behavioral Scientist 43*(5), 767–780. doi: 10.1177/00027640021955586

Weerts, D. J., & Sandmann, L. R. (2010). Community engagement and boundary-spanning roles at research universities. *Journal of Higher Education, 81*(6), 632–657. Retrieved from muse.jhu.edu/journals/journal_of_higher_education/v081/81.6.weerts.pdf

Welch, M., & Saltmarsh, J. (2013). Current practice and infrastructures for campus centers of community engagement. *Journal of Higher Education Outreach and Engagement, 17*(4), 25–55. Retrived from www.jheoe.uga.edu

Wood, R. J. (1990). Changing the educational program. *New Directions for Higher Education, 71,* 51–58. doi: 10.1002/he.36919907107

EDITOR AND CONTRIBUTORS

About the Editor

Lina D. Dostilio is the assistant vice chancellor for community engagement centers at the University of Pittsburgh. In this capacity she leads the university's initiative to establish neighborhood-based engagement centers in a number of Pittsburgh communities. Dostilio is also the scholar-in-residence for Campus Compact's Research Project on the Community Engagement Professional. She previously directed Duquesne University's Center for Community-Engaged Teaching and Research and was the 2012–2013 chair of the International Association for Research on Service-Learning & Community Engagement.

About the Contributors

Jodi Benenson is an assistant professor in the School of Public Administration at the University of Nebraska Omaha. Her primary research interests include social policy, nonprofit organizations, civic engagement, and inequality. Previously, Benenson was a postdoctoral research fellow at the Jonathan M. Tisch College of Civic Life at Tufts University. At Tufts, she worked on several projects in the areas of youth civic engagement, political learning and engagement in higher education, and national service and employment. Benenson received a BS and an MPA from Indiana University and a PhD in social policy from the Heller School for Social Policy and Management at Brandeis University.

J. Shannon Chamberlin has experienced community engagement as a student, student supervisor, college instructor, and researcher. She has conducted survey-based and qualitative research for community engagement professionals. At the International Association for Research on Service-Learning & Community Engagement 2015 conference, she presented a research paper and a poster reporting findings from her PhD dissertation, "College Faculty Experiences Assigning Service-Learning and Their Inclination to Continue." She serves on the Engagement Council at the University of Arkansas at Little Rock and is a higher education service-learning consultant.

Sean Crossland currently serves as the interim director in the Thayne Center for Service and Learning at Salt Lake Community College. Crossland is also an adjunct instructor in the Family and Consumer Studies Department at the University of Utah and in the master of arts in community leadership program in the School of Education at Westminster College. Sean is interested in teaching and research around social change and community engagement.

Ashley J. Farmer-Hanson serves as the director of civic engagement at Buena Vista University in Iowa. In this role Farmer-Hanson coordinates civic engagement learning opportunities in partnership with community agencies. Her research has focused on multiracial identity development and most recently community engagement professionals; she authored the "Organizational Manager" chapter in *Diving Deep in Community Engagement* (Iowa Campus Compact, 2014). In addition, Ashley serves as a commissioner on the Iowa Commission on Volunteer Service.

Kevin M. Hemer is a doctoral student in education at Iowa State University, specializing in higher education. Currently Hemer works in the Research Institute for Studies in Education at Iowa State with the Personal and Social Responsibility Inventory and the Global Perspective Inventory. His research examines the public role of higher education in a democratic society, focusing on undergraduate student outcomes, civic learning, and campus climates. He received an MS in higher education from Florida State University and a BA in government and politics from the University of Maryland.

Kortney Hernandez is a current doctoral student and site manager for a nonprofit, community development, early childhood program under the Center for Engagement, Service, and the Public Good at California State University, Los Angeles. Her research engages the phenomenon of service-learning/community engagement through a critical decolonizing bicultural lens. Her work reflects a decade of practice engaging *with* communities, preschool children, families, undergraduate students, and various community organizations.

Romy Hübler is a recent graduate from the Language, Literacy, and Culture doctoral program at the University of Maryland, Baltimore County (UMBC). She was UMBC's Imagining America Fellow, planning the 2015 national conference in Baltimore, Maryland, and collaborating with local consortium members, cultural and humanities organizations, artists, and community activists to further the democratic transformation of higher education and civic life. Romy is also working with UMBC's Shriver Center to develop a new master's program with a focus on social change leadership. Her research interests are civic engagement, public scholarship, and institutional change.

B. Tait Kellogg is a research affiliate for the Center for Public Service at Tulane University as well as a doctoral student in the interdisciplinary City, Culture, and Community program with a focus in sociology. She has her master's degree in higher and postsecondary education from Teachers College, Columbia University. She currently serves on the steering committee for the Graduate Student Network for the International Association for Research on Service-Learning & Community Engagement. Tait's research interests focus on the relationship between the university and the wider community, including community engagement and college access initiatives.

Laura Martin is the assistant director of the McLean Institute for Public Service and Community Engagement at the University of Mississippi. In this capacity, she works to institutionalize engagement efforts that seek to address poverty and improve quality of life in Mississippi. Martin has worked in the nonprofit sector and in the public policy arena, and she seeks to integrate these perspectives in her community engagement research as a higher education doctoral student.

Kira Pasquesi is an instructor and the program director of the Leadership Studies program at the University of Colorado Boulder and a doctoral candidate in the Higher Education and Student Affairs program at the University of Iowa. Her research examines how colleges and universities use language to represent diversity and inclusion in community engagement. Pasquesi previously served as a community engagement professional at Colorado College where she convened students, faculty, and community partners in difficult dialogues and catalyzed collective action. She is excited to contribute to the future of the field as a codirector for Imagining America's Publicly Active Graduate Education (PAGE).

Lane G. Perry is currently the director of the Center for Service Learning at Western Carolina University in North Carolina and is the coeditor of the *International Journal for Research on Service-Learning and Community Engagement*. He earned his BBA and MEd at the University of Central Oklahoma and from 2008 to 2012 lived in Christchurch, New Zealand, and worked at the University of Canterbury, where he completed his PhD in higher education and served as a faculty member in the College of Education. He has published and presented on the influence of service-learning on student engagement and how service-learning and community engagement can serve as a responsive pedagogy for bridging the space between the community and classroom.

Johanna Phelps-Hillen is a rhetoric and composition doctorate candidate and master of public administration student at the University of South Florida. As an instructor, she utilizes and studies the impact of community engagement pedagogies in technical and professional writing courses. Her recent research projects examine democratic engagement in community-engaged course co-construction. She is currently the institutional review board program coordinator at Utah State University. Her dissertation project is rooted in the nexus of research ethics, public policy, and technical communication. Prior to pursuing her doctorate, Phelps-Hillen served with Utah Campus Compact's AmeriCorps VISTA Project and subsequently worked as Utah Campus Compact's AmeriCorps S&N program manager.

Melissa Quan is the director of the Center for Faith and Public Life at Fairfield University, where she has worked since 2002. Her responsibilities include leading the institutionalization of service-learning at Fairfield University, supporting service-learning course development, building meaningful community partnerships, and managing several research projects for the Center for Faith and Public Life. Quan completed her master's degree in education at Fairfield University with a concentration on service-learning and civic education in 2005 and is currently pursuing a doctoral degree in higher education administration at the University of Massachusetts Boston.

Kara Trebil is a doctoral student in higher education at the University of Denver. Prior to pursuing an advanced degree, she spent five years as the director of civic engagement at Cornell College in Iowa. In this role, she managed community engagement initiatives across campus, collaborated with students to develop ongoing community-campus partnerships, and served on the Iowa Campus Compact advisory board. Her research interests focus on the experiences of traditionally underrepresented students doing community engagement, and identifying ways to make the practice more inclusive and culturally responsive. She received an MEd from the University of Northern Iowa and a BA from Wartburg College.

Laura Weaver is the director of programs and member development at Indiana Campus Compact, where she provides training on and support for the institutionalization of community engagement practices at more than 35 institutions of higher education across Indiana. In this capacity, Laura assists faculty with their teaching and research activities involving reciprocal community-campus partnerships and supports students in implementing an array of engagement activities. Prior to joining Indiana Campus Compact, she spent more than eight years overseeing the Center for Service Learning and Leadership at Purdue University North Central (Northwest), and spent several years working for a national nonprofit organization partnering with college students to build awareness and support for health care initiatives. Weaver received her MSEd from Northern Illinois University and a BS from Bradley University.

INDEX

AAC&U. *See* Association of American Colleges & Universities
AASCU. *See* American Association of State Colleges and Universities
Abes, E. S., 183
Academic Search Complete, 80, 120
ACE Project on Leadership and Institutional Transformation, 102
ACPA. *See* American College Personnel Association
activist scholarship, 5
adaption, 100
Advancing Civic Learning and Engagement in Democracy, 142
Agre-Kippenhan, S., 192, 194
American Association of State Colleges and Universities (AASCU), 43
American College Personnel Association (ACPA), 34
American Democracy Project, 7
American Evaluation Association, 33
American Society for Training and Development (ASTD), 31
armchair activist, 19
Aronowitz, 61–62
asset mapping, 152
Association of American Colleges & Universities (AAC&U), 42, 112
Astin, A. W., 148
ATSD. *See* American Society for Training and Development

attitudes, 29
Auerswand, E. P., 18
authenticity
    CEPs ability for, 68, 149
    dialogue relied on by, 68
    principles of, 66
    in relationships, 67–68
    strive for, 155
authority, 106
Axtell, S., 190

Baartman, L. K., 52
Baer, L. L., 13
Barnhardt, C. L., 150
Bartha, M., 2, 6, 8, 106
Bartram, D., 32
becoming
    as evolutionary learning, 35
    journey of, 8
Bellah, R. N., 56
Better Volunteering, Better Care, 88
Biddix, J. P., 82
Bloomgarden, A., 89
Bonner Foundation, 7, 112
Bornstein, D., 19
boundary spanning, 99, 164
Bowker, M. H., 56, 63
Bowling Alone (Putnam), 56
Bowman, N. A., 8, 144, 151
Boyer, Ernest, 119, 192
Boyte, Harry, 103, 105, 108
Bringle, K. E., 143

207

Bringle, R. G., 85, 143, 163, 170, 172–73, 182
Bruijn, E., 52
budgeting, 91–92
Bush, A., 67
Butin, D. W., 67

Campus Compacts, 87, 91. *See also* Iowa Campus Compact
   founding of, 120
   participation in, 9
   staff of, 4
   support from, 7
Campus Outreach Opportunity League (COOL), 120
campus protest, 82
Cann, C. N., 64
Carducci, R., 15
Carnegie Community Engagement Classification, 11, 89, 93, 125, 192–93
Carnegie Foundation for Advancement of Teaching, 11, 120
Carney, M., 2, 106
CAS. *See* Council for the Advancement of Standards
CEPs. *See* community engagement professionals
chameleon complex, 89
Checkoway, B., 102–3, 105
civic engagement
   civic identity necessary for, 143
   as critical, 57
   democratic engagement compared to, 171
   diversity to related, 151
   service-learning for, 141
   student categories of, 145
civic identity
   for civic engagement, 143
   community engagement framed by, 145
   marginalization influencing, 145
   student expression of, 143–44
civic learning
   background and development in, 141–42
   community engagement impacted by, 155
   competency centered around, 142
   faculty supporting, 151
   goals of, 154
   higher education as support system for, 143
   minority experience of, 153
   pedagogies of, 147–49
   persistence of, 151
   positive impacts on, 150
   responsibility fostered by, 148
   for students, 139
civic-minded graduate model (CMG), 143
Clark, A. Y., 148
Clayton, P. H., 7, 143, 163, 170, 176, 187
CMG. *See* civic-minded graduate model
Coalition of Urban and Metropolitan Universities (CUMU), 7, 42
cocreative organizing
   CEPs familiarity with, 109
   institutional change requiring, 108
   methods for, 108–9
collaboration
   as CEPs strategy, 67, 150–51
   communication, innovation and, 105
   institutional change requiring, 107, 129
   with stakeholders, 130–33
   trust necessary for, 175–76
collective labor
   CEPs engaging in, 57, 63
   commitment to, 62–63
communication
   of CEPs for community-campus engagement, 125
   collaboration, innovation and, 105
   consensus from, 175
   models of, 91
   skills in, 132

as two-way, 174–75
community-campus engagement, 5
   CEPs communication skills for, 125
   critical practice in, 59
   institutionalization of, 118
   leadership requiring, 29
   practices of, 1, 2
   quality of, 174
   social entrepreneurship related to, 19
   social justice in, 70
   student behavior influencing, 144–45
   support necessary for, 3, 53
   survey instrument for, 12
community-campus partnerships, 131, 152
   CEPs cultivating, 162
   competencies of, 165, 176, 191
   as high quality, 161, 188–91
   leadership styles for, 176
   qualities of, 163
community engagement. *See also* community-campus engagement
   administrating of, 40
   assessment data as tool for, 129
   as brand position, 128
   capital required for, 92
   characteristics of, 11–12
   civic identity framing, 145
   civic learning impacting, 155
   commitment to, 124, 133, 169
   coordination sites for, 12
   creative destruction in, 18
   critical practice, power and, 63
   critical theory in, 57
   in curriculum development, 121
   diversity influencing, 146–47
   Eurocentric approaches to, 64
   evolution of, 10
   faculty developing, 181, 182–85, 192
   generations of, 79
   goals and values for, 119, 153
   in higher education, 80, 120–21
   history of, 104
   initiative expansion in, 190
   institutionalization of, 40, 121–22
   as integrative, 121, 193
   measuring of, 89
   orchestration for institutionalization of, 14
   practice in, 69
   preparation for, 188
   racial identity influencing, 152
   as reciprocal, 161
   relationships necessary for, 86, 168
   scholarship promoted in, 120
   service-learning, research and, 10, 57
   significance of, 105
   as social change tool, 98
   supporters necessary for, 126
   transformative approach to, 13
community engagement centers, 12
   evolution of, 98–99
   leadership in, 13
   relationships fostered by, 112
   responsibilities of, 126
   Saltmarsh and Welch study on, 36, 112
   studies on, 36
   training development for, 85
community engagement professionals (CEPs), 1
   academic professionals compared to, 27
   assessment skills of, 131
   authenticity ability of, 68, 149
   backgrounds of, 134
   boundaries of, 106
   central work themes for, 123
   challenges for, 90
   cocreative organizing familiar to, 109
   collaboration as strategy for, 67, 150–51
   collective labor engaged by, 57, 63
   community-campus engagement communication from, 125
   community-campus partnerships cultivated by, 162

competencies for, 35–36, 53n1, 100, 113, 123, 142, 164, 179, 185
competency model for, 30, 46–51
context influencing, 141
credentials for, 42
critical commitments for, 44, 56
curriculum development assisted with by, 83
definition of, 38
democratic engagement as focus of, 99, 110
demographic information of, 38–39
dialogue influencing, 69, 150
difficulties for, 66, 70
diplomacy in, 193
diversity among, 52
evaluation by, 89–91, 124
faculty development by, 179, 181, 184, 186, 190, 197
faculty support by, 192
flexibility of, 188
grant writing of, 87, 127
habits of, 107
in higher education, 57
human resource skills of, 128
identity politics navigated by, 67
institutional change contributions from, 113, 121–23, 126
institutional policy understood by, 81–82
international service opportunities for, 88–89
investments of, 79–80
landmark statements of, 11
leadership frameworks for, 14, 21
marginalization countered by, 151
marketing skills of, 124, 128
networking as responsibility of, 91
partnership development by, 85–86, 162, 168, 188
personal attributes of, 93, 103, 105, 109, 110, 152–54
perspectives influenced by, 189
planning strategies of, 102
political capital of, 125
power understood by, 63–64, 88
practice environments of, 5–6
principles for, 58–59, 69
privilege, power, oppression and, 65
professional identity development in, 7–8
reciprocal relationships of, 84
research potential for, 168
as resource providers, 87–88
rights taught by, 82
risk management as role of, 83, 127
role of, 98, 101–2, 188–89
self-awareness of, 149
skills required of, 84–85, 104, 105, 132, 149–52
socialization of, 45
student engagement by, 152
support for, 113
two-way communication of, 175
community service directors (CSDs), 4
compartmentalization, 111
competency
for CEPs, 35–36, 53n1, 100, 113, 123, 142, 164, 179, 185, 196
civic learning centered by, 142
as common group skill, 28
in community-campus partnerships, 165, 176, 191
concept of, 28
context as critical for, 30
critiques of, 29
definitions of, 28–29
diversity in forms of, 197
ethical orientation in, 52, 164–65, 170
for faculty development, 183, 191
framework for, 80–81
in higher education, 31
for institutional change, 101–2, 106, 114
in partnership development, 176
pathways to, 45

Index 211

profession influencing models of, 30
in program administration, 81
ranking of, 42, 44, 52
as skill based, 127
types of, 122–23, 140
competency model, 38. *See also* Great Eight competency model
of ASTD, 31
for CEPs, 30, 46–51
critical consciousness for, 42
critiques of, 58
for groups and individuals, 41
literature informing, 53
missing areas of, 40–41
as preliminary, 46–51
professional evaluators methods for, 36
refining of, 42–45
competency model surveys
demographics of, 43
participants and respondents for, 43–44
results of, 45
Comprehensive Model for Assessing Service-Learning and Community-University Partnerships, 90
conflict resolution, 171–72
consensus, 175
context
CEPs influenced by, 141
competencies requiring, 30
as external, 104–5
faculty development depending on, 180
as historical, institutional, and environmental, 165–66
institutional change needing, 103–5, 110
of self, 103
unified voice developed through, 111–13
contextualized practice, 180–82
Contreras-McGavin, M., 15

COOL. *See* Campus Outreach Opportunity League
Council for the Advancement of Standards (CAS), 34
creative destruction, 18
critical commitments, 42
for CEPs, 44, 56
contradictions to, 58
in leadership, 9
to partnerships, 133
prioritizing of, 30
to social justice, 61
of students, 150
unique nature of, 37
visibility of, 45
critical consciousness, 42, 61–62, 64
critical practice
literature for, 36
as not formulaic, 70
power, community engagement and, 59, 62–63
critical race theory, 66, 84
critical theory, 15, 57, 70n1
A Crucible Moment: College Learning and Democracy's Future, 142, 148
CSDs. *See* community service directors
Cuban, L., 102, 104
culture
intentional change in, 108
leadership influenced by, 15
as power form, 108
CUMU. *See* Coalition of Urban and Metropolitan Universities
curriculum development, 45, 83, 121

Darder, A., 57, 59, 63
d'Arlach, L., 67
Dean, J. W., 122
Delphi method, 32
democratic engagement
as CEPs focus, 99, 110
civic engagement compared to, 171
in higher education, 104

partnerships built on, 166
principles of, embraced, 106–7
value of, 107–9
Democratic Engagement White Paper
(Saltmarsh, Hartley, Clayton), 170
Dempsey, S. E., 65, 66
Denson, N., 144
Dewey, John, 61–62
dialecticity, 60
dialogue. *See also* peer-to-peer dialogue
authenticity relying on, 68
CEPs influenced by, 69, 150
partnerships assisted by, 175
promotion of, 107
disability, 67
diversity
awareness of, 59–60, 70
among CEPs, 52
civic engagement related to, 151
community engagement influenced by, 146–47
of competency forms, 197
in higher education, 111
Diving Deep in Community Engagement (McReynolds and Shields), 80
Diving Deep: Institute for Experienced Civic and Community Engagement Practitioners (Jacoby and Mutascio), 1–2, 35
Diving In: Institute for New Community Service-Learning Professionals (Jacoby and Mutascio), 1–2
Doberneck, D. M., 187
Donahue, D. M., 66, 146
Dostilio, L., 83, 166, 176, 189, 190
Driscoll, A., 121, 130, 192–93
Duck, S. W., 169
Duin, A. H., 13
Dunlap, M. R., 67

Eatman, T., 67
Eckel, P. D., 100, 102, 107, 111
Education Resources Information Center (ERIC), 80, 120
empirical scoping study, 32
Endres, D., 60
engaged scholarship, 111
Engagement Scholarship Consortium, 4, 7
Engstrom, C. M., 87, 90
Enos, Sandra, 21n1, 163, 165, 174
ERIC. *See* Education Resources Information Center
ethical commitments, 5, 8–9
Etzioni, A., 6
evaluation
by CEPs, 89–91, 124
as effective, 94
program administration and, 79
Evans, S. Y., 67
Evett, J., 8

faculty development
activities for, 194, 196
by CEPs, 179, 181, 184, 186, 190, 197
of community engagement, 181, 182–85, 192
competency for, 183, 191
concerns for, 192
as contextual, 180
customization of, 185–87
incentives used in, 193
as journey, 187
literature for, 36
recruiting necessary for, 189
strategies for, 184, 185
tenure and workload reflection for, 191, 194–95
training and support for, 185–88
false generosity, 68
Ferman, B., 133
Foucault, M., 64
Freire, Paolo, 60–61, 62, 65–68
Friedson, E., 27
full participation, 67
Furco, A., 121

Gale, S., 2, 106
Gallant, T., 100
Garrison, J. D., 68, 187
GASP. *See* Global Activities by Students at Pre-Health Levels
Gelmon, S. B., 90, 192, 194
gender, as survey demographic, 44
Gent, P. J., 67
Gibson, C. M., 92
Gillon, K. E., 150
Glass, C. R., 187
Global Activities by Students at Pre-Health Levels (GASP), 88
globalization, 88
Goodhue, E., 2, 106
Goodman, P. S., 122
Google Scholar, 80, 120
Gould, M., 60
Gouthro, K., 85
grant management, 91–92
grant writing, 87, 127
grassroots change leaders, 99, 106, 109, 111
Great Eight competency model, 32–33
Green, M., 102

Habits of the Heart (Bellah), 56
Harden, T., 66
Hart, S., 70
Hartley, M., 104, 107, 170
Hatcher, J. A., 85, 172–73, 182
hegemony, 63
Henry, S. E., 153
Hicks-Peterson, T., 60–61
higher education
 CEPs in, 57
 civic learning supported by, 143
 community engagement in, 80, 120–21
 competency identification in, 31
 complex structures in, 107–8
 current practices of, 11
 democratic engagement in, 104
 diversity in, 111
 faculty support in, 130
 mission of, 56
 norms and traditions in, 101
 political environments of, 124
 purpose of, 100
 reframing of purpose of, 10
 responsibilities of, 119
Hilgendorf, A., 190
Hill, B., 102
Hill, T. L., 135
Hillman, A., 65
holistic learning, 7, 110
Holland, B. A., 121, 152, 173, 190
Howard, A., 2, 106
How Colleges Change: Understanding, Leading and Enacting Change (Kezar), 100
Hoy, A., 112
Hoyle, E., 6
humanization, 68
human resources, 128

IA. *See* Imagining America
IARSLCE. *See* International Association for Research on Service-Learning & Community Engagement
Ibarra, H., 7
Ibrahim, B. L., 88
identity politics, 66, 67, 69
Imagining America (IA), 7, 43, 82
inclusive practice, 4
individualism, 63
Ing, M., 144
innovation
 for change, 100
 collaboration, communication and, 105
institutional change
 CEPs contributions to, 113, 121–23, 126
 cocreative organizing required for, 108
 collaboration required for, 107, 129
 competency for leading, 101–2, 106, 114

as complex, 101
context necessary for, 103–5, 110
external factors for, 104
innovation for, 100
integration necessary for, 111
leadership for, 106, 125
as multifaceted, 100
networking for, 102
for public good, 98
stalling of, 104
strategies for, 110, 112
support and resources for, 127–29
institutionalization
as behavior experimentation, 122
common model for, 122
of community engagement, 40, 121–22
funding for, 127
key terms for, 119–20
knowledge bases for, 129, 133
institutional philosophy, 124–25
institutional policy, 81–82
integration, 52, 111–12
integrity, 170
intercultural differences, 84
International Association for Research on Service-Learning & Community Engagement (IARSLCE), 3–4, 9
Iowa Campus Compact, 35
isomorphism, 100
Israel, B. A., 163

Jackson, G., 183
Jacoby, B., 1–2, 91, 163, 183, 184
Jaeger, A. J., 187
John, P. D., 6
Joint Committee on Standards for Educational Evaluation, 33
Jones, S. R., 85, 183
Jordan, J. W., 164
JSTOR, 120

Kecskes, K., 63
Keith, Novella, 4, 52
Keith, N. Z., 2
Kellogg Commission, 109, 120
Kettering Foundation, 103, 107
Kezar, Adriana, 15, 102, 103, 105, 106, 110, 111
Kiely, R., 89
Kim, J., 84
Kindred, J., 175
Kinefuchi, E., 61, 62
King, J. A., 33
Kliewer, B. W., 58, 64, 84
knowledge base
definition of, 29
as evolving, 6
forms of, 143–49
identifying of, 80–81
for institutionalization, 129, 133
in intercultural differences, 84
on learning trajectories, 143
for partnership development, 165
of resources, 167–68
of student growth, 90
Kolb, D. A., 61
Kretzmann, J. P., 152
Kuh, G. D., 147

Lantz, P., 163
leadership. *See also* grassroots change leaders
approaches to, 17
CEPs frameworks for, 14, 21
as change-oriented, 15
commitments in, 9
community-campus engagement vital for, 29
community-campus partnerships styles of, 176
in community engagement centers, 13
culture influencing, 15
as distributed, 13
for institutional change, 106, 125
PVCs level of, 32–33
students developing skills in, 86

Index   215

as transformational, 15–17
learning goals, 34–35
Leavitt, L. H., 83
Leiderman, S., 166, 173
Lester, J., 100
Liang, J., 12

MACR. *See* multiattribute consensus reaching
Maher, F. A., 149
marginalization, 68
    CEPs countering, 151
    civic identity influenced by, 145
    harm from, 70
marketing
    CEPs skills in, 124, 128
    elements of, 92
Massey, J., 85
Masucci, M., 57
McCloskey, E., 64
McKnight, J. L., 152
McLellan, J. A., 143
McReynolds, M., 2, 35, 80, 93
Meisel, W., 112
memoranda of understanding (MOU), 172
Meyerson, D. E., 15–16, 106
Michigan Journal of Community Service Learning, 148
Miller, D. S., 67
Mitchell, J. J., 150
Mitchell, Tania, 57, 60, 66, 68, 146
Molchan, K., 83
Moore, D., 59
Morton, K., 60, 163, 165, 170, 174
MOU. *See* memoranda of understanding
Mull, C. D., 164
multiattribute consensus reaching (MACR), 33, 37, 43
Mutascio, P., 1–2, 91

NASPA. *See* Student Affairs Administrators in Higher Education
National Service-Learning Clearinghouse, 83
National Task Force on Civic Learning and Democratic Engagement, 148
NCA. *See* North Central Association
neoliberalism
    acknowledgment of, 58
    forces of, 63
    manifestations of, 64
NERCHE. *See* New England Resource Center for Higher Education
networking
    as CEPs responsibility, 91
    goals of, 91
    for institutional change, 102
    partnerships in, 173
"New American College," 119
New England Resource Center for Higher Education (NERCHE), 43
new frontier, 21
North Central Association (NCA), 120
Nugent, M., 148

Oates, K. K., 83
Obama, Barack (President), 142
O'Meara, K., 187
Omerikwa, K., 84
oppression
    elimination of structures of, 58
    experiences with, 147
    forms of, 65
    in populations, 84
    power, CEPs, privilege and, 65
orchestration
    instruments in, 14
    as integrated, 20
O'Steen, W. L., 187
Outreach and Engagement Practitioners Network, 4

Palmerton, A., 85
Palonen, T., 7
partnerships. *See also* community-campus partnerships
    ability to create, 150–51

CEPs developing, 85–86, 162, 168, 188
commitment to, 133
for community-campus engagement, 131, 152
competency for development of, 176
democratic engagement building, 166
dialogue assisting in, 175
faculty assisting in, 189
interdependence in, 176
knowledge base for development of, 165
management of, 172–73
in networking, 173
organizational strength in, 173–74
passion for, 169
as reciprocal, 131
reflection integration in, 172
relationships compared to, 163
with students, 86–87
Pascarella, E. T., 150
Pasquesi, K., 150
Pedagogy of the Oppressed (Freire), 61
peer-to-peer dialogue, 149–50
PEP. *See* Political Engagement Project
personal responsibility, 4
Petrescu, C., 175
Pigza, J. M., 91, 92
Plater, W. M., 16
pluralistic orientation, 144
Political Engagement Project (PEP), 142
Polman, J. L., 82
positionality, 149
postmodernism, 15
power
CEPs, privilege, oppression and, 65
CEPs understanding, 63–64, 88
critical practice, community engagement and, 63
culture as form of, 108
disrupting of, 65
dynamics of, 62
perspectives of, 84

principles of, 63–64, 69
redistribution of, 57, 65
structures of, disrupted, 65–66
views of, 63
pracademics, 7
practice-scholar communities, 5–7
"Preliminary Competencies of Second-Generation Community Engagement Professionals," 28
Price, M., 163
privilege. *See also* White privilege
CEPs, power, oppression and, 65
construct of, 65
professional epistemology, 7
professional evaluators
competency methods used by, 36
complex role of, 33
methods for, 34
professionals
as civic-minded, 154
definition of, 8
generations of, 9–13
practitioner compared to, 3
for training and development, 31
professions
elements of, 5–9
problematic idea of, 30
as socially constructed, 9
as true, 6
program administration
competency in, 81
evaluation and, 79
grassroots change leaders and, 109
literature for, 36
tasks for, 81
ProQuest, 80, 120
pro-vice chancellors (PVCs), 32–33
Putnam, R. D., 56
PVCs. *See* pro-vice chancellors

Quadir, I. Z., 18
Quinn, L., 58

racial identity, 153
racism, 64, 69

Ramaley, J. A., 13
Rand, Ayn, 21
Reason, R. D., 150
Regan, P. Y. L., 68
Renner, A., 57
request for proposals (RFP), 172
resource provider, 87–88
RFP. *See* request for proposals
Rhoads, R. A., 57
risk management, 83, 127
Ronca, J. M., 127
Rosenberger, C., 57
Ryder, A. J., 150

SAGE, 80
Saltmarsh, J., 79, 126, 170
    arguments by, 98, 104
    community engagement centers study by, 36, 112
    on full participation, 67
    literature analysis by, 11
    recommendations from, 107
    training and development analysis by, 85
Sandmann, L. R., 12, 16, 84, 164, 167, 169
Sandy, M., 152, 173, 190
Scanlon, L., 7, 8, 35, 37
Schutz, A. J., 7, 163
Schweitzer, J. H., 187
Scully, M., 15–16, 106
Seedat, M., 60, 62
Seider, S. E., 65
semiprofessionals, 6
service-learning, 5
    best practices of, 149
    for civic engagement, 141
    community engagement, research and, 10, 57
    critical approach to, 57, 148
    as high-impact practice, 10–11, 147
    opportunities for, 83
    as privilege, 146
    questioning of, 148
    student experience of, 146–47

service-learning directors (SLDs), 4
Sheets, A. G., 150
Shields, E., 2, 80, 93
SLDs. *See* service-learning directors
social change
    community engagement as tool for, 98
    dialecticity in, 60
    principles of, 59–60, 68
    White privilege linked to, 60
social constructivism, 15
social entrepreneurship, 15, 18–20
social justice
    commitment to, 61
    in community-campus engagement, 70
    issues of, 18
    move towards, 58
    orientation to, 148–49
social media, 105
social responsibility, 4
SocINDEX, 120
SOFAR model, 163
Somers, P. A., 82
Spendlove, M., 32
Sperling, R., 60, 69
Steinman, E., 68
Stewart, T., 59
Stoecker, R., 170, 190
Student Affairs Administrators in Higher Education (NASPA), 34, 43
student affairs professionals, 34–35
Student Affairs Standards, 35
Sturm, S., 67
survey instrument, 12

Taylor, C. M., 67
technical competency, 52
technical skills, 8
tempered radicals, 15–16, 20
Tenure Team Initiative, 82
Terenzini, P. T., 150
Tetreault, M. K. T., 149
third-space professionals, 6

transformation
  in community engagement approach, 13
  as distress, 89
  of leadership, 15–17
  radical belief of, 59
Troppe, M. L., 91, 92
Tryon, E. A., 170, 190

Vaccaro, A., 153
Valentine, T., 164
Van Velsor, E., 58
Veloria, C. N., 65
Verjee, B., 66
visionary skills, 93, 105

Ward, E., 122
Webster, N., 59
Weerts, D. J., 92, 127, 145, 167, 169
Weick, K. E., 122
Weiner, L., 34
Welch, M., 79, 126
  arguments by, 98

community engagement centers
  study by, 36, 112
  literature analysis by, 11
  training and development analysis by, 85
Wenger, E., 7
Western Association of Schools and Colleges, 120
Whitchurch, C., 5–6
White privilege
  normalization of, 67
  social change linked to, 60
Williams, E. P., 32
Wingspread Declaration on Renewing the Civic Mission of the American Research University, 103

Yates, M., 143
Young-Law, C., 66
Youniss, J., 143

Zlotkowski, E., 86